Shaping Sustainable Change

T0292914

Multi-actor partnerships are promoted as central to the achievement of sustainable development. However, these relationships are not always easy, and calls are being made for more guidance on how partners can work together effectively to deliver results and achieve meaningful change.

Shaping Sustainable Change explains the growing and significant role of partnership brokering in shaping these relationships. Drawing upon the work of the Partnership Brokers Association, it uses evidence-based materials to show how the work of partnership brokering contributes to the management of collaborative relationships so that they are better positioned to have a positive and sustainable impact. As well as making the case for partnership brokering, the publication explores the profile and key activities carried out by partnership brokers, and the skills required to undertake this role. Examples are also provided to illustrate how partnership brokering works in practice in relation to different contexts, sectors and themes.

This book will appeal not only to partnership brokers but also to professional and academic readers interested in achieving sustainable development.

Leda Stott is a specialist in multi-stakeholder collaboration and Associate of the Partnership Brokers Association.

"An excellent introduction to partnership brokering; this book will be invaluable to any organisation that uses brokers or is thinking of using them in the future. Part 1 examines the roles taken by brokers in facilitating collaboration. Part 2 features a collection of real-life examples of brokering in action."

Judith Nichol, Head of Factual Partnerships, BBC

"Collaborating across boundaries is needed for humanity to survive the challenges of the 21st Century. Partnership brokering is emerging because some brilliant people have realised this. Their words are in this book. I urge you to read it and join them."

Sean Lowrie, Director, Start Network Consortium

"A thought-provoking dive into the core and complexities of partnering, and an engaging journey to real-life practice all around the globe, from Nepal to Spain, Poland to Zambia, and Canada to Papua New Guinea. A must-read and a treat for partnering-passionates!"

Mathieu Hermans, Senior Policy Advisor, Partnering and Capacity-Building, PAX

"Our world increasingly requires groups and individuals with competing interests to collaborate and find common ground. The partnership brokering process outlined in this book provides practical advice on how we can achieve this."

Kwasi Amponsah Boateng, Social Performance Manager, Tullow Oil Plc

Shaping Sustainable Change

The Role of Partnership Brokering in Optimising Collaborative Action

Edited by Leda Stott

LONDON AND NEW YORK

First published 2019
by Routledge
2 Park Square, Milton Park, Abingdon, Oxon OX14 4RN

and by Routledge
711 Third Avenue, New York, NY 10017

Routledge is an imprint of the Taylor & Francis Group, an informa business

British Library Cataloguing-in-Publication Data
A catalogue record for this book is available from the British Library

Library of Congress Cataloging-in-Publication Data
A catalog record has been requested for this book

ISBN: 978-1-78353-814-0 (hbk)
ISBN: 978-1-78353-736-5 (pbk)
ISBN: 978-0-429-44683-2 (ebk)

Typeset in Sabon
by codeMantra

Contents

Figures

Tables

Images

Case studies

Acknowledgements

We would like to thank the Alumni and Associates of the Partnership Brokers Association for providing the catalyst for this publication. Without the learning derived from their experience of partnership brokering in diverse contexts, this book would not have been written.

Our very special appreciation goes to all the authors who have shared their knowledge and ideas so generously; and to Andrew Acland, Joanne Burke, Ken Caplan, Trish Hall, Marieke de Wal and Helga van Kampen for their thoughtful peer reviews of different chapters.

We are grateful to PBA's Coordinator, Marta Serafin, for proofreading with such admirable skill and patience; to PBA Managers, Dianne McLay and Dolores Puxbaumer, for their ongoing support during the preparation process, and to Emily Wood for her input at the start of this project.

Thanks are also extended to Rob van Tulder and colleagues at the Partnerships Resource Centre, Rotterdam School of Management, Erasmus University, with whom it has been our pleasure to work in recent years.

Our work on this publication has been supported by the PBA Board: Ken Caplan, Ian Gray, Judith Nichol, Tanuja Pandit and Emily Poupart, and the International Advisory Group: Sam Aiboni, Amponsah Boateng, Maria Bobenrieth, Ian Dixon, Tim Draimin, Marieke Hounjet, Ian Lobo, Rafal Serafin, Sbaba Olukayode Somemekun and Sasha Torsi.

Last but not least, our profound gratitude to Ros Tennyson for her pioneering work in this field and her unremitting efforts to deepen our understanding of the role of partnership broker.

Leda Stott
on behalf of the Partnership Brokers Association

Contributors

Bulbul Baksi is an Accredited Partnership Broker and PBA Associate, based in India. She studied social sciences (History) and has been trained in psychological counselling. As well as working with the public health and mental health to help organisations change practices and implant new ways of working, Bulbul has also worked with grassroots NGOs and CBOs, and international aid and development agencies that have partnered with government ministries and CSOs. She currently works as an independent professional, mainly in Southeast Asia, to broker partnership building by designing partnering agreements and supporting review and capacity development processes.

Joanne Burke has held senior-level positions in the international sector working on issues related to capacity development for reducing disaster risk and for humanitarian response. Currently a consultant with the Humanitarian Futures Platform, she previously held positions with King's College London's Humanitarian Futures Programme, and with UNDP Geneva to launch the Capacity for Disaster Reduction Initiative (CADRI). She has experience of working in the private sector, with international NGOs and managed the global training programme for USAID's Office of US Foreign Disaster Assistance. Joanne has been affiliated with PBA since 2010 and works as an independent broker and PBA Associate.

Marcia Dwonczyk has over 30 years of experience in Government and non-Government sectors, across Australia and overseas. She is currently working as an independent innovation and change specialist with a focus on partnership and engagement. Marcia works nationally and internationally to increase effective partnering. She is a PBA Associate and Authorised Practitioner Trainer. Specialising in working with diverse stakeholders around complex issues, Marcia works with people to build their knowledge and skills in partnering and engagement to develop new approaches to address these issues.

Rachel Houghton has over 20 years' experience in the international development and humanitarian sectors. For the past 15 years, she has specialised in developing and leading collaborative initiatives with some of the world's foremost international humanitarian organisations. Her most recent post was as the Director of the global CDAC network. She has an MSc, with distinction, in Social Policy and Social Research, and a BA (Hons) in English and American Literature. She is an Associate of PBA and believes passionately in the power of collaboration. Rachel is also a keen collaborator outside of her professional environment, and runs women's wisdom and artistic circles.

Surinder Hundal, after a career in the corporate sector, is now working specifically in the field of cross-sector partnerships, partnership brokering and partnership evaluation. She works as an independent Accredited Partnership Broker and as a specialist in corporate social responsibility. She holds a postgraduate certificate in Cross-sector Partnership from the University of Cambridge. Surinder has worked in Asia Pacific, Europe, the USA, the Middle East and Africa, principally in telecommunications businesses such as Nokia and BT, where she led multifaceted communications, strategy, marketing, corporate responsibility and partnership development roles. She also led policy and communications at the International Business Leaders Forum.

Timo Kahlen is Senior Associate at Strategy& and member of its digital team and public sector practice in Germany. He holds a Master's Degree and CEMS Diploma from the Rotterdam School of Management, Erasmus University. His Master's Thesis was on the topic of cross-sector partnership brokers.

Martin Kalungu-Banda is a consultant in organisation and leadership development; a designer and facilitator of innovation and organisation change processes; a trainer; coach and author. He works with the Presencing Institute, supporting clients such as the Global Alliance for Banking on Values (GABV), the Rand Merchant Bank (RMB), Accenture, WWF and the German International Development Agency (GIZ). He has also worked with 3M, HSBC Bank, the World Bank, World Health Organisation, the University of Cambridge Institute for Sustainability Leadership, the Said Business School at Oxford and the London Business School. From 2005 to 2008, Martin served as Special Consultant to the President of Zambia and, since September 2010, has been an adviser to the Tony Blair Institute for Global Change.

Moses Laman is a Principle Research Fellow and current Head of the Vector Borne Diseases Unit at the Papua New Guinea Institute of Medical Research. He is a general paediatrician, a Young Affiliate of the Third World Academy of Science and an adjunct senior research fellow at the School of Medicine and Pharmacology, University of Western Australia. He has led multiple studies of malaria and other health-related issues since 2003. Dr Laman has worked continuously with international donors over the past 12 years and has an in-depth understanding of Melanesian culture, perspectives, relationships and politics.

Donna Leigh Holden is an international development practitioner who has lived and worked for over 30 years in Asia and the Pacific. She has extensive experience in leading design and evaluation teams for Australian and New Zealand aid programmes, and other donors such as the EU, World Bank, UN and national and international NGOs. She has a special interest in working in challenging and complex situations including conflict and disaster-affected areas or on issues of exclusion and marginalisation. Donna sees partnership brokering as a natural extension of her work as a development practitioner, and one which has the potential to strongly enhance the quality and relevance of development efforts through rethinking the ways we do business and creating new types of relationships between all development actors.

Sarah MacCana has been working as a Project Manager for the Australia–China–Papua New Guinea Pilot Cooperation on Malaria Control Project since 2015. She completed her PBA accreditation as a partnership broker in 2016 and has recently joined PBA's network of international Associates. Sarah holds a BA (Hons) from the University of New South Wales Australia and has worked in the international development sector for 12 years, with a focus on Papua New Guinea (PNG) and the Pacific region. She commenced service with the (then) AusAID in 2006, and served as an aid official within the Australian High Commission in PNG from 2008 to 2012. Sarah has also strengthened monitoring and evaluation and partnership-related capacities in PNG through her work with a range of international and local not-for-profit organisations.

Carlos Mataix is a Professor in the Department of Industrial Engineering at the Technical University of Madrid (UPM) and the Director of the Innovation and Technology for Development Centre at the same university (itdUPM). Carlos has a long history of collaboration in the fields of technology and international development cooperation. He co-founded the Spanish NGO Engineers Without Borders (now ONGAWA) and was responsible for the Planning Quality Support Unit at the Spanish Agency for International Development Cooperation (AECID).

Marion McCahon is a rural community development practitioner who has spent the last 15 years working with communities in Scotland and Canada. Originally from Northern Ireland, she now calls Nova Scotia her home. She holds a B.Tech (Hons) in Rural Resource Management from the University of Edinburgh and an MSc in Sustainable Rural Development from the University of the Highlands and Islands. Her interests include community planning, public engagement, partnership building, resource management and food security. Having worked for many years with National Parks in

Scotland, she also has a special appreciation for community development in protected areas. Marion became an Accredited Partnership Broker in 2011.

Nina Mitchelmore has spent the last 16 years doing community development work on the Northern Peninsula of Newfoundland and Labrador, Canada. With the exception of completing post-secondary education elsewhere, Nina has lived her entire life on the Northern Peninsula. She holds a BA (Hons) from Memorial University of Newfoundland. Nina started her career in the public sector in 2006 and currently works for the Communications and Public Engagement Branch, Government of Newfoundland and Labrador. Through her position with the Provincial Government, Nina is able to work at both a regional and provincial level.

Jaime Moreno Serna is the Technical Director of the Innovation and Technology for Development Centre at the Technical University of Madrid (itdUPM). He holds a Master's degree in Human Development and Cooperation and a Diploma in Industrial Engineering from a double award scheme between the Technical University of Madrid and the Ecole Nationale Supérieure de Techniques Avancées (ENSTA ParisTech). He previously worked as Project Director for the NGO Movimiento por la Paz (MPDL).

Julie Mundy is passionate about both the potential and reality of diverse groups of stakeholders working together to 'do business differently' and achieve real, sustainable change in the world, and believes that effective partnerships provide a framework within which this can genuinely happen. An international development practitioner and independent partnerships specialist for over 25 years, Julie has worked in government, academia, the private sector and with international NGOs in a variety of leadership, governance and project roles. Her focus over the past eight years has been negotiating agreements, reviewing partnerships, resolving conflict, building capacity and advising a broad spectrum of partnerships. Julie holds a key global leadership role with PBA as Director of Training and is a PBA Accreditation Mentor.

Sara Beysolow Nyanti is an Accredited Partnership Broker and development practitioner. She has held senior project management and representational roles within the UN. As an internal broker, she has played most of the functions of a partnership broker. She has coordinated, negotiated and facilitated partnerships with multilateral funds such as the Global Fund for AIDS, Tuberculosis and Malaria among other bilateral and multilateral funding mechanisms. She has supported many community-based organisations and start-ups with technical support and has wide experience of partnership brokering in complex environments.

Gillian Pearl has 17 years of experience in strategic planning, cross-sector partnership development and program management. Founder of Pearl Consulting, she leads the team to conceptualise and deliver social impact programmes and services. Gillian previously chaired the Corporate Citizenship Committee at Singapore's American Chamber of Commerce, represented Singapore abroad at the UN and has served on non-profit boards. Gillian and Pearl Consulting were named as finalists in the 2014 Public Affairs Asia 'Gold Standard Awards' for NGO Engagement and most recently, Gillian became an Accredited Partnership Broker.

Joanna Pyres For the last 14 years, Joanna has been working globally to support government, business, NGO and UN organisations to build effective multi-stakeholder partnerships for sustainable development through training and consultancy with PBA and the Partnering Initiative. Recognising the inequities inherent in the development industry and based in rural Goa, India, Joanna has co-founded circlewallas.net, an NGO that builds the capacity of community members to use participatory methods and partnership brokering to support place-based multi-stakeholder collective action for sustainable futures and green transition. Joanna works to strengthen individual, community and organisational capacities and confidence to collaborate in the spirit of partnership and shared leadership.

Leanne Robinson is a Senior Research Fellow and Head of the Vector Borne Diseases and Tropical Public Health Group in the Disease Elimination Program at the Burnet Institute in Australia. Her research focuses on malaria epidemiology and implementation research for control/elimination of malaria and neglected tropical diseases. Leanne has worked on international collaborations with foreign funding for the past 12 years. She has an ongoing appointment with the Papua New Guinea Institute of Medical Research (PNG IMR) and also works with the Division of Population Health and Immunity at the Walter and Eliza Hall Institute of Medical Research. Leanne is an Honorary Fellow of the University of Melbourne and an Adjunct Senior Research Fellow at the School of Public Health and Preventive Medicine at Monash University.

Rafal Serafin has been an active enabler of civil society, community-based sustainable development, cross-sector partnership and engaging with business since the 1980s. Working with the Polish Environmental Partnership Foundation and the International Business Leaders Forum, he pioneered partnering approaches in Poland and other parts of Central and East Europe. Since 2011, he has brokered local food systems that bring together small farmers, consumers and other stakeholders to provide quality, tasty and authentic food. Rafal is a founding member and Associate of the Partnership Brokers Association (PBA) and experienced mentor. He is currently working with PBA's Partnering with Donors initiative – www.partnering withdonors.org

Sara Romero is part of the coordination team at Innovation and Technology for Development Centre at Technical University of Madrid (itdUPM). Her academic profile combines anthropology, public relations and sustainability.

Her current research centres on the relationship between social innovation and social change using an ethnographic approach. Sara has a background in communications and previously worked in this area in the private sector and with digital advertising agencies.

Leda Stott has over 25 years of experience working in international development, mostly dedicated to the promotion, management and evaluation of multi-actor partnerships. She holds a PhD in Social Policy from the University of Edinburgh and teaches on a variety of postgraduate programmes relating to multi-stakeholder collaboration. Leda has directed partnership research and training programmes for UN agencies, the World Bank, European Commission and Inter-American Development Bank, as well as for a number of bilateral development agencies, NGOs and businesses. An Associate of itdUPM and PBA, Leda currently works as the Thematic Expert for the Transnational Network on Partnership in the European Social Fund.

Ros Tennyson was originally trained in theatre, started her career as a lecturer in theatre studies and later worked in community development culminating in three years as Chief Executive of an experimental primary health care project, Marylebone Centre Trust. She subsequently completed postgraduate courses in action research and in coaching and mentoring. Between 1992 and 2011, Ros led the cutting-edge partnership work of the International Business Leaders Forum. During that time, she co-created both the Partnering Initiative and the Partnership Brokers Project. A prolific author and widely recognised trainer, advisor and thought leader in the field of partnerships for development, she has worked for a range of agencies in all sectors and in many locations across the globe. Since 2012, Ros has also been PBA's Director of Strategy and Innovation.

Rob van Tulder is Full Professor of International Business-Society Management at RSM Erasmus University Rotterdam. He holds a PhD degree in social sciences from the University of Amsterdam. He has been a Visiting Professor in a number of universities and consultant to international organisations, multinational enterprises, NGOs and government ministries around the world. He is the Co-founder of the Department of Business-Society Management, one of the world's leading units for studying and teaching about the contribution to society of business and leaders. Dr van Tulder is presently the Academic Director of the Partnerships Resource Centre at the Rotterdam School of Management, which studies cross-sector partnerships for sustainable development between firms, NGOs and government.

Ning Xiao is the Deputy Director and Professor of National Institute of Parasitic Diseases, Chinese Centre for Disease Control and Prevention. He was a visiting scholar in the University of Tokyo, Japan with focus on malaria during 1997–1998, and pursued his PhD in Asahikawa Medical

University, Japan. Dr Xiao serves on a range of international health committees; as Strategic and Technical Advisory Group member for the World Health Organisation's Neglected Tropical Diseases; Regional Steering Committee member for the Global Fund's Regional Artemisinin-resistance Initiative and as a member of the Joint Coordinating Board for the TDR (Special Programme for Research and Training in Tropical Diseases). He works as a technical lead on two international cooperation projects for malaria control: the China–UK–Tanzania pilot project and Australia–China–PNG trilateral project.

Abbreviations

BATNA	Best Alternative to Negotiated Agreement
CBO	Community-Based Organisation
CCM	Country Coordinating Mechanism
CLLD	Community-led Local Development
COP	Community of Practice
CSO	Civil Society Organisation
CSR	Corporate Social Responsibility
DFID	Department for International Development (UK)
EC	European Commission
ECCP	European Code of Conduct on Partnership
ESF	European Social Fund
ESIF	European Structural and Investment Funds
EU	European Union
GFATM	Global Fund to Fight Aids, Tuberculosis and Malaria
IBLF	International Business Leaders Forum
INGO	International Non-Governmental Organisation
itdUPM	Innovation and Technology for Development Centre, Technical University of Madrid
MDG	Millennium Development Goal
M&E	Monitoring and Evaluation
MSA	Management Support Agency
NGO	Non-Governmental Organisation
NPM	New Public Management
ODI	Overseas Development Institute
PBA	Partnership Brokers Association
PBAS	Partnership Brokers Accreditation Scheme
PNG	Papua New Guinea
PPP	Public Private Partnership
SDG	Sustainable Development Goal
SWOT	Strengths, Weaknesses, Opportunities and Threats
UN	United Nations
UNICEF	United Nations Children's Fund
UPM	Technical University of Madrid

Foreword

How do we know where an idea comes from? What brings it into being? Whether it is truly 'ours' or whether we are merely the articulator of an idea whose time has come?

I don't have an answer to any of these questions but I do remember a colleague saying to me, many years ago now, that the best ideas are always 'ahead of the evidence'. This seems particularly pertinent in a book that aims to bridge knowledge and experience.

An idea based on evidence is, essentially, a hypothesis waiting to be proved, adjusted or disproved. An idea based on a 'hunch' or an intuition about what might be needed in future is, essentially, an opportunity to explore what we know we don't yet know.

What does it take to achieve truly effective, ground-breaking, partnerships? This was my burning question in the mid-1990s and was the direct result of observing many examples of 'partnerships' for sustainable development that seemed to fall so far short of both their stated ambition and their potential. The answer to the question suddenly became unexpectedly but utterly clear: become more intentional about partnership process management.

Some 20 years later, 'partnership brokering' (a more concise term than 'partnership process management') has become a globally recognised phenomenon and the role of the 'partnership broker' is increasingly accepted as a legitimate professional discipline underpinned by training and a formal accreditation procedure.

This publication is the first attempt, as far as we know, to capture the emerging partnership-brokering story. We have done our best to dance between art and science, ideas and evidence and to share our collective and individual understandings and insights. What we offer here is rooted in both research and practice – but, above all, it is a story. In the words of the writer, Ben Okri, in his meditation on storytelling, *The Mystery Feast*:

> A story exists in language, but lives in the imagination, in the memory. When does a story live? It only lives when it is read or heard. A story

is part telling, part hearing. Part writing, part reading. It dwells in the ambiguous place between the teller and the hearer, between the writer and the reader. The greatest story-tellers understand this magical fact, and use the magic of the in-between in their stories and in their telling.

None of us as contributors to *Shaping Sustainable Change: The Role of Partnership Brokering in Optimising Collaborative Action* believe that we are great storytellers, nor do we believe that we have all the answers, but we do have questions, experiences and ideas and we share them open-heartedly. What we rely on you, the reader, to bring is the magic of your imagination to penetrate the 'in-between' elements, drawing from your own evidence and intuitions.

This is what will breathe life into our words. This is where the magic and energy for the next instalment of the partnership brokering story will come from.

Ros Tennyson
North Wales
January 2018

Introduction

Leda Stott

'Partnership' is promoted globally as an essential requirement for the achievement of sustainable development.[1] While there is no standard definition of the term, the central premise of partnership is that by pooling their diverse resources, different social actors are able to achieve more together than they would by working alone. According to the United Nations:

> A successful sustainable development agenda requires partnerships between governments, the private sector and civil society. These inclusive partnerships built upon principles and values, a shared vision, and shared goals that place people and the planet at the centre, are needed at the global, regional, national and local level.[2]

Working in partnership, or what is commonly translated as 'working together',[3] is clearly not new; however, over the last 30 years, it has been refigured as an effective (and sometimes 'the' most effective) way of addressing development challenges.[4] This resurgence of interest in partnership has been linked to globalisation and the changing roles of the public and private sectors, and civil society.[5] A number of writers have argued that the rolling back of the state has created a push for stronger relationships between international agencies, governments and the private sector in order to cover service and funding gaps.[6] Public Private Partnerships (PPPs), in which the public sector contracts businesses to provide services or construct infrastructure, are highly mentioned in this regard.[7] Increasingly, however, attention is being paid to less transactional partnership arrangements involving a more diverse selection of stakeholders.[8]

This focus on multi-stakeholder partnerships is closely linked to the drive for imaginative solutions to address 'wicked problems' relating to complex issues such as resource limitations and ecological thresholds, poverty, inequality and social exclusion. Coupled with the promotion of democratic governance and citizen's participation in decision-making processes, an ambitious partnership agenda is emerging that seeks transformation at systems level through creative, horizontal relationships among a larger range of players and access to a wider resource base. With their 'broader, more collaborative and innovative approaches',[9] it is these multi-actor partnerships that are positioned as central to the United Nation's post-2015 development agenda and the achievement of the Sustainable Development Goals (SDGs).[10]

Although partnerships have the potential to transform through increased opportunities to harmonise, innovate and enhance sustainability, the actual process of building collaboration is often a challenge. Working across different sectors, organisations, groups and individuals can be both challenging and risky for those involved. As well as power differentials and 'unresolved or unstated competition'[11] between partners, the embedding of horizontal accountabilities requires a substantial investment of time and energy. It is no surprise then that, alongside demands for collaborative initiatives to demonstrate a positive impact, calls are also being made for more careful consideration of how partners can work together effectively to achieve results.[12] It is here that partnership brokering is critical.

The term 'partnership broker' was first coined by Ros Tennyson and Luke Wilde in 2000 to describe individuals or organisations that worked to steer and support the building of partnerships.[13] A few years before, Tennyson had referred to the importance of intermediaries who worked 'behind the scenes', often with little or no acknowledgement, to manage partnerships.[14] At the same time, writers such as David L. Brown outlined the role played by 'development bridging organisations' that could 'span the gaps among diverse stakeholders to promote social change',[15] while Huxham and Vangen drew attention to a new kind of leader working in collaborative initiatives.[16]

The role of partnership broker was formalised by Ros Tennyson and Michael Warner in 2003 when, working on behalf of the International Business Leaders Forum (IBLF) and the Overseas Development Institute (ODI), respectively, they established the Partnership Brokers Accreditation Scheme (PBAS). The aim of this initiative was to promote 'professionalism and integrity in brokering multi-stakeholder partnerships for sustainable development'.[17] The PBAS training programme included a short 4-day course followed by a period of workplace practice with support from a partnership mentor. In 2012, PBAS was absorbed in an independent Partnership Brokers Association (PBA) with an expanded remit to offer new training opportunities, share learning and offer services relating to partnership brokering. Over the last 15 years, 2,500 participants from a huge variety of different organisations, sectors and countries have completed training courses in partnership brokering and over 400 have been formally accredited as professional partnership brokers.[18]

This publication draws upon PBA's pioneering work to improve collaborative arrangements by acknowledging and professionalising the work of partnership brokers in stimulating, shaping, managing and tracking the process of working together. It aims to respond to the growing demand for information on the process side of building partnerships. To do this, the book uses materials, generated primarily from practice, to examine how partnership brokering contributes to the management of collaborative relationships so that they are better positioned to have a positive and sustainable development impact. As well as PBA's extensive international network, including its alumni, trainees and the organisations with which it works, it is hoped that the contents will also be of interest to academic institutions and business schools where partnership modules are taught, and to international agencies, government departments, businesses and NGOs that promote partnership brokering within their work.

Most of the authors have undergone PBA's partnership broker training and are familiar with PBA and its work. However, while PBA's practitioner orientation is at the core of the book, efforts have also been made to include wider perspectives and inputs from the academic arena. Indeed, a core objective of the publication is to try and bridge the gap that exists between academic and practitioner literatures on partnership so that they are mutually reinforcing. For practitioners, the fact that academic literature on partnership is dispersed across a range of disciplines, and largely inaccessible to those working outside university circles, poses enormous challenges. There is also a sense that academics need to go to greater lengths to draw from 'grey literature' pertaining to the cutting edge of partnership practice in order to enhance their theoretical work. Conversely, while noting a lack of detailed academic papers on the topic of partnership brokering, Rob van Tulder and Timo Kahlen observe in Chapter 3 that practice-based materials in this field tend not to be based on validated research. A heartfelt appeal is thus made for efforts to address these challenges through stronger connections between these two 'learning' worlds, particularly as sustainable development solutions that build upon the combined knowledge of both are so urgently required.

The book is divided into two parts: Part 1 explores the profile and key activities that may be carried out by partnership brokers, and the competencies and skills required to undertake this role. Part 2, meanwhile, shares examples of how partnership brokering works in practice in relation to different contexts, sectors and themes.

Part 1 begins with a chapter that positions the case for partnership brokering. Leda Stott suggests that, as well as creating a 'whole picture' from different partnership pieces, partnership brokering seeks a balance between contextual, interdisciplinary and technical knowledge and the use of skills such as connectivity, empathy, strategic thinking and diplomacy. Alongside the careful use of appropriate methodologies and tools, the promotion of these competencies can do much to ensure that development challenges are addressed more sustainably. Ros Tennyson follows this with an overview in Chapter 2 of the activities undertaken by partnership brokers, the skills and attributes they draw upon for their work and the challenges they may face. She distinguishes between internal and external partnership brokers, and explores their potential roles during a partnering cycle that includes phases of scoping and building; managing and maintaining; reviewing and revising, and sustaining outcomes.

The ensuing chapters in Part 1 of the book look at different aspects of partnership brokering and the knowledge, skills and competencies that these may require. In Chapter 3, Rob van Tulder and Timo Kahlen focus on the scoping phase of partnership-building. They suggest that partnership brokers can assist in creating a proper 'fit' between the type of 'wicked problems' that partnerships seek to address and an appropriate partnership form. Bulbul Baksi then looks more broadly in Chapter 4 at how partnership brokers can support the continuous formal and informal negotiation processes involved in building and managing partnerships across diverse partnership layers. As well as sharing information on the values that underpin partnering negotiations, Baksi suggests that partnership brokers may also develop skills such as active listening and empathy in order to promote dialogue where there is difference. She also endorses the usefulness of partnership principles when engaging in partnership negotiations. Julie Mundy builds upon this endorsement in Chapter 5 with an examination of how partnership brokering can be enhanced by adherence to a set of collaborative principles that include valuing diversity, equity, openness, mutual benefit and courage. Beyond simply positioning these principles as standard markers, however, Mundy emphasises that partnership brokering is about ensuring that they are fit for purpose in the different contexts in which partners work. She also outlines the ten principles of partnership brokering that PBA has developed in order to embed good practice.[19]

While the so-called 'soft' or interpersonal skills are clearly important for effective partnership brokering, Surinder Hundal makes clear in Chapter 6 that partnership brokering also depends upon technical competencies that ensure coherence and consistency in collaborative systems and processes. Noting that this requires much more than simple project management skills, Hundal suggests that partnership brokers who assume a 'managerial role' require the ability to ascertain when to be directional and when to be supportive or facilitative. This is a notion that is further explored by Ros Tennyson and Rachel Houghton in relation to leadership in collaborative arrangements. In Chapter 7, the authors question the relevance of traditional 'top-down' leadership models for partnership initiatives and, following an enquiry into other perspectives, suggest that partnership brokers may assume leadership responsibilities that are more fluid and diverse.

Working effectively in partnership clearly depends upon much more than the management of relationships between partners. In Chapter 8, Leda Stott, Marcia Dwonczyk and Joanna Pyres note that partnership brokers have a key role to play in encouraging the stronger participation of local actors in partnerships, as both potential partners and key external stakeholders. By promoting inclusion, reinforcing respect for diversity and building collaborative capacity, the authors suggest that partnership brokers can do much to ensure that collaborative relationships facilitate, inspire and 'empower rather than control and thereby disempower'.[20] This topic is also explored in Chapter 9 which focuses on review, revision and reflection processes in partnerships. Here, Joanne Burke reinforces the importance of a partnership broker's role in helping partners strengthen their collaborative mindsets and skills by promoting reflection on how partnership activities have been undertaken; assisting co-creation with diverse partners; supporting self-assessment by partners for partners and, in so doing, encouraging a dynamic process of continuous learning.

The second part of the book mirrors many of the issues and challenges raised by the authors in Part 1 with a selection of accounts from partnership brokers in practice. Several of these pieces are drawn from *Betwixt and Between, The Journal of Partnership Brokering*.[21] This journal was established by PBA in 2013 to provide a public platform for thought leadership, critical analysis and insights into partnership brokering practice from across cultures, sectors and geographies. Other examples included in this section of the book are derived from papers developed for PBA accreditation and from those wishing to share their experiences of partnership brokering more widely.[22] As a result, the reader is offered a flavour of the richness and diversity of partnership brokering experiences in relation to particular thematic, geographical and sector settings. Some centre on the roles assumed by internal or external partnership brokers (and sometimes both) working as individuals, teams or organisations in particular contexts, while others look at the application of partnership principles and the use of tools and methodologies by partnership brokers during different phases of partnership-building.

Part 2 begins with a set of specific sector challenges encountered by partnership brokers. Sara Nyanti's account in Chapter 10, of the accelerated implementation of a multilateral fund partnership programme for HIV and AIDS services in Nepal, highlights some of the ethical issues that a partnership broker might need to consider around capacity-building, monitoring and sustainability. In Chapter 11, Gillian Pearl explores the requirements for carrying out the dual role of project manager and internal partnership broker in private sector partnerships. She identifies some of the skills needed to deliver on both sets of responsibilities and explores how awareness and greater recognition can be given to partnership brokering in a private sector context. The third account comes from Spain where the Innovation and Technology Centre for Development at the Technical University of Madrid (itdUPM) operates as both an internal and external partnership broker. In Chapter 12, Carlos Mataix, Jaime Moreno Serna and Sara Romero outline itdUPM's efforts to generate an interdisciplinary environment for the co-creation of innovative technical and organisational solutions to address sustainable development challenges within a traditional academic setting.

The stories shared by Rafal Serafin and Martin Kalungu-Banda in Chapters 13 and 14, respectively, concern partnership brokering experiences related to small-scale agriculture and food systems. Serafin describes a partnership, brokered by the Polish Environmental Foundation in the Malopolska region of south Poland, to build a local food system and revitalise rural development, while Kalungu-Banda tells the story of his involvement in developing community capacity to provide fruit and vegetables for a South African supermarket outlet in a remote part of Zambia. While both authors emphasise the importance of particular contextual drivers in their work, they also draw attention to a series of generic factors that partnership brokers may find useful to take note of, including the importance of reflection, review and learning from the process of partnership-building. This is a thread that is discussed further by Marion McCahon and Nina Mitchelmore in Chapter 15. They describe how a review was designed by two external brokers to evaluate and strengthen partnerships within a cluster of heritage organisations in Newfoundland, Canada. In this case, the results of the review were used to build a new partnership model that drew from partnership brokering and positive community development practices.

A recurrent theme in many of the stories and experiences shared in this section of the book is how partnership brokers seek to address power dynamics that might limit the potential of different actors to maximise their participation. Small or local players, many of whom are perceived by traditional power holders as lacking in capacity, confidence or resources, often fall into this category. In Chapter 16, Donna Leigh Holden looks at this issue in relation to partnerships in the international development sector where power imbalances between key delivery partners and local civil society organisations often exist. She suggests that partnership brokers working in this field need to think creatively about how they can endorse principles of equity, openness and mutual benefit while also working to promote systems change at the highest levels. The need for action at policy level, particularly with the increasing emphasis in the development sector on engaging in more meaningful partnerships to deliver sustainable outcomes, is a theme that is taken up by Sarah MacCana, Moses Laman, Ning Xiao and Leanne Robinson in Chapter 17. Sharing lessons from their work within the trilateral Australia–China–Papua New Guinea Pilot Cooperation on Malaria Control Project, they suggest that positive and sustainable development impact in cooperation models of this nature can be enhanced through a development framework that adopts a well-designed partnership-based approach supported by a dedicated partnership broker.

We are reminded throughout this book that if collaborative working is to be sustainable, it cannot rely perpetually on partnership brokers, no matter how efficient or effective they may be. As well as partners stepping up to assume greater responsibility for the work of a partnership, it is also essential that the innovations developed through working collaboratively, and supported by partnership brokers, are integrated into standard systems and practices so that they become the *de facto* way of doing things. This process of institutionalisation, and the integration of change at individual, organisational and policy levels, rests significantly upon the exchange of partnership knowledge and information-sharing. If working in partnership is to deliver on its expectations for supporting a more sustainable world, learning about the process of partnership-building must be shared more deeply and systematically. To do this, increased efforts are needed to develop more creative learning frameworks and methodologies for capturing the process side of building collaborative experiences, with ample opportunities for reflection on what works and what does not. It is the intention of this book to make a contribution to this process.

Notes

1 See for example the United Nations: https://sustainabledevelopment.un.org/partnerships/ (accessed 9/2/2018).
2 http://www.un.org/sustainabledevelopment/globalpartnerships/ (accessed 9/2/2018).
3 See: Rein, M., Stott, L., Yambayamba, K., Hardman, S. & Reid, S. (2005) *Working Together, A Critical Analysis of Cross-Sector Partnerships in Southern Africa*, Cambridge: University of Cambridge Programme for Industry.
4 Tennyson, R. *The Partnering Toolbook*, London: IBLF; Nelson, J. (2002) *Building Partnerships: Cooperation between the United Nations System and the Private Sector*, New York: United Nations.
5 See: Rein et al. (2005) Op.cit.
6 See: Utting, P. & Zammit, A. (2009) United Nations–business partnerships: Good intentions and contradictory agendas. *Journal of Business Ethics*, 90: 39–56.
7 See: Miraftab, F. (2004) Public-Private Partnerships. The Trojan horse of neoliberal development? *Journal of Planning Education and Research*, 24: 89–101.
8 Caplan, K. & Stott, L. (2008) Defining our terms and clarifying our language. In L. Svensson & B. Nilsson (Eds.), *Partnership – As a Strategy for Social Innovation and Sustainable change*, Stockholm: Santérus Academic Press: 23–35.
9 Australian Public Service Commission (2012) Tackling wicked problems: A public policy perspective, available on: http://www.apsc.gov.au/publications-and-media/archive/publications-archive/tackling-wicked-problems (accessed 9/2/2018).
10 https://sustainabledevelopment.un.org/sdgsproposal (accessed 9/2/2018).
11 Caplan, K, Gomme, J., Mugabi, J. & Stott, L. (2007) *Assessing Partnership Performance: Understanding the Drivers for Success*, London: Building Partnerships for Development.
12 Ibid: 1.
13 Tennyson, R. & Wilde, L. (2000) *The Guiding Hand: Brokering Partnerships for Sustainable Development*, Turin: United Nations Staff College & London: Prince of Wales Business Leaders Forum.

14 Tennyson, R. (1998) *Managing Partnerships: Tools for mobilising the public sector, business and civil society as partners in development*, London: International Business Leaders Forum: 63.
15 Brown, D.L. (1999) Development Bridging Organizations and Strategic Management for Social Change, *IDR Reports*, 10 (3): 4.
16 Huxham, C. & Vangen, S. (2000) Leadership in the shaping and implementation of collaboration agendas: How things happen in a (not quite) joined-up world. *Academy of Management Journal*, 43 (6): 1159–1175.
17 See: http://partnershipbrokers.org/w/about/history/ (accessed 9/2/2018).
18 See: www.partnershipbrokers.org/training
19 See: http://partnershipbrokers.org/w/brokering/principles-of-good-practice/
20 Eisler, R. (2014) Cultural Transformation: Building a Partnership World, *Kosmos*, Spring-Summer, 2014: 52.
21 See: http://partnershipbrokers.org/w/journal/ (accessed 9/2/2018).
22 In some cases, due to sensitivities around content, identities and place, names have been removed and general lessons have been drawn out for the reader.

Part I

Partnership brokering
Why, what and how?

Chapter 1

The case for partnership brokering

Leda Stott

The systems scientist and cultural historian, Rianne Eisler, views the tensions between social systems that are based upon domination and those that are based on partnership as having shaped human history.[1] She describes the former as a top-down system that relies upon physical, psychological and economic control and the latter as a democratic and egalitarian model based upon relations of mutual respect, accountability and benefit. It is Eisler's belief that the espousal of a partnership model is essential for building a sustainable future and that the momentum towards this is accelerating.[2]

There has certainly been heightened interest in working in partnership in recent years. Partnership solutions are widely promoted as the key to addressing societal challenges, particularly 'wicked problems'. These are problems that, because of their complexity, require collaboration between different individuals, organisations and sectors. Indeed, multi-actor partnerships are positioned as central to the achievement of the UN Sustainable Development Goals and post-2015 development agenda,[3] and collaborative arrangements are being adopted within and across an enormous range of sectors and settings: in both development and humanitarian contexts; among businesses, NGOs, international agencies and public authorities; addressing themes such as education, water and sanitation, health and employment; and operating at local, national, regional and international levels. The benefits of pooling the resources, knowledge and expertise of a diverse range of societal actors include the development of more innovative, coordinated and focused approaches to pressing challenges.[4]

However, while the case for partnership has clearly been made, less attention has been given to how collaborative initiatives are shaped and supported so that they can maximise their potential. Senge, Hamilton and Kania[5] believe that the success of such arrangements rests upon 'system leaders' who are able to 'catalyse and guide' systemic change by helping people to build a shared understanding of complex problems, foster reflection and 'more generative conversations' and move away from 'reactive problem-solving to co-creating the future'.[6] Although Nelson Mandela is used as an example of someone encapsulating these attributes, they stress that the core capabilities for promoting effective collective action can also be learnt and developed by less renowned individuals. This affirmation is echoed by a growing number of partnership researchers and practitioners who have noted the important role played by 'bridging agents', 'bridge builders', 'boundary spanners', 'change agents', 'engagers', 'facilitators' and 'intermediaries' to support collaborative arrangements in diverse contextual settings.[7] Here, we use the overarching term **partnership brokering** to describe the work of those who provide the 'connective tissue' that enables the partners involved in collaborative alliances to work together optimally and augment their ability to achieve positive societal transformation.

What is partnership brokering?

Partnership brokering is fundamentally about providing and nurturing an enabling space for the development of successful partnerships.[8] Early references to the role of 'partnership broker' describe it as one that may be assumed by an individual or an organisation that mediates between different parties to promote the work of a partnership.[9] As Ros Tennyson explains, partnership brokers may be internal, those who work from within a partnership, and external, those who operate from outside a partnership.[10] Whatever the form assumed, evidence suggests that collaborative arrangements will require and draw upon the services of a partnership broker at some stage in their lifetime.[11] Tennyson further states that their role is often low key and may sometimes not be obvious, '...but without it the partnership would have been significantly less successful if, indeed, it had got started at all'.[12]

Why is partnership brokering needed?

Partnership brokering is critical for a range of reasons. As well as getting the process of partnering started, it is central to the building and maintaining of partnerships, and important for the promotion and sharing of learning about how partnership works (or does not) in different contexts. According to Manning and Roessler, the support of 'bridging agents' 'who interact across multiple boundaries and translate ambiguous conditions into collaborative opportunities and constraints' is central to the development of effective long-term alliances.[13] The implication is that, in a fast-changing world where the development problems we face are increasingly stark and where spaces for debate are contested, identifying and navigating spaces for collaboration is more necessary than ever. By keeping abreast of contextual developments and variations, and anticipating, diagnosing and responding to situations rapidly, partnership brokers are needed to assist prospective partners to read different environments, make decisions about whether or not to work in partnership and adapt collaborative efforts to changing circumstances so that they become more sustainable.[14]

Michael Warner asserts that the complexity and challenges of building cross-sector relationships require a form of 'neutral' support to achieve consensus and clarity throughout the relationship,

> ...particular where there are large numbers of partners involved, or where partners have conflicting work cultures and ethics. In these circumstances, an invitation to a mutually acceptable third party to broker consensus at strategic points in the partnering process, such as identifying potential partners or negotiating a Partnering Agreement, becomes not only defensible, but often decisive.[15]

Partnership brokering, however, entails much more than simply bringing partners together at particular junctures; it is also about guiding, supporting and challenging those involved to develop solutions that add value to their work and to society as a whole. Increasingly, this requires promoting 'innovative' and 'transformative' approaches to partnering. Such approaches incorporate methodologies that seek to question and reflect upon standard ways of doing things. In this sense, partnership brokers can play a role that moves collaboration beyond simple exchanges and transactions that are ad hoc or short-term in nature to connections that support lasting systems change. Partnership brokering is thus not just about fostering partnership initiatives but also involves testing and challenging so that we move beyond 'business as usual' models and develop opportunities for the achievement of more sustainable solutions to development challenges. This work inevitably requires a delicate balancing between 'the ideology of collaborative working and the pragmatism needed to get things done'[16], and is likely to require dedication to a range of different issues, some of which are outlined below.

Providing contextual understanding

Partnership brokering can assist an understanding of complex problems in particular contexts. The ability to see the 'bigger picture' and assess how collaborative efforts that address systemic issues might be developed within specific operational context is central to this. Leadbeater describes this as the capacity to be 'rooted and cosmopolitan', possessing deep familiarity with the local context while also connecting to international ideas and insights.[17] Partnership brokering can therefore offer what might be described as a translation service in which both top-down and bottom-up connections are enhanced as international or national requirements are made sense of at regional and local levels, and given coherence.[18] Such a liaison role also involves making linkages between policy and practice, and between geographical, sociohistoric, sectoral, organisational and individual contexts.

This ability is similar to Gladwell's depiction of the role played by connectors who promote innovation: 'They are the translators: they take ideas and information from a highly specialised world and translate them into a language the rest of us can understand'.[19] As well as assisting coordination among different players and supporting the promotion of multi-level governance that partnership ostensibly espouses, Waddock notes that this cross-boundary connecting function is central to the promotion of 'new ways of understanding the world'.[20]

Partnership brokering can also assist in ensuring that partnership initiatives work within relevant policy and regulatory environments, particularly when partnership aims relate to achieving national development goals and country targets. In recent work on partnerships that address access to basic services, for example, partnership brokers have played a crucial role in ensuring that linkages are developed with national, regional and local levels of government.[21] By engaging with the public sector in this way, an enabling environment has been promoted in which partnership is favoured by more progressive legislation for collaborative endeavours tackling access to services such as energy, waste management, maternal health and water and sanitation.

Facilitating meaningful dialogue

Warner believes that partnership brokering can play a role in assisting a move away from 'adversarial' approaches towards more respectful forms of communication and interest-based negotiation.[22] Richard Sennett takes this a step further by suggesting that cooperation demands a process of communication that goes beyond win–win scenarios to the pursuit of 'dialogic exchange' in which emphasis is placed on understanding rather than convincing those who have different viewpoints to one's own.[23] This kind of connection relies upon active listening and the ability to step into the shoes of others. According to Krznaric, such empathy is central to collaboration and vital for '...shifting us from a *self-interest frame* of thinking to a *common-interest frame*, where our underlying mode of thought is structured by a concern for both ourselves and others'.[24]

Endorsing principled behaviour

Tennyson and Mundy suggest that 'people of stature and integrity who understand the value of compromise for a greater good' are needed to help address increasingly complex mutual challenges.[25] There are echoes here of Greenleaf's call for 'servant leaders' who possess personal morality and integrity, and who are able to engage in 'self-reflection that counters personal hubris'.[26] This requires a commitment to inclusivity and an ability to assist those working in partnership to 'understand the issues underlying the challenge and to build their capacity to address them collaboratively'.[27] Scharmer and Kaufer further suggest that such individuals must be willing to undertake the journey 'from ego-system to eco-system awareness, or from *me* to *we*'.[28] Within this transition, the ability to let go of 'self' and accept that others will take the work forward is essential: 'System leaders need to have a strategy, but the ones who are most effective learn to "follow the energy" and set aside their strategy when unexpected paths and opportunities emerge'.[29] Put more simply, 'good brokers aim to work themselves out of a job'.[30]

Promoting accountability

Simon Zadek[31] has consistently argued that partnership arrangements need to demonstrate accountability if they are to be effective. According to Caplan, this involves partners being accountable to one another, to external stakeholders and, if they exist, to relevant national or thematic regulatory frameworks.[32] Promotion of accountability to partners and stakeholders demands the following: compliance – so that partners know what is required of them to achieve objectives; transparency – so that information is available on partnership decisions and related actions, performance and expected outcomes; and responsiveness – so that stakeholder feedback is carefully considered and responded to, and reasons why a particular decision or action has been taken can be publicly demonstrated.[33] Ensuring that these different elements are addressed is a central part of partnership brokering and requires particular skills in the complex processes of planning, communication and management across different individuals and groups. As well as being perceived as fair by the parties involved, partnership administrative systems also need to be clear and functional so that collaborative activities can be carried out efficiently.

Bringing in unheard voices

Working in partnership demands a move away from hierarchical organisational or traditional project-based ways of working to espousing horizontal processes in which decision-making and outcomes are shared by partners and, where appropriate, respond adequately to the needs of other stakeholders, particularly those who may bear risks as a result of the activities of a partnership. While power dynamics are always likely to be present, collaborative relationships rely upon concerted efforts to ensure full participation of all their members in decision-making processes and the equitable valuing of resources that each partner may bring to the table.[34] Such an approach demands that, where relevant, the voices of local, marginalised or vulnerable stakeholders also need to be included appropriately in partnership-building, particularly when they are the focus of collaborative activities. This focus builds upon Scharmer and Kaufer's premise that 'the goal must be to co-sense, co-inspire, and co-create an emerging future for their system that values the well-being of all rather than just a few'.[35]

Leading differently

Partnership brokering has been positioned as a 'new' form of 'cross-boundary leadership' that promotes collective thinking and bridge-building[36] and as 'integrative leadership' across individual, group, organisational and inter-organisational levels.[37] Tennyson further suggests that partnership brokering is needed to create clarity in a complex world, facilitate interaction between diverse groups of people, carry a level of risk on behalf of others and inspire with a vision of a more cooperative future.[38] She views these as attributes of a 'non-directive leadership' that is fundamental to good partnership brokering and sees parallels between partnership brokers and 'servant leaders'[39] who, as well as encouraging the growth and development of others, also 'initiate action, are goal-oriented, are dreamers of great dreams, are good communicators, are able to withdraw and re-orient themselves, and are dependable, trusted, creative, intuitive, and situational'.[40]

Eisler suggests that the embedding of a partnership culture requires leaders and managers that 'seek and consider input from others' as opposed to those that 'give orders that must be obeyed'.[41] This does not mean that a firm, directive hand is not needed. As observed by Huxham and Vangen, partnership brokering combines pragmatism and idealism by blending both a facilitative and a directive role at different phases of partnership-building.[42] Partnership brokers thus have an important shaping and steering role to play. Escobar describes this as a process of 'scripting' in which provision is made for 'a structuring force intended to foster certain forum dynamics and an overall narrative for participants to take away'.[43] In the spirit of collaboration, it is also true that leadership may be assumed by different individuals over time and that partnership brokering is '...typically a collective process involving multiple individuals from both inside and outside partnering organisations'.[44]

Reviewing, reflecting and learning

Partnership brokering is also crucial in another way: it can facilitate learning by promoting deeper understanding of partnerships. An essential part of this involves partnership brokers allowing as much space as possible for experimentation and ensuring that an ongoing review of both partnership results and processes is in place. Partnership brokering is also about providing a 'safe space' for meaningful dialogue through exchanges that are both respectful and challenging. Such conversations stimulate reflection and deeper learning from both diverse approaches, and from perceived successes and failures. Partnership brokers also have another role here, that of supporting the construction of a partnership narrative and building its institutional memory so that the learning from collaborative experiences is not lost.

Conclusion

In her article on memes[45] and values in a fast-changing world, Sandra Waddock describes the important role played by those who are able to assist sense-making processes that promote long-term system change. In order to undertake the important task of reframing, rethinking and reshaping how people view and connect with the world around them, Waddock suggests the need for 'intellectual shamans (along with shamans in other realms)'.[46] As well as being sense-makers and connectors, shamans are also described as healers: 'underlying their work is the notion of creating a better world, discipline, theory, or set of practices'.[47] The notion of a healing function is one that is increasingly central to the process of partnership brokering as now, more than ever, our sustainable future depends upon individuals and organisations that are able to reconcile, restore and replenish through collaboration.

Notes

1 Eisler, R. (2008) Our great creative challenge: Rethinking human nature – and recreating society. In R. Richards (Ed.), *Everyday Creativity and New Views of Human Nature: Psychological, Social, and Spiritual Perspectives,* Washington, DC: American Psychological Association, xiii: 275.
2 Ibid: 277.
3 United Nations. (2014) The road to dignity by 2030: ending poverty, transforming all lives and protecting the planet. *Synthesis Report of the Secretary-General on the Post-2015 Sustainable Development Agenda,* New York: United Nations.
4 See Tennyson, R. (2004) *The Partnering Toolbook,* London: International Business Leaders Forum: 5.
5 Senge, P., Hamilton, H. & Kania, J. (2015) The dawn of system leadership. *Stanford Social Innovation Review,* Winter: 27–33.
6 Ibid: 28–29.
7 For the use of 'bridging agent' see: Manning, S. & Roessler, D. (2014) The formation of cross-sector development partnerships: How bridging agents shape project agendas and longer-term alliances. *Journal of Business Ethics,* 123 (3): 528; for 'bridge-builders' see Brown, D.L. (2015) Bridge-building for social transformation. *Stanford Social Innovation Review,* Winter: 34–39; for 'boundary spanner' see: Williams, P. (2010) Special agents: The nature and role of boundary spanners. *Paper to the ESRC Research Seminar Series-Collaborative Futures: New Insights from Intra and Inter-Sectoral Collaborations,* University of Birmingham; for 'engagers' see: Escobar, O. (2015) Scripting deliberative policy-making: Dramaturgic policy analysis and

engagement know-how. *Journal of Comparative Policy Analysis: Research and Practice*, 17 (3): 269–285.

8   Ibid: 11.

9   Tennyson, R. & Wilde, L. (2000) *The Guiding Hand, Brokering Partnerships for Sustainable Development*, Turin: United Nations Staff College & London: Prince of Wales Business Leaders Forum: 33.

10 Tennyson, R. (2005) *The Brokering Guidebook, Navigating Effective Sustainable Development Partnerships*, London: The Partnering Initiative, International Business Leaders Forum: 11–12.

11 Ibid: 8.

12 Ibid.

13 Manning & Roessler (2014) Op.cit.

14 Stott, L. & Scoppetta, A. (2013) Adding value: The broker role in partnerships for employment and social inclusion in Europe. *Betwixt & Between, The Journal of Partnership Brokering*, (1).

15 Warner, M. (2003) Partnerships for sustainable development: Do we need partnership brokers? *Paper for Overseas Development Institute*, London: Overseas Development Institute: 8–9.

16 Huxham, C. & Vangen, S. (2004) Doing things collaboratively: Realizing the advantage or succumbing to inertia? *Organizational Dynamics*, 33 (2): 199.

17 Leadbeater, C. (2014) *The Frugal Innovator, Creating Change on a Shoestring Budget*, London: Palgrave Macmillan: 145.

18 Stott & Scoppetta (2013) Op.cit.

19 Gladwell, M. (2000) *The Tipping Point*, London: Abacus: 200.

20 Waddock, S. (2015) Reflections: Intellectual shamans, sensemaking, and memes in large system change. *Journal of Change Management*, 15 (4): 270.

21 Stott, L. (2014) *Partnerships for Innovation in Access to Basic Services*, itdUPM & MIF, IaDB, Madrid & Washington, DC: 32.

22 Warner (2003) Op.cit: 9.

23 Sennett, R. (2013) *Together, The Rituals and Pleasures of Cooperation*, London: Penguin Books: 78–83.

24 Krznaric, R. (2014) The empathy effect, how empathy drives common values, social justice and environmental action, *Paper for Friends of the Earth*: 4.

25 Tennyson, R. & Mundy, J. (2017) *Partnership Brokers in Action, Skills, Tools, Approaches, Partnership Brokers Training, Course Workbook*, 2nd Edition. London: Partnership Brokers Association: 21.

26 Definition of Servant Leadership, http://toservefirst.com/definition-of-servant-leadership.html (accessed 9/2/2018), and see also: Greenleaf, R.K. (1977) *Servant Leadership – A Journey into the Nature of Legitimate Power and Greatness*, New York: Paulist Press.

27 Tennyson & Mundy (2017) Op.cit: 22.

28 Scharmer, O. & Kaufer, K. (2013) *Leading from the Emerging Future: From Ego-System to Eco-System Economics*, San Francisco: Berret Koehler Publisher: 16.

29 Senge, Hamilton & Kania (2015) Op.cit: 32.

30 Tennyson & Mundy (2017) Op.cit: 22.

31 Zadek, S. (2007) Collaborative governance: The new multilateralism for the 21st century. *Global Development 2.0*, Washington, DC: Brookings Institute.

32 Caplan, K. (2005) Partnership accountability: Unpacking the concept. *Practitioner Note Series*, London: Building Partnerships for Development.

33 Ibid.

34 Huxham & Vangen (2004) Op.cit: 193.

35 Scharmer & Kaufer (2013) Op.cit: 12.
36 Brown (2015) Op.cit.
37 Crosby, B.C. & Bryson, J.B. (2010) Integrative leadership and the creation and maintenance of cross-sector collaborations. *The Leadership Quarterly*, 21: 228.
38 Tennyson (2005) Op.cit: 9.
39 See Greenleaf (1977) Op.cit, and https://www.greenleaf.org/.
40 See: http://toservefirst.com/definition-of-servant-leadership.html (accessed 9/2/2018).
41 Eisler, R. (2007) *The Real Wealth of Nations: Creating a Caring Economics*, Berrett-Koehler Publishers: 113.
42 Huxham & Vangen (2004) Op.cit: 199.
43 Escobar (2015) Op.cit: 278.
44 Manning & Roessler (2014) Op.cit.
45 The ideas, behaviours and ways of doing things that spreads between people within a culture.
46 Waddock (2015) Op.cit.
47 Ibid.

Chapter 2

What do partnership brokers do?

Ros Tennyson

Having explored the case for partnership brokering, it is now appropriate to define the role, activities, skills and attributes of those operating as partnership brokers and to consider partnership brokering as a distinct and different professional vocation. The concept of a 'partnership broker' was first coined by Tennyson and Wilde in 2000,[1] eight years after the Rio Earth Summit (1992) saw governments, businesses and NGOs meeting together for the first time at a strategic global level to address the issue of sustainable development. In Rio, the 'why' and the 'what' of the partnership imperative were articulated quite clearly. What was almost entirely ignored was the 'how'. Which may explain why, after the Summit was over, very little changed.

It is clear that whilst partnering has become the default mechanism for delivering aid and development programmes and is now a 'Sustainable Development Goal' in its own right, there is still a long way to go in optimising partnership potential. Partnering is practised by many as if it is simply 'business as usual' with a new name, instead of a significantly different way of planning and operating that requires: changes in mindset, courage to challenge assumptions and willingness to break habitual behaviour patterns. Alongside this, there is the additional challenge that many of those operating as 'partners' claim to be too busy to dedicate the time it invariably takes to partner well. With these prevailing conditions, it is hardly surprising that partnerships have made somewhat disappointingly slow progress. With so much working against them, how then can they be expected to get anywhere near achieving the hoped-for goals and impacts that the world so desperately needs?

Partnerships that work effectively vary considerably in their characteristics and ways of operating, but the one thing they seem to have in common is that somewhere, if you delve deeply enough, there is someone busily co-ordinating, quietly driving, systematically working through challenges and tirelessly process-managing the relationship, without which the partnership might never have got beyond the signatures on the collaboration agreement (if, indeed, there is one). Often unacknowledged, and rarely the person in the limelight, these individuals provide the hidden glue or connective tissue that holds the partnership together. Sometimes, they themselves do not recognise the significant role they are playing; they are just getting on with it, doing what they see is necessary to the best of their ability. Indeed, one common characteristic of those in this role is modesty.

What is a 'partnership broker'?

A partnership broker is an active "go-between" who supports partners in navigating their partnering journey by helping them to create a map, plan their route, choose their mode of transport and change direction when necessary.[2]

This is the first definition of a partnership broker ever used and to date no others that we know of have replaced it. Based on the metaphor of partnering as a journey, it is quite general and perhaps a little whimsical but this does, we believe, convey a reasonable starting point for an understanding of the role. The term 'partnership broker' was chosen to imply something more multi-dimensional than either facilitation or coordination.[3] Although facilitating and coordinating are very important partnership brokering roles, the term 'broker' implies a more proactive and comprehensive form of engagement.[4]

Naming and defining the role were intended to help frame and highlight both its purpose and why it matters. This has been critically important in giving the role coherence and status. Now, nearly 20 years later, the term is increasingly understood and internationally recognised. Those operating as partnership brokers are being taken seriously and more than 2,500 people from all sectors (business, non-profit, international agencies and the public sector), and from widely different contexts, have completed a specialist Partnership Brokers Training.[5] Of these, more than 400 have become formally accredited as professional partnership brokers. It is more than a start.

Types of partnership broker

Every partnership is unique and the expectations and requirements from those acting as partnership brokers, as well as the possibilities and opportunities for partnership brokering, vary enormously. There is an important distinction to be made between those operating from within one of the partner organisations, acting as both a partner representing their own organisation's interests and as the partnership broker working for the benefit of the whole partnership, and those working as independent partnership brokers contracted by the partnership or one of the partner organisations on behalf of the partnership. The differences between the two types of partnership broker and the types of challenges each might face are explored below.

Internal partnerships brokers are those who carry the responsibility for shaping and supporting the partnership itself whilst also preparing their own organisation to be effective partners. They are therefore accountable to both their own organisation and to other partners. This is likely to be an ongoing arrangement, often with the same person in the role. One common challenge of being an internal partnership broker is the wearing of two hats: one, as a representative of their own organisation in the partnership and the other, as someone trying their best to work with partners in ways that are equitable and do not favour their own organisation. This can be quite a 'dance' but it can be done. Of course, an advantage of being an internal partnership broker is knowing the context and the partners well and being there for the long (or, at least, medium) term, thereby providing both genuine insights and continuity.

The tasks that an internal partnership broker typically undertakes, whether formally or informally, include the following:

- supporting their organisation to be effective partners;
- representing their organisation in a partnership;
- working to shape/build the partnership and manage the partnering process;
- coaching partners in order to build their partnering capacity;
- helping partners decide when an external partnership broker may be useful or necessary.

External partnership brokers are those operating as independent third parties contracted to undertake specific tasks because they bring specific expertise and/or a form of external 'authority'. This is likely to be an episodic arrangement with partnership brokers being contracted in only as and when needed. The challenges of being an external partnership broker are rather different (in some ways, the opposite) to those faced by their internal counterparts; they may be perceived as being (and, perhaps, truly are) non-aligned in their relationship to each partner but this is, at least in part, because they know far less about the context and the history than an internal partnership broker would. Even though they may bring rich and diverse experience of partnering to the task, they invariably have less personal involvement and are more distant from the realities that partners face.

An external partnership broker typically undertakes tasks that include assisting an initiating/lead organisation or the partners as a group with:

- scoping the early stages of a partnership;
- problem-solving and facilitating difficult conversations;
- coaching and mentoring key individuals;
- advising on or undertaking health checks or partnership reviews;
- writing learning case studies;
- helping partners to explore moving on options.

External Broker	
ANIMATOR	PIONEER
Reactive	**Proactive**
Mandate	**Mandate**
COORDINATOR	INNOVATOR
Internal Broker	

Figure 2.1 Types of partnership broker defined by where they are 'located'.

Interestingly, the majority of those seeking training in partnership brokering skills operate as internal partnership brokers at the time of their training.[6] This may be due to lack of funding available for external partnership brokers or to a level of 'consultancy fatigue' which leads organisations to try and work with 'in-house' rather than seek 'bought in' solutions. Our contention is that, since they can be seen as having different functions, both are important to fulfil different purposes.

The separation of 'internal' from 'external' may help to demystify some elements of the partnership brokering role but there are other ways of viewing the different types of partnership brokering approaches that exist. How much licence or authority should a partnership broker have? Can they, for example, initiate and shape a partnership? Or is their role always that of supporting a partnership that has been initiated by others? We describe this as the difference between a 'proactive' and a 'reactive' mandate. This is not related to their personal preferences, characteristics or competencies per se (though it might be good to know that the mandate they have aligns well with their preferences and partnership brokering style) but to do with the position in which they find themselves (see Figure 2.1).

Some partnership brokers (those with a reactive mandate) are expected to 'serve' the partnership and some partnership brokers (those with a proactive mandate) are expected to 'lead' the partnership (See Chapter 7).

What do partnership brokers actually do?

The partnering cycle (see Figure 2.2) is a useful framework through which to consider the changing roles and tasks any partnership may require from the partnership brokering function since it helps to remind partners that a **partnership** goes through a clear cycle of activity as much as the **projects** the partnership is undertaking.

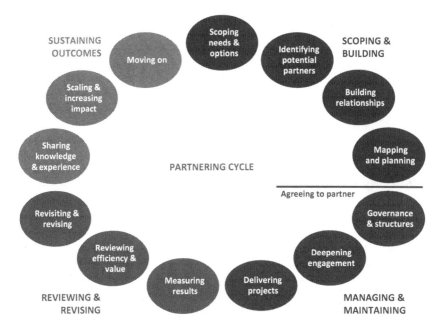

Figure 2.2 The partnering cycle.
Source: PBA.

Partnership brokering means far more than making connections and managing relationships – though these are both important. It can involve a wide range of activities during the life of a partnership that may run over many years (see Table 2.1).[7] It is worth noting, however, that it will not, or even should, always be the same person undertaking all partnership brokering tasks. In this regard, it may be better to consider what partnership brokering roles and tasks may be necessary at different stages and how different individuals can best take on the partnership brokering role, handing over to others as necessary.

In addition to these roles and tasks within the partnership, partnership brokers may also need to think more laterally about other areas of work and stakeholders beyond the partner group itself. A wider view of partnership brokering roles can be summarised as follows:

Within a partner organisation:

- **Enabling** internal teams to collaborate more effectively themselves;
- **Building** more coherence within the organisation for a partnering approach;
- **Creating** 'fit for purpose' systems to support partnerships appropriately.

Table 2.1 Potential partnership brokering roles and tasks during the partnering cycle

Phase	Potential roles	Potential tasks
Scoping and building	• Scoping the partnering possibilities • Exploring drivers, expectations and underlying interests of proposed partners • Modelling core partnering principles to help build good partnering behaviour • Conveying the importance of differentiating between the partnership and its projects • Assisting potential partners in working through challenges and build genuine alignment out of their diverse values and approaches	• Making the case for a partnership approach to key stakeholders (including potential partners/ donors/decision-makers/ beneficiaries) • Exploring options (potential partner organisations, activities, models) • Energising and engaging key players in the partnering process • Managing expectations of partners and other stakeholders • Negotiating an appropriate collaboration agreement for the partnership
Managing and maintaining	• Ensuring partners are contributing to the partnership and its project(s) as agreed • Encouraging partners to co-create and abide by appropriate governance arrangements • Building partner capacities to partner effectively and to optimise the partnership • Deepening engagement of partner organisations • Helping partners to work through complex internal and external challenges • Assisting in continually improving the partnership's performance • Enabling partners to explore new ways of transforming systems	• Securing agreed resource contributions from partners/donors • Embedding governance arrangements • Developing a comprehensive communication plan • Building individual and organisational partnering capabilities • Helping partners to secure internal buy-in and navigate internal barriers • Working constructively to address both simple and complex challenges • Agreeing benchmarks for partnership reviews • Fostering innovative thinking and helping partners take and manage risks when it is necessary to be innovative and transformative

(*Continued*)

Phase	Potential roles	Potential tasks
Reviewing and revising	• Encouraging partners to adopt an attitude of enquiry whereby learning is seen as a central partnership • Supporting partners in reviewing the partnership's added value and effectiveness • Encouraging partners to capture and share their partnership's story with others • Helping partnerships to become more efficient and effective • Building understanding of successful partnering by encouraging partners to share their lesson learned • Guiding partners to plan for sustaining outcomes and moving on	• Agreeing and co-creating review procedures • Exploring added value to partners and unexpected benefits/costs/outcomes • Helping to draw out lessons and capture deeper layers of information • Making any changes to the partnering arrangements deemed necessary • Assisting in revising the collaboration agreement • Brainstorming new ideas/developments • Agreeing what to share in the public domain and how • Encouraging partners to think about sustainability and moving on options
Sustaining outcomes	• Exploring moving on options and supporting agreed decisions • Ensuring closure/moving on processes are implemented collaboratively • Helping partners celebrate, learn from and share their partnership's story and their partnering experiences • Checking out that project outcomes are on course to be sustained/embedded/transferred and/or scaled	• Co-creating a sustainability action plan and supporting implementation • Bringing a range of 'moving on' options to the table for discussion • Recognising and celebrating the partnership's achievements • Reaching agreement on communications/information for the public domain • Identifying further spheres of influence and champions • Managing all closure/moving on procedures with care and attention to detail

Source: Adapted from PBA (2012) *What do Partnership Brokers Do? An Enquiry into Practice*, London: Partnership Brokers Association.

Between the partners:

- **Operating** continuously between the partners (and sometimes, on behalf of partners, with their own stakeholders) – as outlined in Table 2.1.

Beyond the partnership:

- **Explaining** the partnership to the partnership's own stakeholders (e.g. donors, policymakers, target groups, etc.);
- **Intermediating** between partners and non-partner organisations;
- **Positioning** the partnership in relation to other initiatives.

Key skills for partnership brokers

Whether a partnership broker is operating in an internal or external capacity or to a reactive or proactive mandate, there are some key skills that, to a greater or lesser extent, they will all need (Table 2.2).

Table 2.2 Partnership brokering skills

Skills	Notes
Negotiation in ways that reveal underlying interests and build on diversity	Assisting partners in working through differences of opinion, approaches and values in ways that explore their underlying interests, vision and aspirations. Negotiating in ways that help them develop insight, empathy and understanding for each other's perspectives. This is fundamental for building greater equity and added value out of diversity.
Facilitation of meetings, working groups and workshops	Promoting a strong and effective working relationship between partners by building on principles of equity, transparency, mutual benefit and embracing diversity. This is likely to require the facilitation of some difficult conversations and even the management of conflict/confrontation in a measured and skilled way.
Management of groups and group processes	Understanding something of the nature of groups and how group dynamics can assist or destabilise a partnership is an important element for partnership brokers to take on. This does not mean managing groups to be compliant; rather, it requires a level of confidence in managing group processes so that those in the group (partners) feel safe enough to challenge each other and penetrate more deeply into underlying issues and tensions.
Understanding and managing complexity	Helping partners to 'de-layer' issues as well as managing and recording sometimes complicated, sometimes complex data requires really astute listening and sense-making skills. It also entails developing a frame of reference that is acceptable to the partners together and relies upon the ability to think, speak and write concisely and clearly.

(Continued)

Skills	Notes
Communication (oral and written) within and beyond the partnership	Communicating with precision in order to fully represent the nuances of a discussion or the range of views on a particular issue. Partnership brokers need to understand and articulate the frames of reference used by the partners. They may also need to present partnering concepts, frameworks and examples so that partners have access to the knowledge and experience of others.
Coaching and mentoring	Working collaboratively and role modelling effective co-working, shared responsibility in action and collaborative decision-making processes. As a partnership progresses and, hopefully matures, the partnership broker will transfer responsibilities to partners (or project staff). This involves stepping back from a front-line role and working in the background to support and coach others as they build partnering and partnership brokering skills.
Strengthening institutional capacity to partner effectively	Increasing and deepening the engagement of partner organisations as well as supporting their efforts to become more 'fit for purpose' in their partnering approach. Partnership brokers will also need to help partners build governance and accountability procedures as the partnership itself becomes more 'institutionalised'.
Advising on how to conduct health checks, reviews and revisions to the partnering arrangements	Promoting the idea of regular health checks and reviews to ensure that partners remain engaged and that the partnership is still animated, productive, achieving its intended results and generating value for the partners. As someone with close knowledge of the partnership, the partnership broker may be uniquely placed to facilitate such reviews themselves or to brief and support an external reviewer. They are, in any event, likely to have a critical role in helping the partners to revise the partnership.

Desirable attributes in a partnership broker

> The success of any intervention is entirely dependent on the interior condition of the intervener.[8]

Good partnership brokers work consciously and conscientiously on their 'interior condition'. Partnership brokering is more than just a combination of skills and a simple list of skill sets does not adequately capture the more nuanced aspects of the role. One could argue, as suggested by the quote above, that it is as much **who you are** as **what you do** or **how you do it**. Partnership brokers (perhaps comparable in some ways to mediators or peacekeepers) will, ideally, bring subtle additional attributes to the role, some of which are outlined in Table 2.3.

Table 2.3 Attributes of a partnership broker

Attribute	Description
Capacity for empathy	Being fully present, paying attention and using observation and active listening skills to understand the diverse perspectives, desires and concerns of partners. Getting inside their perspectives to help them to process these through a partnership lens. It is also a capacity for warm engagement.
Confidence to hold space	Enabling partners to work through ambiguities and/or challenging issues that may have no immediate or obvious solutions. This can involve encouraging the partners to be more reflective and to let new thinking emerge when the time is right. It can also involve helping partners to differentiate between issues and decisions that are straightforward or relatively simple and others that are more complex or unpredictable.
Authenticity and integrity	Partnership brokers are, of course, only human and can make errors of judgement that impact the partnership. It is important to be open about intentions and honest about mistakes. What is not acceptable is to try and gloss over things or to become manipulative in managing things that have taken an unfortunate turn. Partners will grow to respect the work of the partnership broker in a direct ratio to how far they feel the individual has integrity and is trustworthy.
Patience and persistence	It is easy to give up when things become difficult and partners can quite quickly cool off in terms of their enthusiasm and willingness to give time and effort when they feel it is only uphill work. The partnership broker may well be the person most determined to get through challenges and work through difficulties. Patience is not a virtue we all naturally possess, but a willingness to be there for the 'long haul' and to accept that things will take time and sometimes be exasperating is part of the change process partnering needs. A good sense of humour also helps!

(Continued)

Attribute	Description
Genuine interest in learning from, and sharing, experience	The best partnership brokers are endlessly curious and relentlessly keen to know more and to understand things better. They know that they don't know what they don't know and they are eager to grow their practice and push their own boundaries. It can make a big difference if a partnership broker can also bring this way of thinking to the partners so that they too become action researchers into their own and others' experience. Every partnership has lessons for others and partnership brokers can encourage partners to get validation and/or added value from sharing their stories and experiences beyond their partnership.
Willingness to 'let go' when the time is right	The greatest testimony of success in the partnership brokering role is when partners adopt and manage partnering processes themselves – in this scenario, a designated partnership broker is no longer necessary. An ethical partnership broker is always striving to build the confidence and capacity of others and working themselves out of the partnership brokering role.

Partnership brokering archetypes

To take this one step further, we also consider archetypes and how they may help us understand how differently individuals will take on the partnership brokering role. Whilst the concept of archetypes in understanding character traits can be controversial,[9] we believe that they can provide additional useful insights into understanding approaches to partnership brokering. They can also, like metaphors, move us beyond analytical thinking, into more intuitive and cultural realms (Table 2.4).

Of course, human beings are complex and never fall neatly into a single 'type'. Considering archetypes or any other kinds of 'typologies'[10] may be most useful as a lens to assist partnership brokers to reflect on their approaches and tendencies. They may help to identify their own (or others') strengths and weaknesses and assist in building complementarity out of diversity. People do, of course, change over time (though it is clear that some people are more flexible and willing to change than others). Such changes are often highly influenced (consciously or unconsciously) by the context in which we are living and working. We are also undoubtedly deeply shaped as partnership brokers by our partnering histories and experiences (whether these have been productive or challenging). Typologies can be helpful when

Table 2.4 Archetypes and different partnership brokering approaches

ARCHETYPE	Characteristics as demonstrated in partnership brokering approaches
Guardian	Nurtures the partnership and mentors partners to enable them to take on more partnering responsibilities.
Teacher	Natural inclination to inform and to share knowledge and experience to build confidence and capacity in partners and the partnership.
Judge	Someone who arbitrates and helps partners to balance actual or perceived contradictions.
Inventor	A pioneer who believes that if what is needed doesn't exist, it should just be invented.
Builder	Gets on with the task and organises things with a strong focus on practical action, delivery and results.
Magician	Helps partners to imagine and believe in the possibility of transformation.
Seer	A capacity for foresight and an ability to assist partners in working towards a visionary goal.
Sage	Brings insights into the task that come from deeply internalised experience and a quiet wisdom.
Warrior	Is courageous and gives partners confidence to do things differently and to challenge norms where necessary.
Peacemaker	Able to mediate between partners with different perspectives and strong views.
Healer	Understands what underlying issues may need to be addressed before pressing problems can be solved.
Explorer	Brings a sense of adventure and going into the not-yet-known and helps partners to navigate uncharted territory.

they provoke us into modes of self-enquiry and they are unhelpful when they are used as an excuse for being inflexible in our ways of working.

How much should partnership brokers do?

Whatever their levels of skill and whatever their archetype(s) or preferences, partnership brokers need to constantly monitor their relationship to partners (individually) and to the partnership (as an entity). Are they doing too much (and letting the partners get away with doing too little)? Or are they doing too little (by taking the line of least resistance and thereby unwittingly colluding with poor partnering practices)? Indeed, an important question is how much responsibility can/should partnership brokers carry? They often carry quite a lot as the quote from a case study below reveals:

> Perhaps it is fair to describe the partnership brokers as both "warriors" and "worriers" at one and the same time. This is to be expected since warrior-ing and worrying are characteristics of many of those operating in this role.[11]

Whether they are 'warriors' or 'worriers' (or both), it is becoming clear that partnership brokers require:

- physical and emotional stamina;
- the ability to be reflective and self-critical;
- an openness to receiving constructive feedback;
- a willingness to hold tension and juggle contradictions.

Risks and challenges for partnership brokers

Being a partnership broker can be tough. From the perspective of their personal well-being, parnership brokers often feel considerable pressure from partners and, in the case of internal brokers, from their line managers to be 'all things to all people'. They can suffer from burn out and/or from a sense that the brokering role can be quite a lonely one.

It is also quite common, especially where a partnership broker carries out their role in a way that gives credit to others and does not draw attention to themselves, for those they work with and for decision-makers not to recognise the importance of the job they do. In this scenario, it can mean that partnership brokers have too little authority to challenge the status quo or make the changes they deem necessary for the partnership to work optimally. It can also mean that few resources are allocated to support the partnership brokering role and/or partnering processes and/or capacity-building, so little changes and the partnership brokers get blamed for lack of progress or failure.

There can be additional challenges connected to the position of the partnership broker in relation to the partnership. In the case of 'internal' partnership brokers, their brokering work is very often simply an add-on to an existing role which can mean too little time available to dedicate to the many tasks. They also grapple with conflicting accountabilities (to their own organisation/line manager as well as to the partners) – which will take precedence when their requirements are divergent.

In the case of 'external' partnership brokers, their relationship to the partnership may simply be too short-term to be able to really penetrate partnering dilemmas and challenges and the partnership may suffer from a lack of continuity.

Risks and challenges for partnerships

It is not just those in the partnership brokering role that face risks and challenges; the very fact of having someone designated in the role may pose risks for the partnership itself. As much as there is a case for partnership brokering (see Chapter 1), there may also be a case against it. For example, where partners see the partnership broker working well on their behalf, there can be a tendency that they simply sit back and 'leave it to the expert' – they do not see any need for them to push themselves to partner more effectively. In addition to this holding back the potential of the partners and the partnership to achieve more, it can also lead to an unhelpful level of dependency on the partnership broker.

Allied to this, there can be situations where the partnership broker becomes too necessary for the well-being of the partnership. It can also happen that the partnership broker becomes too attached to the partnership and/or to their own importance within the partnership and is (secretly) glad when partners do not take on partnership brokering tasks. This is an understandable human response but poor partnership brokering. If partners do not 'step up' and take on partnering roles and responsibilities, they are less likely to embed partnering lessons and partnership-friendly practices within their own organisations and systems so things that need to change, don't. Where this occurs, the partnership brokering function (perhaps inadvertently) inhibits rather than promotes transformational change.

Conclusion

The profession of partnership brokering is still in its early stages. There is much more to explore, test out and understand. Having said this, a growing number of leading agencies in all sectors now use the term 'partnership broker' in job profiles and ask for partnership brokering experience and/or qualifications as either a prerequisite or as desirable.[12]

What is clear is that those operating in the partnership brokering role require a rich mix of skills, approaches and attributes to do it well. It seems that 'mastery' as a partnership broker is not easily achieved. Indeed, it may well take a lifetime to get anywhere near it: partnership brokering pioneers, who have been operating in the role for 20 years or more, often comment on how much they still need to learn. It may also be that the very moment a partnership broker stops self-questioning and stops striving to be better is the exact moment when they should stop operating in the partnership brokering role.

We have discussed how a partnership broker should always regard their role as a temporary one, being willing to hand over and let go when the time is right. It may also be that the concept of partnership brokering is itself a temporary phenomenon, demonstrating the importance of investing time and money in effective management of partnering processes. When such investment becomes the norm, partnership brokers may become unnecessary because partners themselves will bring the skills, clarity of purpose, time and imagination necessary. We are not there yet, but that may be the right direction of travel.

Notes

1 Tennyson, R. & Wilde, L. (2000) *The Guiding Hand: Brokering Partnerships for Sustainable Development*, Turin: United Nations Staff College & London: Prince of Wales Business Leaders Forum.
2 Definition adapted from Tennyson & Wilde (2000). Op.cit.
3 Those in the partnership management role are sometimes called 'partnership facilitators' or 'partnership coordinators'.
4 Partnership Broker is the term used internationally but it can be problematic in certain contexts. Alternative terms are: process manager, change leader, intermediary, bridge-builder, animator or partnership manager.
5 See: www.partnershipbrokers.org/training.
6 Roughly 80% of those participating in PBA training courses are internal brokers.
7 This table has been informed by PBA (2012) *What do Partnership Brokers Do? An Enquiry into Practice*, London: Partnership Brokers Association, which analyses 250 logbooks written by those working as partnership brokers. It is always a 'work in progress' as the partnership brokering role is still relatively new and we are all learning more about it over time. It now forms a core part of the 4-day Partnership Brokers Training (www.partnershipbrokers.org/training).
8 Scharmer, C.O. (2007) Addressing the blind spot of our time: an executive summary of the book by Otto Scharmer *Theory U: Leading From the Future as it Emerges*. http://www.presencing.com/sites/default/files/page-files/Theory_U_Exec_Summary.pdf (accessed 9/2/2018).
9 People have very mixed views about archetypes. Some find them extremely helpful in understanding strong tendencies in themselves and others that explain why they respond/behave/feel the way they do. Others are concerned that they may tend towards a too simplistic perspective and to fixing people (either in their own perceptions of themselves or their perceptions of others) in a way that can make them resistant to changing.
10 For example, the Team Role Preferences adapted from Belbin (http://www.belbin.com/about/belbin-team-roles) (accessed 9/2/2018): Innovator, Strategist, Mobiliser, Coordinator, Nurturer, Shaper, Implementer or Completer as used in the 4-day Partnership Brokers Training course (www.partnershipbrokers.org/training).
11 Tennyson, R. & Wood, E. (eds.) (2013) *Dealing with Paradox: Stories and Lessons from the First Three years of Consortium-building*, London: Partnership Brokers Association.
12 Often through the accreditation offered by the Partnership Brokers Association.

Chapter 3

Creating a better fit

A scoping role for partnership brokers

Rob van Tulder and Timo Kahlen

Since the turn of the millennium, multi-actor partnerships for sustainable development have gained popularity. The plethora of problems that can arise before, during and after the formation of these partnerships[1] provides a logical call for 'partnership experts' who can convene potential partners and support them during the partnering process.[2] For many centuries, brokers and brokerage firms have functioned as acknowledged intermediaries in buying and selling transactions within the same sector or supply chain but in multi-actor partnerships, they present a relatively recent phenomenon. Nevertheless, they are generally considered of great importance for successful partnerships by practitioners and academics alike.[3]

As noted in Chapter 2, partnership brokers can be more than one person at a time; they can be organisations or people from within or outside of an organisation;[4] from any sector;[5] while taking different positions inside and outside organisations.[6] As mediators, partnership brokers facilitate the interaction between partners as well as with other external stakeholders. As learning catalysts, partnership brokers can help partnerships improve their functioning and increase the impact of multi-actor partnerships by sharing knowledge and experience in cross-sector partnerships.[7] In addition, partnership brokers can also assume the role of partnership manager (see Chapter 6).[8] Each of these different roles has its advantages and disadvantages.

The relevance of partnership brokers has increased tremendously over the past two decades due to recognition that the problems that society has to address belong more and more to the realm of complex or so-called 'wicked problems': problems that are not only difficult to address because of different interests among stakeholders but also because of difficulties in defining the actual problem.[9] Wicked problems exist because solutions cannot be found to address them by traditional sectors of society (civil society, state and market) and thus require the engagement of actors from multiple sectors working together in partnerships.[10] Wicked problems create so-called 'institutional voids' in which none of the societal actors has been able – or willing – to take action and create new formal or informal 'rules of the game'.[11] Thus, a particularly relevant dimension for defining the effectiveness of partnership brokers is to check whether they actually assist partners to have an impact on addressing these wicked problems. Making this question practical requires a clear understanding of what partnership brokers actually do and how they can align different interests around a common vision.[12] This applies particularly to the role that partnership brokers might assume in the start-up or formation phase of partnerships which is generally acknowledged to be the most important phase of any partnership aimed at generating transformational change.[13]

A number of academic publications recognise the potential of partnership brokers in addressing cross-sector challenges.[14] Partnership brokers are described as 'boundary-spanning leaders with credibility',[15] as 'social agents',[16] as 'a key factor facilitating collective action',[17] as 'change makers who span cross-sector boundaries'[18] and as conveners of partnerships,[19] intergovernmental collaboration,[20] networks[21] and mediators in conflicts.[22] Despite the increased importance given to the role of partnership brokers, however, a systematic search reveals relatively few detailed academic papers on the topic.[23] Insights into the actual practice of partnership brokers can be found in publications by organisations engaged in partnership brokering and in relation to their own research activities. However, hardly any of these publications are based on validated research. Although they often contain compendia of research in adjourning areas that can indeed be considered 'established', they are largely anecdotal or case-based. There also exists a considerable degree of self-reinforcement in which guides refer to the same source.[24]

The terminology surrounding partnership brokers is not without ambiguity either. Many names are used interchangeably in practice[25] which, in turn, hints at the ambiguous position of these intermediaries. Some of these apparent synonyms include: mediator,[26] negotiator,[27] facilitator,[28] process manager and partnership intermediaries,[29] change leader,[30] co-coordinator[31] or connectors, co-designers and learning catalysts.[32] In the end, most of these can be regarded as role descriptions a partnership broker might hold. In practice, they can lead to confusion as well as conflict when not understood and carried out appropriately.

The present state of knowledge on partnership brokers presents an interesting clash among practical insights, established training practices and modest scientific research. This makes a systematic discussion on enhancing the function of partnership brokers particularly challenging. Partnership brokers, moreover, present a moving target as they can be engaged in a large number of activities for many different stakeholders under very diverse circumstances. Extant academic and practitioner literature on partnership brokers presents a spaghetti bowl of techniques, insights and visions on what partnership brokering might entail.[33] The number of validated ideas on which techniques work best, who should undertake them, under what circumstances, for which problem and in which phase of the partnering cycle, remains limited. Most of the insights that guide the actual practice of partnership brokers are prescriptive and practitioner-oriented rather than based on systematic scientific research.[34]

The 'fit challenge'

Bearing in mind these concerns, we argue that the question of how partnership brokers can improve the way they work can best be addressed by considering the various roles they can adopt in the formation phase of a partnership and then link this to the different types of partnering that an effective approach towards an issue requires. We call this the 'fit challenge'. This challenge involves both a better understanding of the roles partnership brokers can adopt and the particular fit partnership brokers can help to establish among the issues to be addressed, the partners involved and the context in which they operate. In the partnership broker literature, this challenge is often referred to as the 'scoping' or 'convening' function of partnering. It is our belief that when a proper fit between a partnership and the issue it seeks to address can be established, the impact of a partnership broker throughout the entire partnering cycle, and ultimately the impact of the whole partnership, can be enhanced.[35]

It has been widely acknowledged that the way partnership brokers create trust, discover shared interests and expectations,[36] use social capital and bridge structural holes due to 'weak ties'[37] is located in the earlier phases of partnership-building. This is also where the majority of challenges to effective partnership formation appear.[38] During this time, partnership brokers often encourage the application of scoping and resource/capability mapping to assess whether partnering is a viable and attractive possibility in comparison to traditional 'going-it-alone' solutions or other forms of collaboration. Good scoping, however, requires a correct assessment of the wickedness of the issue that is of concern and the type of partnership that is most appropriate to address it. Partnership brokers thus need to promote consideration of an 'issue fit' and an 'organisational fit'. To identify the most relevant skills and techniques for assessing these 'fits', the type of 'institutional void' partners are trying to overcome needs to be defined.

Defining the initial challenge

Multi-actor partnerships aimed at addressing a wicked problem ideally build upon the complementary strengths of each partner, compensate for mutual weaknesses, share risks and/or define areas for the articulation of shared interest. All partnerships involve the pooling of a large number of divergent characteristics such as: ideas; visions; capabilities and competencies; commitment; risks; values; responsibilities; networks of weak and strong ties; power relations; mindsets; individuals, and organisational cultures.[39] What partnership brokers have to broker, therefore, is a large variety of all the different dimensions needed (in various combinations) for the successful formation of a partnership. Ultimately, the most important of these dimensions can arguably be considered to be the brokering of interests[40] that enable the creation of value through social coalitions.[41] The fundamental question partnership brokers have to address in the formation phase thus relates to a proper identification of where and why the creation of value in societies is underserved.

Addressing specific scoping challenges

Scoping contributes to setting realistic and common expectations of the current situation, necessary efforts, risks and probable outcomes.[42] Not much research has been carried out on the effectiveness of particular scoping exercises for partnerships.[43] Though partnership practitioners recognise the importance of scoping, it is noted that they often do not devote sufficient time to it in practice.[44] In addition, limited attention is often focused on elaborate due diligence analyses which are strongly influenced by the importance attached to (perceived) power and interest differences.

We have identified six key challenges faced by partnerships during the scoping phase, all of which can be addressed with the support of careful partnership brokering. These include the following:

Difficulty in assessing whether partnering is actually the best way to go forward

A partnership broker can assist exploration of whether a partnership indeed presents the best approach for addressing an issue as compared to 'going-it-alone' or engaging in other forms of collaboration, e.g. establishing platforms for dialogue. In the partnering cycle, this question is faced twice: at the very beginning of the initial, situational analysis and after a thorough and collective problem analysis to decide if partnering is still the best way forward.

Partnering is currently often consciously chosen and promoted because traditional solo approaches have not been sufficiently successful and the prospects of combining all types of resources to achieve greater efficiencies and effectiveness, for commercial as well as social goals, are combined with the sharing of risks and long-term commitment.[45] Even though such reasoning may be implicitly shared, a partnership broker can check on and restate this understanding. This will give legitimacy to the ensuing partnering activities. If partnering is deemed necessary, partnership brokers can then support explorations of which parties should be involved and in what constellation. When comparing different collaborative models, partnership brokers can also do much to make sure that a common understanding of the exact terminologies and specifications of different approaches exists. During this process, it is also important for partnership brokers to be honest and not create their own jobs by suggesting partnerships when this may not be appropriate.

Dealing with multiple problem 'owners'

This issue is easily amplified in multi-actor collaborations due to scepticism or even outright hostility between the sectors.[46] Hostilities are based on the positions of actors in the societal triangle among the three sectors of business, government and civil society and the fulfilment of their roles. When actors fail in their primary responsibility or 'fiduciary duty', it can be difficult to establish respect between them and others. Partnership brokers can do much to promote and establish an appreciation of the other parties' viewpoints upon which a joint problem analysis and solution generation can be based.[47]

Screening for an organisational and cultural fit between potential partners

When aiming at innovative solutions that bring transformational change to wicked problems, an organisational and cultural fit between partnering organisations is critical. Assessing a potential match, however, remains largely theoretical. A partnership broker can play an important role in customising each partnership's unique requirements so that they are understood, tested and advanced coherently with partners.

Including a thorough joint problem analysis early in the process

One of the biggest challenges currently faced in partnership practice is the failure to engage in a thorough joint problem analysis. An integral part of the Logical Framework Approach, critical problem analysis is usually disregarded in both academic- and practitioner-partnering literatures, which means that they do not start with a problem definition or diagnosis of the need for a partnership project but immediately leap to the intended outcome and design.[48] Partnership brokers can support a stance that resists the temptation to jump to ostensible solutions without conducting a joint problem analysis. As well as not falling prey to such time pressures, it may be useful to use a general framework for analysing wicked/complex problems (see below).

The transition from a problem analysis to specific partnership objectives that do justice to the complexity of the actual problem

Another challenge for partnership scoping and more sophisticated partnership brokering in practice is the transition from a common problem understanding to a specific partnership objective. This challenge incorporates other challenges, e.g. issues regarding multiple ownerships or arriving at a common problem understanding and ultimately a shared vision. Partnership brokers can do much to encourage partners to develop and incorporate a shared vision that will assist them to act together in concert.

Including capacity-building and continuous learning possibilities in partnership set-ups

A final challenge in scoping relates to the inclusion of capacity-building in partnering processes and the promotion of continuous learning.[49] The more complex a challenge addressed by a partnership, the more initial capacity should include advanced provisions for (mutual) learning. This type of intervention is supported by the so-called 'developmental evaluation' techniques that stimulate partners to improve the Theory of Change of the partnership along the various phases of the partnering cycle and focus on monitoring and learning rather than on control.[50] Partnership brokers can thereby seek to incorporate dimensions of flexibility and continuous (loop) learning into partnership design and processes. This should also help to avoid the development of action plans that are too technical with complicated procedures which are often an outcome of scoping.[51]

Tackling wicked problems with the right partnership fit

Each of the challenges outlined above is impacted by the complex nature of the wicked problems that multi-actor partnerships try to resolve. Sources of wickedness can be linked to the three sectors that 'surround' these issues: governments (state), firms (market) and citizens (communities). Each sector can offer both a different and a complementary approach to an issue, partly because the primary responsibility of each and their value propositions are different: markets provide private goods on an exclusive for-profit basis; communities provide social goods for communities (that can be partly exclusive for others) and governments create public goods (that are provided to all) on a non-profit basis. Well-functioning societies are 'balanced' societies in which each of these sectors plays a constructive and complementary role. The better each sector functions, the easier it becomes to address wicked problems.

A successful partnership configuration should thus encourage each sector to fulfil its fiduciary duty.[52] Problems tend to become 'wicked' when the parties involved do not address them adequately and/or when organisations from other sectors engage in 'crowding out' by voluntary taking over the primary responsibilities of other actors, e.g. when citizens or governments clean up the waste produced by companies, they provide a perverse incentive for the latter not to take up their own responsibility or fiduciary duty. These problems then become wicked for the other parties in society. The wickedness of these problems is thus primarily related to the inability or unwillingness of a primary sector to coordinate its activities with others in the same sector and restore 'trust' in the public perception of the sector.

The nature of wicked problems can be further categorised into different areas:

Sectoral failure: When sectors do not fulfil their primary role, e.g. market failure exists when firms do not supply goods that people want; governance failure exists when governments do not create laws and sufficient regulation; civic failure exists when communities do not organise sufficient mutual support and trust.

Lack of responsibility: When a sector creates negative effects or costs for society. These 'negative externalities' include: pollution, citizens that do not clean up their waste (and create health issues), corrupt or inadequate governments. The sector can solve this issue itself, but very often is not able or willing to do this.

Insufficient creation of positive externalities: Problems that can be addressed by sectors, but run the risk of being under provided if left to the initiating sector itself (so-called 'Merit goods'). Examples are education, vaccination, employment effects, sufficient investments for innovative public products and services.

Systemic challenges: So-called 'common pool' problems that are nobody's responsibility. They are also called 'tragedy of the commons' and should be considered the most 'wicked'. So-called 'bystander effects' appear in which everybody sees the problem but nobody is able or willing to act. Systemic problems are also called 'collective action' problems, because they require the joint action of all societal sectors at the same time.

Organisations in each sector can assume four different roles in response to these societal challenges (see Table 3.1).[53] These include the following:

- taking up their primary role or fiduciary duty;
- dealing with negative externalities;
- trying to create positive externalities;
- engaging in collective action to solve systemic problems.

By analysing a wicked problem in relation to the categories outlined in Table 3.1, a partnership broker can assist potential partners to ascertain

Table 3.1 Issue-partnering fit

Nature of wicked problem	Sectoral failure	Taking responsibility for addressing a problem		Systemic challenges
		Lack of responsibility	Weak positive externalities	
Roles that can be assumed by:	Take up of primary role by:	Dealing with negative externalities by:	Trying to create positive externalities by:	Engaging in collective action to solve problem by:
State	Making laws and enforcing regulation (mandating)	Facilitating subsidies and regulation against public 'bads' such as corruption and power abuse	Endorsing and facilitating other organisations to create positive effects	Trilateral cross-sector partnering to change the system
Market	Competitive production of goods and services	Minimise negative effects (e.g. pollution)	Optimise positive effects in products and value chains	Fixing system together with whole sector, involvement of communities and application of innovation
Communities/Civil Society	Creating social value through mutual support	Advocacy within and towards other sectors	Service delivery to create positive effects	Trilateral cross-sector partnering to create systems change
Most appropriate partnership approach	Intra-organisational/ sectoral (involving partners within a sector)	Intra/bi-sectoral (involving partners from two sectors)	Bi/tri-sectoral (involving partners from two or more sectors)	Tri-sectoral (multi-actor/ cross-sector)

to what extent a trilateral partnership (across all sectors) is needed or whether a single sector or bilateral sector option might be more appropriate. A further assessment can then be carried out to assess the degree of commitment among participating organisations to address the problem using the most relevant approach. Five core options are proposed:[54]

- A full trilateral fit in which the relevant actors from different sectors are likely to wholeheartedly combine their partnership strategies.
- A partial trilateral fit in which most parties embrace a partnership strategy while others consider themselves more dependent on the other actors considering the problem addressed by the partnership.
- A weak trilateral fit where only a few partners recognise interdependence on the problem while other parties view the issue as quite distant and are disinclined to take action or responsibility for it.
- An optimal bilateral fit where players from two sectors engage in an equally committed partnership.
- A partial bilateral fit where only parties in one sector are supportive of a partnering approach.

By classifying the various 'partnering fits' in terms of full to partial or weak to optimal, a partnership broker should be better able to assist in identifying the challenges that they may need to work on in a future collaboration (see Table 3.2). In a full trilateral partnership, for example, the task for a partnership broker is likely to centre on the balancing and coordination of the – in principle – equal commitment of each party. In an optimal bilateral fit partnership, a partnership broker may be suited to a 'liaison' role.[55] Where there are partial and weak fits, one can expect considerably more tasks for the partnership broker. In these cases, partnership brokers must assist an assessment of whether partnership implementation and the generation of a significant impact on the issue are realistic. They will then need to help identify and raise the topic of unequal commitment among potential partners, including a discussion of the possible consequences of this for and during the partnership. Expectation management, one of the greatest challenges for partnership brokers in general,[56] is amplified in unbalanced partnerships. The task of managing expectations will include addressing risks, such as changes in political agendas that may alter the commitment of state agencies in partnerships, for example, during elections. In such cases, partnership brokers can suggest partnership frameworks with flexible governance configurations that can help improve a partnership during its implementation, for instance, by adding new partners (moving from a 'coalition of willing' to a 'coalition of needed'). Even in flexible governance configurations, however, a clear assignment of roles and responsibilities for each one of the possible configurations is important.

Table 3.2 Partnership broker roles and fits

	Full trilateral fit	Partial trilateral fit	Weak trilateral fit	Optimal bilateral fit	Partial bilateral fit
Partnership broker role	Convener Mediator Learning catalyst		Convener Mediator		Convener
Core aim	Balance and clearly separate roles and responsibilities according to capabilities.	Acknowledge 'sector' failure and need for action/commitment – not just reliance on other players.	Ensure full understanding of difficult set-up and promote commitment of all parties.	Regular brokering as convenors, mediators or learning catalysts.[57]	Critically question whether this is really the desired solution.
Addressing attitudinal challenges	Assist parties to acknowledge that their failure to address a specific issue is part of problem. Ensure full and balanced commitment of each partner. Promote clear roles and responsibilities in line with organisational capabilities/resources. Have these integrated into a clear governance framework.	Acknowledge differing degrees of commitment and indicate possible consequences. Watch out for risk of over commitment and crowding out.	Address limited commitment by getting parties to acknowledge failure in own sphere and responsibility for solution. Assess realistic impact of partnership when only one organisation fully commits to it.	Matchmaking between two committed parties. Facilitation to reach inter-organisational synergies with analysis of capabilities, division of roles and responsibilities, and enforcement of good governance. Support knowledge creation and management.	Work to promote motivation, particularly as it may be unjust to characterise this project as a partnership. Ensure real commitment. Assess realistic impact of partnership.

	Identify specific organisational capabilities needed for partnership and detect potential for synergies.		Are there synergetic organisational capabilities to bridge gap?
			Manage expectations (particularly as chance of high impact is low).
Addressing formal challenges	Ensure that parties do not mix up intentions and roles.	Promote strong governance measures in order to handle sizeable risk of free-riding.	Promote formalisation of roles so that commitment is enhanced.
	Watch out for free-riding or abandoning partnership leading to risk of loss (or decrease) of resources/capabilities essential for functioning of the partnership.	Work to ensure governance arrangements enable partnership to reach full potential.	
	Assist with development and support for institutional and facilitative legal frameworks.	Suggest frameworks (agreements, contracts, etc.) to mitigate and protect against loss of resources.	

In addition to the above, there are also a range of general challenges and tasks that partnership brokers may assume which are relevant for all types of fits and roles. The first is the correct identification of each party's organisational capabilities and resources, and the detection of potential synergies in relation to these. Even with a high organisational fit between potential partners, honest commitment to the partnering approach (which should be explained and separated, for example, from mere sponsoring activities) needs to be thoroughly assessed. Potential partners may have a big incentive to present themselves as motivated in order to engage in partial or weak partnership configurations where there are opportunities for free-riding. A partnership broker can do much to avoid this by assisting an investigation of underlying interests and the existence of genuine motivation for partnering. To do this, the negotiation strategies discussed in Chapter 4 offer useful pointers. An indication of the 'true' engagement of an organisation in a partnership is the amount and degree of responsibility that they are willing to take on as a partner. For this reason, and to ensure effective implementation of the organisational fit and related synergies identified, a third key task for the partnership broker is to promote commitment via written agreements for partnership governance.[58] In the case of wicked problems, rather than detailed control measures and key performance indicators, this commitment should be aimed primarily at learning and a collective vision of partnership development.[59]

Conclusion

As most partnerships are formed on the basis of 'coalitions of the willing' rather than 'coalitions of the needed', partnership brokers can do much to promote synergistic value creation by promoting a high organisational fit among partners and the issues that they aim to tackle.[60] A more sophisticated scoping process would include a problem analysis and then identifying and screening appropriate stakeholders. Using a process of 'societal triangulation' that relates the source and nature of the wickedness for which a partnership is intended to its sectoral origins, potential partners can be encouraged by a partnership broker to confront the degree of wickedness of a problem and the degree of their commitment to addressing the issue.[61] Different degrees of commitment are likely to create an unbalanced partnership and create difficulties in partnership formation, and certainly continuation. A partnership broker can support changes in partner commitment by assisting partners to recognise the interdependent and wicked nature of the problem to be addressed and the need to participate in a more active way in its solution.

Because issues change, so the necessary partnership configuration may also change. The increasing emphasis on adaptive partnerships in collaboration literature suggests that a proper issue-partnership fit should ideally provide room for a dynamic relationship to develop. The partnering process and the measurement of its effectiveness then become primarily performance-based rather than impact-based.[62] Within this scenario, the partnership broker's role is crucial.

Notes

1 Kolk, A., Van Tulder, R. & Kostwinder, E. (2008) Business and partnerships for development. *European Management Journal*, 26 (4): 262–273; Stöteler, I., Reeder, S. & van Tulder, R. (2012) Cross-sector partnership formation-what to consider before you start. Partnerships Resource Centre, May.

2 Selsky, J.W. & Parker, B. (2005) Cross-sector partnerships to address social issues: Challenges to theory and practice. *Journal of Management*, 31 (6): 849–873; Stadtler, L. & Probst, G. (2012) How broker organizations can facilitate public-private partnerships for development. *European Management Journal*, 30 (1): 32–46.

3 Manning, S. & Roessler, D. (2014) The formation of cross-sector development partnerships: How bridging agents shape project agendas and longer-term alliances. *Journal of Business Ethics*, 123 (3): 527–547; Stadtler & Probst (2012) Op.cit.

4 Tennyson, R. (2005) *The Brokering Guidebook. Navigating Effective Sustainable Development Partnerships*, London: The Partnering Initiative.

5 PBA. (2012) *What Do Partnership Brokers Do? An Enquiry into Practice*, London: Partnership Brokers Association.

6 Gould, R.V. & Fernandez, R.M. (1989) Structures of mediation: A formal approach to brokerage in transaction networks. *Sociological methodology*: 89–126.

7 Ibid.

8 Serafin, R. (2006) Five key things I have learned about partnership brokering: Over 20 years of professional practice in Canada, UK. Café Conversations: 41.

9 Rittel, H. & Webber, M. (1973) Dilemmas in a general theory of planning. Policy sciences, 4 (2): 155–169; Van Tulder, R. & Keen, N. (2018) Capturing collaborative complexities – Designing complexity sensitive theories of change for transformational partnerships. *Journal of Business Ethics* (forthcoming).

10 Austin, J.E. & Seitanidi, M.M. (2012b) Collaborative value creation a review of partnering between nonprofits and businesses. Part 2: Partnership processes and outcomes. *Nonprofit and Voluntary Sector Quarterly*, 41 (6): 929–968; Selsky & Parker (2005) Op.cit.; Kolk et al. (2008) Op.cit.

11 North, D. (1993) Institutions and economic performance. *Rationality, Institutions and Economic Methodology*: 242–261.

12 Kahlen, T. & Van Tulder, R. (2015) How Do Partnership Brokers Actually Broker? From Interest-based Scoping to Vision-based Negotiation. Rotterdam: Partnerships Resource Centre at RSM Erasmus University.

13 PBA (2012) Op.cit.; PrC (2015) Cross-sector partnership formation – What to consider before you start, Partnership Resource Centre.

14 Bryson, J.M., Crosby, B.C. & Stone, M. (2006) The design and implementation of cross-sector collaborations: Propositions from the literature. *Public Administration Review* (Special issue), 66 (1): 44–55; Googins, B. & Rochlin, S. (2000) Creating the partnership society: Understanding the rhetoric and reality of cross-sectoral partnerships. *Business and Society Review*, 105 (1):127–144.

15 Bryson et al. (2006) Op.cit.: 46.

16 Serafin (2006) Op.cit.
17 Selsky & Parker (2005) Op.cit.: 856.
18 Waddock, S. (2010) From individual to institution: On making the world different. *Journal of Business Ethics*, 94: 9–12; PBA (2011) Appointing a partnership broker, London: Partnership Brokers Association.
19 Sharma, A. & Kearins, K. (2011) Interorganizational collaboration for regional sustainability: What happens when organizational representatives come together? *The Journal of Applied Behavioral Science*, 47 (2):168–203.
20 Lackey, S.B., Freshwater, D. & Rupasingha, A. (2002) Factors influencing local government cooperation in rural areas: Evidence from the Tennessee valley. *Economic Development Quarterly*, 16 (2): 138–154.
21 Brass, D.J., Galaskiewicz, J., Greve, H.R. & Tsai, W. (2004) Taking stock of networks and organizations: A multilevel perspective. *Academy of Management Journal*, 47 (6): 795–817.
22 See for example Bardach, E. (1998) *Getting agencies to work together: The practice and theory of managerial craftsmanship*, Washington, DC: Brookings Institution Press.
23 Kahlen & Van Tulder (2015) Op.cit.; Lee, L. (2015) Understanding the role of the broker in business non-profit collaboration. *Social Responsibility Journal*, 11 (2): 201–220.
24 The most renowned of these sources are *The Partnering Toolbook* (2004) and *The Brokering Guidebook* by Tennyson (2005) Op.cit. Successive publications by the Partnership Brokers Association (PBA) generally build further on these publications to explore 'what partnership brokers do' (PBA, 2012. Op.cit.), what their profile is (PBA, 2011. Op.cit.), or give examples on how the concepts help in practice, see: Pyres, J. (2013) Good for Business? An enquiry into the impact of Microsoft's investment in partnership brokers training. Enquiry, unsRWS; and: Tennyson, R. & Wood, E. (2013) *Dealing with paradox stories and lessons from the first three years of consortium-building*. London: Partnership Brokers Association.
25 PBA (2011) Op.cit.
26 Ansell, C. & Gash, A. (2007) Collaborative governance in theory and practice. *Journal of Public Administration Research and Theory*, 18 (4): 543–571; PBA (2012). Op.cit.; Tennyson, R. & Wilde, L. (2000) *The Guiding Hand: Brokering Partnerships For Sustainable Development*. Turin: United Nations Staff College and London: Prince of Wales Business Leaders Forum.
27 Meyer, M. (2010) The rise of the knowledge broker. *Science Communication*, 32 (1): 118–127.
28 Stadtler & Probst (2012) Op.cit.; Fife, E. & Hosman, L. (2007) Public private partnerships and the prospects for sustainable ICT projects in the developing world. *Journal of Business Systems, Governance and Ethics*, 2 (3): 53–66.
29 PBA (2011) Op.cit.
30 PBA (2011) Op.cit.; Tennyson (2005) Op.cit.
31 PBA (2012) Op.cit.
32 Lee (2015) Op.cit.
33 Kahlen & Van Tulder (2015) Op.cit.
34 Ibid.
35 Stadtler & Probst (2012) Op.cit.; Van Tulder, R., Seitanidi, M., Crane, A.W. & Brammer, S. (2016) Enhancing the impact of cross-sector partnerships. Four impact loops for channelling partnership studies. *Journal of Business Ethics*, 105 (1): 111–130.
36 McEvily, B. & Zaheer, A. (2004) Architects of trust: The role of network facilitators in geographical clusters. In R. Kramer & K. Cook (Eds.), *Trust and distrust in organizations*, New York: Russell Sage Foundation: 189–213.

37 Von Schnurbein, G. (2010) Foundations as honest brokers between market, state and nonprofits through building social capital. *European Management Journal*, 28 (6): 413–420.

38 Frost & Sullivan (2013) *Growth Process Toolkit – Strategic Partnerships*. Mountain View, CA: Frost & Sullivan.

39 Selsky & Parker (2005) Op.cit.; Lackey et al. (2002) Op.cit.; Bryson et al. (2006) Op.cit.; Austin & Seitanidi (2012b) Op.cit.; Seitanidi, M.M. & Crane, A. (Eds.) (2013) *Social Partnerships and Responsible Business: A Research Handbook*, London: Routledge; Kahlen & Van Tulder (2015) Op.cit.

40 Van Tulder, R. & Pfisterer, S. (2014) Creating partnering space – Exploring the right fit for sustainable development partnerships. In: Seitanidi & Crane (Eds.) (2014) Op.cit.; Tennyson, R. (2004). *The Partnering Toolbook*, London and Geneva: The International Business Leaders Forum (IBLF) and the Global Alliance for Improved Nutrition (GAIN); Gray, B. & Purdy, J. (2014). Conflict in cross-sector partnerships in Seitanidi & Crane (Eds.) (2013) Op.cit.: 60–78.

41 Lee (2015) Op.cit.

42 PBA (2012) Op.cit.

43 Studies on the scoping practice have primarily been performed for environmental projects Mulvihill, P.R. (2003) Expanding the scoping community. *Environmental Impact Assessment Review*, 23 (1): 40.

44 Austin & Seitanidi (2012b) Op.cit.; Austin, J.E. (2000) Strategic collaboration between nonprofits and businesses. *Nonprofit and Voluntary Sector Quarterly*, 29 (1): 69–97.

45 Wang, C. & Ahmed, P. (2003) Organisational learning: A critical review. *The Learning Organization*, 10 (1): 8–17.

46 Gombra, N. (2013) How the "Partnership Brokerage" concept could address management expectations & create new opportunities for the MMF, *Partnerships for International Sustainable Development*: 53. Tennyson (2005) Op.cit.; UNGC (2013) *UN-Business Partnerships: A Handbook* [e-book], New York: UN Global Compact Office.

47 IBN is a main tool for brokers for such mediation, but with considerable limitations as analysed in a separate paper (Van Tulder & Kahlen 2015); PrC (2016) Wicked Problems Plaza, Partnerships Resource Centre, and see also Chapter 4.

48 Van Tulder, R. (2010) Partnering skills – The basic philosophy. Partnership Resource Centre. *Working Paper Series*, 005.

49 See for example: Abrahamsson, M. & Becker, P. (2010) *Scoping study for partner driven cooperation in disaster risk management between Sweden and Botswana*, LUCRAM, Lund University; World Vision. (2013). *Local partnering for development programmes – The essentials*. Monrovia, CA: World Vision International; GIZ (2011) *Capacity Works – The Management Model for Sustainable Development* [e-book]. Eschborn: Deutsche Gesellschaft für Technische Zusammenarbeit (GTZ) GmbH; UNGC (2013) Op.cit.; Glasson, J. (1999) The first 10 years of the UK EIA system: Strengths, weaknesses, opportunities and threats. *Planning Practice and Research*, 14 (3): 363–375; Abrahamson and Becker's study show how helpful the application of LFA can be for capacity development plans in the case of disaster risk management collaboration. In their work on collaborative value creation Austin and Seitanidi describe the importance for organisations to stay adaptive, and to engage in "deliberate role recalibration" and experimentation on partnering design and substance (2012b: 938).

50 Van Tulder & Keen (2018) Op.cit.

51 See Snell, T. & Cowell, R. (2006). Scoping in environmental impact assessment: Balancing precaution and efficiency? *Environmental impact assessment review*, 26 (4), 359–376.

52 Van Tulder & Keen (2018) Op.cit.; Van Tulder, R. with van der Zwart, A. (2006) *International Business-Society Management*, London: Routledge.
53 Van Tulder & Pfisterer (2014). Op.cit.
54 Using this scoping technique we have identified ten possible positions of part-nerships in the space between public-private-profit-non-profit sectors and six additional combinations more in the periphery outside of this core partnering space (ibid).
55 Gould & Fernandez (1989) Op.cit.
56 Gombra (2013). Op.cit.
57 Stadtler & Probst (2012) Op.cit.
58 Tennyson (2005) Op.cit.
59 Van Tulder & Keen (2018) Op.cit.
60 Austin & Seitanidi (2012b) Op.cit.
61 Van Tulder & Keen (2018) Op.cit.
62 Van Tulder et al. (2016) Op.cit.

Chapter 4

Building on diversity

Negotiation in partnerships

Bulbul Baksi

Building and managing partnerships require almost continuous negotiation. Partnership relishes diversities, which means that it tries to build on differences in opinions, approaches, agendas, mindsets, cultures and experiences. Negotiations are embedded in the processes of co-creating, co-evolving and collaborative problem-solving. These processes entail ongoing collaborative decision-making. The decisions may be relatively minor, such as where to house a meeting, or they may be major ones, such as debating the strategic focus areas for the partnership. Each decision has the potential to reinforce a partnership or generate frustration or disfranchisement among partners. Therefore, a partnership broker plays an important role in assisting partners understand and work through the layers of diversities.

The mediation specialist, Andrew Acland, defines negotiation as '... a process in which parties to a dispute consult directly with each other about possible means of settling it'.[1]

The purpose of negotiation in a partnership involves more than settling a dispute or resolving a conflict.[2] Defined by the Cambridge Dictionary as the process of discussing something with the aim of reaching agreement, or the discussions themselves,[3] negotiation, by encouraging new thinking, can help to implant the principles of partnering and thereby create opportunities for pushing the boundaries of the partners, leading them to new ways of doing things that may result in systemic changes. A central tenet is that partnership brokers must help partners to develop and strengthen their own negotiation skills so that they have enhanced capacities to negotiate among themselves.

The aim of this chapter is not to lay down a model or identify specific steps to be followed in partnering negotiations. Instead, it will share some of the principles that underpin partnering negotiations and provide suggestions for how partnership brokers may approach the negotiation process.

Why do partners negotiate?

Negotiations in partnerships may take place in any of the following contexts:

- When partners co-create a plan – this entails negotiating among diverse experiences and frames of references, agendas and interests.
- When partners take decisions – which means working through their differences to reach agreement.
- When partners are involved in disputes or conflicts – where they need to negotiate to resolve them.

The three contexts are not mutually exclusive and may take place through-out the partnering cycle outlined in Chapter 2 (see Table 4.1):

Table 4.1 Negotiating during the partnering cycle

Phase in the partnering cycle	Key negotiation focus areas
Scoping and building	• Explore common and individual interests to agree on a robust common goal and address individual interests, as long as they do not conflict with the common goal. • Negotiate resource commitments by bringing diverse resources to the table and valuing them. • Secure commitment to the partnership as well as to the project.
Designing agreements	Formalise partnership agreements which, in addition to roles, responsibilities and other standard agreement provisions, often requires significant negotiations around: • Intellectual Property Rights • Branding • Allocation of management or co-ordination fee • Communication conventions • Grievance redress procedures • Reporting processes • Governance arrangements
Managing and maintaining	• Ensure accountability for commitments. • Make the partnership's governance arrangements responsive to emerging needs. • Negotiate with internal systems of respective partners to make them responsive to partnership requirements.
Review and revising	• Design a review process aligning perspectives and needs of all partners. • Address challenging issues that may have been neglected in previous phases.
Sustaining outcomes	• Address different levels of preparedness and motivation for moving on. • Agree on moving on options.

The challenges of partnership negotiation

Dealing with multiple layers of diversities

Partnerships harbour many different layers of diversities. Each partner is an individual as well as an organisational representative and carries multiple selves and identities. Additionally, however rational decision-makers may strive to be, current developments in neuroscience indicate that human brains do not make decisions based on reason alone and that emotion plays a significant role in decision-making.[4] Each self is thus overlaid by emotions which may be intense and even conflicting. This means that partnership decision-making is multidimensional and complex. The role of the partnership broker is to help partners understand the layers of intent behind each standpoint and accept that, while each point of view is legitimate, negotiating effectively also entails a degree of loss of control that can ultimately enhance opportunities for partnership-building. Case Study 4.1 portrays a partnership debate that had substantive issues, which was disrupted by strong emotions that overwhelmed several partners. The negotiations in this case took place after the meeting through one-to-one interactions in which the partnership broker helped partners appreciate the layers of intent behind each standpoint.

Case study 4.1 Finalising partnership governance arrangements

Several partner representatives had worked together in a governance task team for weeks and final consultations on the arrangements proposed were taking place with senior management representatives of the partner organisations. One of these representatives challenged the proposals on the grounds that they were too bureaucratic and might slow down partnering processes. An argument about this ensued which led to division into two camps: the task team, who felt that the arrangements they had proposed should be accepted, and the senior management representatives, who insisted that they had to be heard if they were to be part of the partnership decision-making process.

Managing uncertainty

The many levels of diversity in partnerships generate uncertainties that can lead to fear and anxiety (see Figure 4.1).[5] This fear and anxiety can foment despair and even panic, inducing reactions such as: fighting against a perceived opponent; blaming; mentally withdrawing from a situation or forming subgroups to create small domains of influence. In these situations, people tend to amplify their concerns dramatically and project assumptions

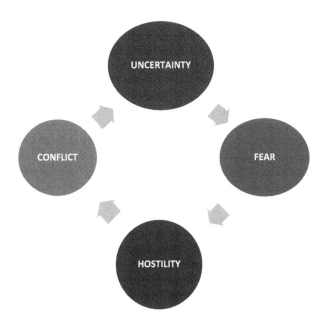

Figure 4.1 The uncertainty cycle.
Source: Acland, A. (2011) Adapted from Friend & Hickling (2005) *Planning Under Pressure*, Oxford: Elsevier Butterworth-Heinemann.

onto others which they then believe to be truths. These reactions may often be unconscious and can be played out actively or passively. When reactions are unconscious, they are difficult to interpret and therefore more problematic to work with, particularly when emotional reactions split people internally. As Figure 4.1 shows, conflicts may result both among and within people, organisations and cultures. A partnership broker may thus need to begin negotiations by helping partners to making uncertainties explicit so that they can be addressed before they escalate into conflict.

Addressing power and influence

If partnerships aspire to move beyond 'business as usual', they must address challenges posed by power imbalances and inequities. A partnership broker often has to explore how differences in power are manifested in a partnership and help partners negotiate these issues from the very start. Power may be visibly demonstrated, such as when partner representatives claim special status or privileges, or it may be invisible and influence discussions surreptitiously. It is sometimes trickier to handle covert power and influence because they are hidden behind what is ostensibly good partnering behaviour. Case study 4.2 shows an overt use of power by the lead partner representative which is layered with the emotional experience of feeling cornered and pressurised.

Case study 4.2 Co-creating a partnership review process

The process of co-creating the design of a partnership review led to disagreement among partners on the length of time this might take and how the process of data analysis might be expedited without diluting the quality of the research. A representative of the lead partner organisation asserted their authority during the negotiations and the other partners turned from actors to spectators. Following this, the partnership broker shared their reflections on what they had observed and suggested a break. Further one-to-one explorations between the partnership broker and the partner representatives revealed that the person who had apparently wanted to influence the process disproportionately by pulling rank was directly answerable to the principal funders of the partnership and was feeling anxious, cornered and slighted. These reactions had to be clarified before the meeting could proceed.

Case Study 4.3, meanwhile, points to the covert power of financing partners which influences negotiations even when they are not sitting at the negotiation table. A partnership broker may need to determine whether a situation involving imbalance of power and influence merits negotiation or whether it requires confrontation.

Case study 4.3 Developing a collaboration agreement

Members of a partnership met in a workshop to develop a collaboration agreement. When it came to intellectual property issues, the partner providing the funds claimed that the intellectual property of products produced by the partnership should belong to them because they were paying for the experts' time and production costs. The rest of the partners did not protest, possibly because they expected this as a norm. However, from a partnering point of view, such an arrangement was inequitable and unfair, and reinforced stereotypical power imbalances. The partnership broker thus made the implicit benchmark and the discomfort with it among partners explicit and shared information on alternative ways of addressing the issue. After a difficult conversation among partners, the funding partner finally negotiated internally for joint ownership of intellectual property rights.

Principles for partnership negotiations

Two assumptions underlie our negotiation approach in partnerships: firstly, negotiations should promote partnering principles (see Chapter 5) and secondly, they should be conducted in a manner that enables partners to optimise the potential for change. Negotiation in partnerships thus refers, explicitly or implicitly, to two questions: How far is the negotiation process promoting partnering principles? And how far is it promoting or undermining a process of real change?

The following key principles for partnering negotiations have been gathered from experience and, aligned with the partnership brokering good practice principles, offer useful guidelines for ways in which a partnership broker can help partners to negotiate:

- Empathy is central to brokering negotiations as it can help to address the challenges of working with diverse perspectives, experiences, interests, values and emotions.
- Partnership brokers have an obligation to expose contentious issues and instigate 'difficult' conversations rather than smooth over them.
- It is important to look for transformative moments which can lead to breakthroughs or generate change processes. Challenge and confrontation are often part of this process.
- Partnership brokers should help partners to build on diversities by conducting reflective conversations across different frames of reference.
- Partnering principles should be promoted throughout the negotiation process.
- Partnership brokers should help partners strengthen their negotiation skills so that they can gradually negotiate among themselves without support from the broker.

Negotiation pointers for partnership brokers

Partnership brokers may choose from a range of interventions to support negotiations. The choice depends upon the context and the key focus of negotiations. Negotiations may entail bouncing ideas off each other to co-create products and processes, conversations on tricky challenges to reach agreement and transformation of conflict, if they emerge, into a generative exercise. Partnering negotiations do not follow a model or predetermined steps. The choice of a method is influenced by the partnership broker's understanding, often intuitive,[6] of what a partnership needs at a particular time. The partnership broker has to be present in the 'here and now' and make rapid choices regarding actions and interventions. They are likely to draw on a repertoire of frameworks and skills which are consistent with key partnering and brokering frameworks. These include helping partners to:

Create a 'brave space' for dialogue and open communication

Daniel Shapiro believes that it is not enough to create a safe space where people can agree to differ.[7] Instead, a 'brave space' is needed where people can express their emotions and work through them. In a partnership context, such a space enables partners to find creative ways of handling their differences so that their diversities contribute to the richness of working together. Creating a 'brave space' involves the same principles as creating a safe space, such as preparing guidelines for working together, ensuring confidentiality and reinforcing the purpose of coming together. Many partnership brokers have also found it useful to reiterate partnering principles and invite people to be courageous and open. The underlying tenet is that a partnership broker should aim to prepare the ground for equitable and productive negotiations from the very start, before disagreements begin to surface. The very promotion of a 'brave space' is to encourage people to be genuine about their discomfort and disagreements.

Make the shift from positions to interests

According to Fisher and Ury, the aim of negotiation is to arrive at 'a good and wise agreement' that, as far as possible: meets the legitimate interests of the different parties involved; resolves conflicting interests fairly; is durable and takes community interests into account.[8] A 'soft' negotiator seeks to avoid personal conflict and tends to allow concessions that may ultimately make them feel exploited or bitter. A 'hard' negotiator wants to win and is likely to take extreme positions to drive a bargain that serves their interests which may ultimately harm a relationship. Fisher and Ury propose a third way to negotiate: interest-based or principled negotiation in which '...you look for mutual gains whenever possible, and that where your interests conflict, you should insist that the result be based upon some fair standards independent of the will of either side'.[9]

In principled negotiation, the parties are helped to shift from positions to explore the interests that lie beneath a stated position. Interests may include needs, desires, fears, concerns and values. In Case Study 4.1, the demand of the senior management representatives that the governance arrangements of the partnership entity should be modified and the counter claim by the task group that they were good enough and should be approved are examples of positions. Underlying these positions were the interests of task force members in finalising the governance arrangements as soon as possible in order to keep momentum, and those of senior management representatives who felt that such haste would lead to serious compromises on quality that would have an impact upon the partnership in the long run. A partnership broker can actively facilitate a shift in focus from positions, usually expressed as what partners think is right, to interests, the needs and concerns that underlie claims. The shift results from empathy and asking meaningful questions to learn about the interests. This involves teasing out the hidden agendas that destroy collaboration and opening up opportunities for creating mutually agreeable solutions.

The hypothesis upon which the interest-based negotiation framework is built is that beneath opposing positions, there are likely to be shared, complementary and compatible interests. In Case Study 4.1, for example, both parties wanted to promote the best interest of the partnership entity so that they could demonstrate a pioneering achievement. By unearthing this common interest, the real points of tension, the opposing interests, could be reduced to one or two issues that were easier to address.[10]

Encourage listening to build empathy

The emotional plane is always active in a decision-making process. It is most visible during difficult conversations among partners where partners may passionately hold divergent views with different implications for decision-making, or where they hold a partner responsible for violating a jointly agreed partnering principle or a jointly taken decision. Such situations generate uncertainties, and partners may begin to find themselves in the grip of intense emotions, assumptions and projections onto each other.

Empathy is the key to addressing emotions in negotiations. Carl Rogers, the humanistic psychologist who made empathy and positive regard the basis of Client Centred Therapy, asserts that:

> The state of empathy, or being empathic, is to perceive the internal frame of reference of another with accuracy and with the emotional components and meanings which pertain thereto as if one were the person, but without ever losing the 'as if' condition.[11]

According to Kohlrieser,[12] empathy generates authentic bonding that can help people to break free of the hostage-like situation or '...mindset (that) involves feeling trapped, helpless, powerless, disconnected, and unable to influence or persuade'.[13] By acknowledging their emotions and concerns, empathy helps them regain command over their emotions and use them more productively for making decisions. Richard Sennett[14] believes that empathy can be promoted through the use of dialogic communication. This involves responding to others on their terms and enables us to gain insights into ourselves. Dialogic communication hinges on listening to what is implied rather than what is said. Although shared agreement may not be reached, Sennett suggests that the process of exchange enables people to increase understanding of their own views and of one another. Sennett also believes that empathy involves curiosity about the other and is assisted by 'the subjunctive mood' which he describes as tentativeness in communication. This is the opposite of the 'fetish of assertiveness' or the impulse to 'ram home your case as though its content is all that counts'.[15] Empathy and the subjunctive mood help people to explore ambiguities and create the space for cooperation to emerge.

A partnership broker can endeavour to strengthen the capacity of partners to empathise by helping them suspend judgement. When people disagree, they are very often caught up in their own frames of reference. They interpret and judge every point of view by comparing it to their own. They therefore need help to make a shift from their own frame of reference to appreciating that of others. Partnership brokers can help partners to do this by listening to the implicit meaning or intent in their statements rather than only to what is being overtly expressed, acknowledging different points of view and articulating their understanding of the different interests, needs, values, emotions and the experiences that inform them. Acknowledgement conveyed tentatively, with due humility, and followed by questions such as, 'is my understanding correct?' or, 'help me understand why you think this is the best solution' can assist in making people feel heard and help them reflect further.

Make substantive (and sometimes unarticulated) issues explicit

According to Kohlrieser, bonding and authentic dialogue can assist people to change their mindsets. In this scenario, the role of a leader (or partnership broker) is to enable authentic dialogue to take place by making issues that create dissonance explicit.[16] Thus, instead of dancing around a tough issue, leaders 'put the fish on the table'. When managed well, authentic dialogue and conflict resolution can build stronger teams and help people feel a much greater sense of engagement.[17] Kohlrieser's advice not to smooth over a challenge, disagreement or conflict is also appropriate for partnership negotiations.

Sam Kaner further suggests that closing a decision too soon, without substantial debate, runs the risk of making solutions unsustainable.[18] Wise decision-making should go through what he calls a 'groan zone' (see Chapter 5, Figure 5.2), which lends it rigour and strength. By enabling partners to work methodically through divergent views, a partnership broker can help to develop shared frameworks and more convergent decision-making.

If partners are locked in a conflict, a partnership broker may have to identify the key substantive issues with reference to underlying frames of reference and conflicting or opposing interests. This may sometimes lead partners to realise that there is underlying common ground or it may expose fundamental differences in values, approach and needs. Either way, the role of the partnership broker is to create the conditions for partners to discuss them. The process of reflection leads to generation of new ways of understanding issues and therefore new ways of resolving them, thereby transforming conflict into a productive process. Reflective conversations may therefore generate transformative moments that allow partners to make breakthroughs. Sometimes, however, confrontation may be necessary to challenge, disrupt and change.

Question assumptions and pose challenges to frames of reference

As challenge helps to generate change, partnership brokers often need to challenge as well as empathise. The idea is not to challenge aggressively but, instead, to adopt Sennett's subjunctive mood to ask tentative questions that encourage the listener to explore their stance. Challenging with the intent of assisting partners may lead to arguments which are then processed for generating a process of change. It is worth noting that, in challenging, a partnership broker will also expose their own frame of reference by explaining her/his intent and reasons for posing a challenge. Partners may thus pose counter-challenges to the partnership broker. This may generate a dialogue between frames of references, including those used by the broker. The broker thus acts as a role model for posing challenges in a way that deepens reflection.

Reframe perspectives

Shapiro believes that Fisher and Ury's interest-based negotiation approach overlooks the role emotions play in conflicts which can be magnified when people feel that their identities are threatened.[19] This can lead to arguments between 'them' and 'us', what he terms the 'tribes effect' which fosters polarised thinking and a sense of self-righteousness in which each party feels that legitimacy stands on their side. According to Shapiro, building bridges requires reframing in order to understand each other's '*mythos*': the set of beliefs and assumptions that shape identity.[20] Reframing requires a high level of skill and entails restating a point of view or a perception using a different lens. It helps people to become 'unstuck' and opens up further opportunities for exploring an issue. It also requires heightened listening – to others and to yourself; both of which generate empathy. In Case Study 4.2, the lead partner pulled rank by creating a narrative around their dominance. Partners were influenced by this *mythos* and were thus wary of challenging her/him. In one-to-one discussions during a break in the meeting, the partnership broker helped both the lead partner and the other partners to reframe this *mythos*. For the lead partner, this meant reframing the emotions manifested to show that her/his stance was indicative of desperation to meet deadlines. For the partners, reframing focused on the significance of their roles and contributions that enabled them to negotiate more equitably with the lead partner representative.

Share information as appropriate

Fisher and Ury suggest the use of objective criteria such as existing standards and benchmarks when seeking to arrive at an agreement, especially when interests are conflicting.[21] While this may be a useful suggestion, as Wolski notes, the acceptability of a benchmark depends upon the priorities and value attached to objects, ideas and processes by different partners.[22] Care thus needs to be taken to ensure that the policy of a dominant partner is not taken as <u>the</u> benchmark. In Case Study 4.3, where partners were debating intellectual property rights in a workshop to develop a partnering agreement, the policy of the funding partner was presented as <u>the</u> benchmark. In this case, the partnership broker used information on alternative practices to challenge this perspective. Sharing relevant information from a large body of references and benchmarks can thus help to promote more layered thinking and enable partners to work through their biases.

There is a risk that a reference in the name of 'objective criteria' may close an issue prematurely because it represents a more powerful or predominant point of view. However, if information is used to deepen understanding or help partners to think creatively about options, it can be very useful. A partnership broker might thus encourage partners to share their own knowledge which may include experience of similar or comparable situations and challenges along with relevant data, research and benchmarks.

Move with agility between a partnership's common goal and individual objectives

A partnership broker provides a holding space for dialogue to take place and is alert to risks of conversations losing focus. This entails nimble navigation between opening up space for dialogue and introducing closure points, and focusing on both the common goals of the partnership and the individual objectives of each partner. This process can be challenging, particularly where power dynamics are involved.

In interest-based negotiation, partners are often advised to develop a BATNA or the Best Alternative to Negotiated Agreement.[23] In Case Study 4.4, where the funding partner unduly influenced the time allocated for action research, a good BATNA for the local organisations might have been to identify alternative funding sources with more flexible timeframes. They could then have argued that they would not accept the international organisation's funding unless the project enabled them to produce fair results. This could compel an otherwise rigid funding partner to reconsider their ostensibly non-negotiable timeframe. A BATNA, however, can also be used as a coercive tool in partnering negotiations and foster an adversarial rather than collaborative mindset. Wolski critiques the strategy of a BATNA on the grounds that while interest-based negotiation calls for candour about interests, it does not ask the parties involved to reveal their BATNAs which largely determine the outcome of a negotiation.[24]

Revealing interests thus merely becomes an avenue for getting more. In such cases, a partnership broker's ability to reposition common goals at the centre of negotiation processes can be crucial. The shared goal often serves as the critical reference point for assessing the relevance and acceptability of different suggestions, opinions, interests and agendas.

Case study 4.4 Addressing time constraints

A group of scientists in an international organisation that supported field-based environmental action research programmes said that the timeframes stipulated for local organisations to engage in action research were inadequate for the achievement of robust results. The international organisation was constrained by the conditions set by the funding partners and compliance with the restrictive timelines which they believed ultimately compromised their work in the field.

Invent and review options for mutual gain

A partnership broker can help partners to invent options for mutual gain by using the partnership's common goal as a reference point. For some issues, a genuine win-win scenario may be found which resolves disagreements. However, this is not always the case. In Case Studies 4.3 and 4.4, there was no win-win for the partners involved. In Case Study 4.3, the partnership broker pushed boundaries so that the financing organisation was forced to consult its policymakers to make room for joint ownership of intellectual property rights. In Case Study 4.4, the local organisations made a compromise, against their will, to ensure that the project went ahead.

As reaching agreement on contentious issues may include an element of bargaining, a partnership broker must help partners think creatively about options, consider their pros and cons and reflect on what they are willing to give up or compromise on. Negotiation may require compromises but partners should feel that they are doing this because of a greater good around which they are aligned. In other words, they should feel that this is the best option rather than that they have no other option but to compromise.

Reach alignment on decisions

Partnering decisions often follow the principle of alignment. Alignment is different from consensus. Consensus has been described by Andrew Acland as a '... a method of finding common ground when there are many different people and interests involved in a situation'.[25] In the experience of partnership brokers, a search for common ground often leads to settling for the lowest common denominator which compromises the potential of a partnership, especially for generating meaningful change. It may also drive compliance because, due to power inequities, partners simply agree, even if the decisions do not satisfy them. Finding an alignment in which everyone 'faces in the same direction' seems to serve partnerships better. Partners can align on underlying principles while actual decision-making can be distributed on the basis of roles and responsibilities. In Case Study 4.5, where local INGO staff took the lead in negotiating a decision regarding risk management, alignment took place around a set of underlying principles: firstly, the project should be adapted to local conditions; secondly, partners would openly discuss risks, both those anticipated and those regarding challenges they were experiencing; and thirdly, they would try to find solutions that were in the best interests of the project. As a result, each partner was able to choose their own secondary partners without going through a complex collaborative decision-making process. Alignment on the principles provided scope for sharing risks and paved the way for more distributed decision-making by creating a reference point for ensuring the accountability of decision-makers which drew upon the strengths of a collaborative approach.

In partnerships, it is critical to base decisions on consistent principles. As well as helping partners develop their frames of reference, a partnership broker can also assist them to agree on the principles that will inform decision-making.

Case study 4.5 Discussing risks

Three partners were co-creating a partnership agreement where there was a significant difference of opinion between a private sector entity and a government agency over the criteria for choosing secondary partners whose participation was critical for the success of the project. The national and international staff of one of the partners, an international NGO, differed on the issue. Ultimately, the national staff of the INGO emerged as internal brokers by explaining how the local conditions constrained choosing secondary partners on the basis of stringent government guidelines. The three partners subsequently discussed the risks around choosing secondary partners from their diverse perspectives. The fact that they openly discussed and argued about these risks reduced the apprehension of reputational risk that the government agency was most concerned about. In the end, the partners embraced the risks by making a commitment to be open about any risk that might jeopardise the partnership or the interests of any one of the partners.

Take heed of partnering principles and goals

It is the obligation of a partnership broker to safeguard partnering principles and alert partners when they are being violated. In Case Study 4.4, the local organisations as well as the scientists in the international organisation agreed on a shared goal for the project: to transfer laboratory-based technology to field level practice. However, by agreeing to an unrealistic timeframe, they compromised on the implicit goal of making the transfer smooth for end users and ensuring that the technologies would be usefully employed by them. They also compromised on the partnership principles of equity and mutuality because donor obligations were prioritised over other issues. The partnership brokering good practice principles oblige a partnership to challenge partners who compromise on key principles. This may sometimes involve an informed choice not to move forward with the partnership. Critics have alleged that partnerships, through a collusive accommodation of interests, can promote a non-confrontational culture and thereby subvert radical change.[26] In some situations, however, confrontation can initiate a change process. This happened in Case Study 4.3 when the funding partner was confronted on intellectual property rights policy that was inconsistent with partnering principles.

Hold space to enable partners to work through their differences

The ability and the skill to 'hold space' is probably the most important skill that a partnership broker can cultivate. 'Holding space' is a widely used phrase in counselling. It owes its origins to Donald Woods Winnicott, a psychoanalyst and paediatrician, who used it to refer to the way a mother 'holds' her distressed child to allow them to express emotions and project the angry and painful emotions without judgement.[27] A similar 'holding' is provided by the therapist to help a patient embrace pain and gradually work towards reframing their perspective. Creating a holding space while partners negotiate means that the partnership broker provides a container for explosive or negative emotions and that, while they are present in time and space, they may choose not to speak or directly intervene. In Case Study 4.5, the partnership broker simply held the space as partners conducted negotiations to resolve the dispute. The act of holding helps to contain and absorb emotions, and enables people to gradually regain their composure. A partnership broker might then try to help reframe the experience without diluting what has transpired. This is a complex skill that draws on both empathy and restraint. While holding the space is an almost continuous task for the partnership broker, it is also important to note that it is sometimes insufficient for enabling partners to resolve their disagreements. The partnership broker uses her/his judgement on whether partners can resolve their differences on their own if they are provided with the 'brave space' to do so or whether other interventions, such as reframing perspectives, are required alongside this to help them move ahead.

Two other aspects of brokering negotiations deserve attention here. The first relates to whether negotiations should necessarily take place when all partners are present.[28] The experiences of many partnership brokers indicate that negotiations often require several sessions in which both plenary and one-to-one meetings and conversations are held. As well as ensuring that these connections are held in strict accordance with partnership principles, a partnership broker will need to decide how best to conduct a meeting for a contentious issue based on an understanding of what will best serve to address this. Final decisions must always be taken with full transparency so that all partners are aware of what has been agreed upon.

The critical role played by a partnership broker in negotiations raises a second issue, that of neutrality of the partnership broker. What does this neutrality entail? Not taking sides? Not having a bias? This is a tricky issue as a partnership broker cannot operate without an opinion or judgement on what might or might not be a 'good' decision. If they have an opinion but withhold it, then they are violating the principle of openness. It is thus advisable for partnership brokers to explicitly put their perspective on the table during negotiations, acknowledging that while they have an opinion it is not an inviolable one and can also be challenged and discussed.

Conclusion

Negotiations are an integral part of the partnering process and are embedded in the processes of co-creation, collaborative decision-making and conflict resolution. Partnerships derive their strength from diversities which invariably leads to disagreements, disputes and even conflicts. Partnerships are complex as they are overlaid with factors such as power differentials, the multiplicity of identities of each partner representative and the emotions and uncertainties that they may carry regarding the partnership. The principle of alignment has been found useful for assisting efficient decision-making in partnerships. Sometimes, confrontations, and resultant conflicts, are necessary for promoting the principles of partnership. If avoided, partnerships can be accused of indulging in collusive accommodation of particular or powerful interests. However, the goal of conflict resolution is not merely to reach an agreement but to strengthen possibilities for transformative changes, moments where partners make a breakthrough and enter a new domain of options or processes that can lead to changes in policy and strategy.

A partnership broker helps partners to negotiate in ways that promote partnering principles and lay the groundwork for change. There is no defined model or predetermined steps that a partnership broker must follow in this process. However, there are underlying principles and frameworks, and a repertoire of methods and interventions that they can draw upon. These include the partnering and partnership brokering principles outlined in Chapter 5 which require partnership brokers to make contentious issues explicit rather than smooth over them. Partnership brokers can also draw on current thinking in the discipline of negotiation and on sociological discourses, adapting the insights offered in these fields for core partnership brokering frameworks.

Notes

1 Acland, A.F. (1995) *Resolving Disputes Without Going to Court*, Century Books: London U.K: 32.
2 Though partnering negotiations do not presuppose the existence of conflict, a situation that continually manages diversities may be more prone to the emergence of conflict.
3 https://dictionary.cambridge.org/dictionary/english/negotiation (accessed 9/2/2018).
4 Damasio, A.R. (1994) *Descartes' Error: Emotion Reason and the Human Brain*, New York: Putnam.
5 The Uncertainty Cycle has been conceptualised by Andrew Acland (2011) based on the work of Friend, J. & Hickling, A. (2005) *Planning Under Pressure*, Oxford: Elsevier Butterworth-Heinemann.
6 Intuition has been defined in two ways: firstly, it is deeply internalised knowledge and experience, the application of which is almost unconscious; secondly, it results from the connection you establish with the other, with the world outside and realise almost unconsciously what is needed now and act accordingly. I think these are not opposing definitions but complementary ones.
7 Shapiro, D. (2016) *Negotiating the Nonnegotiable, How to Resolve Your Most Emotionally Charged Conflicts*, New York: Viking.
8 Fisher, R. & Ury, W. (2011) *Getting to Yes: Negotiating Agreement Without Giving In*, London: Penguin Books (Revised edition).
9 Ibid: Kindle version. Location: 289.
10 Wolski, B. (2012) The 'new' limitations of Fisher and Ury's model of interest-based negotiation: Not necessarily the ethical alternative. *James Cook Law Review*, 19, 127–155.
11 Rogers, C. (1980) *The Way of Being*, Boston: Houghton Mifflin Company: 140.
12 Kohlrieser, G. (2006) *Hostage at the Table – How Leaders Can Overcome Conflict, Influence Others, and Raise Performance*, San Francisco: Jossey-Bass.
13 Ibid:18.
14 Sennett, R. (2012) *Together, The Rituals, Pleasures and Politics of Cooperation*, London: Penguin.
15 Ibid:18.
16 Kohlrieser (2006) Op.cit.
17 Ibid.
18 Kaner, S. (2014) *Facilitator's Guide to Participatory Decision Making*, 3rd Edition, San Francisco: Wiley.
19 Ibid:133.
20 Ibid.
21 Fisher & Ury (2011) Op.cit.

22 Wolski (2012) Op.cit.
23 Fisher & Ury (2011) Op.cit.
24 Wolski (2012) Op.cit.
25 Acland (1995) Op.cit: 20.
26 Poncelet, E.C. (2001) "A Kiss Here and a Kiss There": Conflict and collaboration in environmental partnerships. *Environmental Management*, 27 (1): 13–25.
27 Winnicott, D.W. (1964) *The Child, the Family, and the Outside World*, London: Pelican Books.
28 As many partnerships are conducted remotely, the notion of what this entails is changing.

Chapter 5

Embedding ethical and principled partnering approaches

Julie Mundy

If partnerships are considered to be a means of achieving enduring positive change, the importance of a principled approach is critical in creating and sustaining a just society. Ensuring that all partners are able to contribute, participate and benefit as fully as possible is central to the achievement of deep engagement, system change and, potentially, a wide range of positive outcomes.

There may be many occasions when a more powerful partner at the table will impose their own views, systems, priorities or approaches on other partners, whether out of frustration, a need for control, unquestioned assumptions about how things should happen or a genuine belief that their way is 'best'. In partnerships where there are no agreed operational principles, there is nothing to prevent this from occurring, and what started as a 'partnership' may quickly unravel into a traditional contract management scenario, with, at best, its subsequent loss of value for all concerned, and at worst, the cynical exploitation of one or more partners.

In this kind of scenario, the partnership may shift from a win-win to a win-lose engagement. The longer-term impact of this can be that the partners who are, or who feel, weaker or less important simply 'withdraw' by contributing or participating less. Feelings of disempowerment and sense of a devaluing of what the partnership should be achieving if it was managed optimally, inevitably lead to less effective partnerships. Whilst this is something to be avoided, it is not an uncommon experience for those involved in arrangements described as 'partnerships'. The effective management of power may be therefore to make the difference between a genuine partnership and the one that is a partnership in name only.

Another driver for adopting an approach that is underpinned by agreed core principles is that partners cannot rely solely on their own organisational or personal assumptions about how things will work between people as they strive to achieve collaboratively desired outcomes. Nor are they able to exercise the same degree of control over the process or the other partners compared to a scenario where they are sole owners or contractors.

Agreeing upon principles by which partners will be guided to collaborate and share ownership responsibly can provide a compass for the pathway they are building together.

Partnering principles

What are partnering principles?[1] In fact, it is due to a number of common challenges evidenced across all sorts or different types of partnerships that the fundamental principles of good partnering have emerged. They are explored here in some detail because it falls to partnership brokers to help partners explore, adapt and adopt such principles into the day-to-day working of a partnership.

Valuing diversity

Common partnering challenge:
ANXIETY ABOUT DIFFERENCE

Key principle:
VALUING DIVERSITY

Leads to:
NEW VALUE

Artist: Guy Venables

Partnership broker's role
Disrupting the uncertainty cycle
Providing reassurance
Building understanding of different perspectives and approaches
Demonstrating respect for and acknowledging the challenges and benefits of diversity

One of the main reasons organisations come together is to address problems that they are unable to solve by themselves. They recognise that it is necessary to bring together different actors with complementary or diverse strengths, experiences and approaches. Yet, it is often the reality of working with those who are different from us that causes serious anxiety within partnerships and may hold back progress.

Andrew Acland[2] talks about a cycle where uncertainty, if left unaddressed, escalates into fear, then hostility and eventually erupts into counterproductive conflict.[3] Any number of things can cause partners to feel anxious and uncertain about working together. Uncertainty can be caused by: a lack of information or understanding; different values or experiences; preconceptions and stereotypes about each other; poor prior experiences of partnering; discomfort about how decisions are made; different communication protocols and pressures in the operating environment including time or financial concerns.

An important role for a partnership broker is to help disrupt the uncertainty cycle and thereby protect and build on the diversity that brought the partners together initially. This can be done by building better communication between partners, helping to surface hidden interests and agendas and discussing any differences openly. Sometimes, a partnership broker will need to reassure partners that just because their approaches are different, this does not need to be a cause for alarm, and that in partnerships, we seek alignment rather than agreement in everything.

Ian Dixon, an experienced partnership broker working in Australia, uses the analogy of a piece of rope where each partner represents one of the individual strands; each individually coloured to represent the diverse strengths, skills and expertise which they bring to make up a stronger whole.[4] Partnership brokers need to watch for the more powerful partners in any partnership seeking to change the colour of those strands to reflect their own, particularly as there seems to be an innate desire for some partners, once together, to enforce homogeneity on others (e.g. in terms of reporting requirements or governance) which suits their own needs but may risk losing the very diversity which brought them together in the first place.

Equity

Common partnering challenge:
POWER IMBALANCE

Key principle:
EQUITY

Leads to:
RESPECT

Artist: Guy Venables

Partnership broker's role
Building understanding of each partner's contributions and value
Ensuring all partners have a voice at all stages of the Partnering Cycle
Managing the dynamics of power in the partnership

A constant challenge in all partnerships is maintaining equity. It is important to differentiate between equity and equality. Equality refers to each partner having exactly the same level of contribution and benefit. Since this is not a realistic aim in society, it is similarly unachievable in partnerships. However, adopting the term 'equity', where each partner's voice is heard and their contribution is respected, and where all partners are able to contribute from their unique area of strength, is fundamental to good partnering.

Providing a partnering framework and environment where partners, no matter how powerful or powerless they are, can operate equitably will help to ensure that each partner is able to contribute fully and thus optimise value for all concerned. Power imbalances or inequity in partnerships can result in a lack of respect which, in turn, can impact on partners' willingness to stick at it and work collaboratively when difficulties arise.

A great deal has been written about the deeply layered nature of power in relationships by social psychologists. French and Raven describe six forms of social power: coercive, reward, referent, legitimate, expert and informational.[5] All these forms of power may play out in complex partnerships (see Table 5.1). In partnerships, power can be attached to a situation, an organisational partner (often the funding partner) and an individual's status, role, expertise, reputation and even personality. It is therefore important for a partnership broker to be able to penetrate and understand the layers of individual and group dynamics and how they impact on the overall partnership, helping to manage them accordingly.

In addition, it is vital to understand that power in any partnership can be both real and perceived. For example, donors, with the weight of their funding or influence behind them, may choose not to exercise their power but other partners may expect them to wield it, and behave accordingly. Where power is present in an obstructive way, a partnership broker can assist partners to acknowledge and address the types of unhelpful behaviours that will, over time, reduce the effectiveness of the partnership. This may not be a one-off conversation: power imbalances, both real and perceived, are ever-present threats to good partnering, and need to be acknowledged and discussed in an ongoing manner. New Zealand-based partnership broker, Trish Hall, asks two overarching questions of partners and/or partnership brokers that are designed to uncover and address power dynamics. These invite them to consider what types of power they have in any collaboration, and what types of power they perceive others to have.[6]

In order to manage issues of power, a partnership broker can help partners achieve equity by ensuring that they each have a voice in meetings and providing opportunities to build understanding of what each of them contributes. Partners can, for example, develop a resource map that captures both financial and non-financial contributions each brings to the table. This, in turn, can help partners to understand that much more than financial contributions are required for a partnership to be successful. Where partners with

Table 5.1 Collaboration and different forms of power

Type of power	Impact on collaboration
Legitimate power/ formal authority	Legitimate power belongs to a person who holds a position or a role (e.g. project manager) within an organisation. An individual can exercise legitimate power when they carry out tasks with the authority their position gives them (e.g. formal chain of command). Partnerships need this authority at times. If people use this power inappropriately in partnerships, the results will be constrained and the commitment of others to the partnership could be minimised.
Reward power	Reward power is the ability to give rewards to individuals. Rewards in a partnership can be a public acknowledgement, or recognition, praise or asking for input on other initiatives.
Charismatic power	Charismatic power is based upon the engagement and appeal of individuals who inspire others. It depends on personal flair, but also on skills acquired through training and practice. People with charismatic power are respected for their competence as well as their personal characteristics regardless of their formal authority in the organisation. Partnerships need this sort of power to be used to build a collaborative team.
Expert power	Within organisations and partnerships, a person who has expert knowledge, ability or skill can influence others. Expertise may be obtained through special training, experience, access to specialist information, exceptional abilities or a general aura of competence. Partnerships need expert power that is exercised with generosity rather than control.
Information power	Anyone who possesses information of any type desired by others has information power. Collaborators exercise information power because everyone brings their information about the initiative.
Connection power	The ability to network and build and maintain relationships is central to the success of partnerships. Everyone in a partnership will need to exercise and expand this power. Some people have super-connector abilities that will be invaluable to a partnership.

Source: Adapted from French & Raven (1959) and Raven (1965) by Trish Hall.

less confidence or experience may not be able to identify what they bring to a partnership, a partnership broker can encourage partners to help each other to draw out and value the many different kinds of contributions. Partnership brokers can help partners to think very broadly about contributions using a visual tool such as the one developed by Tennyson (see Figure 5.1).[7]

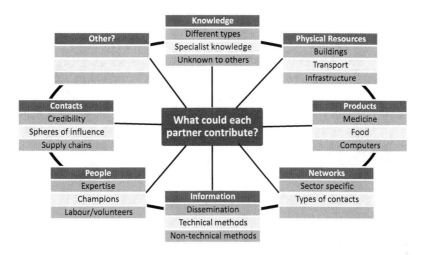

Figure 5.1 Partnership resources mapping.
Source: Adapted from Tennyson, R. (2004) *The Partnering Toolbook*, London & Geneva: IBLF and GAIN: 12.

Openness

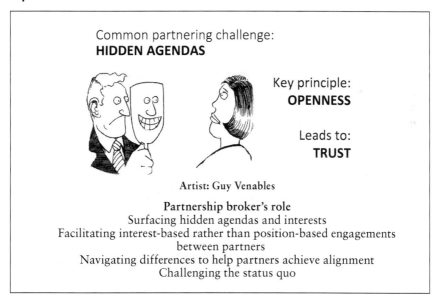

Although transparency is often cited as a key partnership principle,[8] this can be a difficult concept to promote, particularly as in some contexts it is quite a politically charged term that may be linked to societal perceptions of fraud and corruption. It may thus be helpful for partnership brokers to focus on promoting and encouraging openness between partners, so that there are no hidden surprises – especially unwelcome ones – as a partnership progresses. In addition to consideration of a partnership's common goals and objectives, a good way to do this is to help partners to identify and disclose their individual organisational motives and drivers for engaging in a partnership from the very start. Facilitating full and frank discussion of these drivers can assist partners in assessing whether there is any conflict that will potentially prevent the partnership from achieving its goals. Well-honed negotiation skills and the courage to challenge strongly held views are also key attributes a partnership broker may need to bring in order to preserve this principle.

Case study 5.1 The elephant in the room

At the end of a successful day's negotiations to develop a detailed partnership agreement among a travel company, an investor and an environmental NGO, who were partnering to develop and deliver ecotourism initiatives to benefit local villagers, the partnership broker asked whether there was anything else which was important for the partners to know about each other in order for them to work successfully together. At this point, the partners had been collaborating together for some months to develop the concept and design of the partnership. The investor mentioned its anti-fraud and child protection requirements, which everyone was aware of and understood. The travel company then stated that its organisational values meant that it could not support elephant rides or related tourism in any form. The NGO was surprised by this as its own principles straddled the government policy towards positive ('chain free-pain free') use of elephants in research and anti-poaching and local tourism entrepreneurs who could have included elephant rides as part of the tourism offering. The travel company, in turn, was surprised as it had thought it had made its intent on the matter of elephants clear from the start of discussions. The investor was neutral on the matter. Given that the issue was linked to organisational values, this was potentially a 'deal breaker' moment for the partnership. It involved patient subsequent exploration of organisational values, motivations and modus operandi which took many months to navigate, both at head office and in-country, before the partnership could proceed. A clear understanding of and alignment between the respective organisational values of partners can be fundamental to effective partnering.

Mutual benefit

Common partnering challenge:
COMPETITIVENESS

Key principle:
MUTUAL
BENEFIT

Leads to:
COMMITMENT

Artist: Guy Venables

Partnership broker's role
Helping partners to identify and maximise the value-add
for each partner
Identifying and measuring indicators of success for the
partnership overall and for individual partners
Assessing value-add (benefits versus costs) during review processes

When partners stop turning up to partnership meetings, or send junior delegates, or do not do what they have committed to do, it may be a flag for partnership brokers to check that there is still 'enough in it' to keep the partners engaged. The most successful partnerships are those where there is very clear mutual benefit for all partners concerned so they are prepared to commit organisational resources to the partnership. When partners are only interested in achieving their own organisational goals, at the cost of others, a partnership will not be successful. A key role for partnership brokers can thus be to help partners identify the potential and actual value-add of working in a partnership by developing indicators of success for both the partnership and individual partners at the outset, and by ensuring that these are measured and reviewed regularly. If this is done at an early stage, a partnership broker can assist partners to assess whether their individual objectives are similar or aligned *enough* with those of others in order for the partnership to succeed. Where objectives appear to be in conflict, a partnership broker can help partners to explore these differences and consider how far there is a basis to proceed with the partnership (see Chapter 4). What is needed and what is important to each partner may evolve as partnerships (and organisations) progress, so this may not be a static consideration. Sometimes too, partners will not identify all the value-add at the start of the partnership, as this may emerge as the partnership unfolds, so asking questions during review processes such as 'what are the unexpected and intangible benefits of working in this partnership for your organisation?' can be important.

Courage

Common partnering challenge:
UNCERTAINTY

Key principle:
COURAGE

Leads to:
**Breakthrough
results**

Artist: Unknown

Partnership broker's role
'Holding the space' when things become unclear or difficult
Asking the tough questions
Reminding partners of purpose and progress
Facilitating discussions on risk appetite and risk management

Partnerships are increasingly being created to solve genuinely complex and often intractable problems, those which have stymied society for decades: gender violence, climate change, terrorism, water resource management, economic empowerment, homelessness, recidivism, etc. These types of challenges are of a nature and seriousness that they cannot be solved by organisations or sectors working in isolation, no matter how good the intent or how deep their pockets. By their very nature, partnerships working in these spaces require a wide diversity of resources combined with the ability to adopt new ways of thinking and innovative approaches and plans.

As suggested earlier, this way of working can breed uncertainty and requires quite new thinking. It can be useful for partnership brokers working in innovative partnerships to facilitate a conversation around risk as each partner's appetite or tolerance for risk is likely to be different. Governments, for example, are often seen as risk averse due to reputational or political considerations. This can become problematic when partnering with NGOs or the private sector that may be used to operating more nimbly and with increased appetites for risk.[9] The resulting disconnect can cause considerable difficulty in partnerships, and may be a vital conversation to have upfront.

As noted in Chapter 4, a partnership broker may need to help 'hold the space' for partners to reflect and take time to generate new ideas and strategies, especially when they get stuck in the 'groan zone'[10] (see Figure 5.2) and want to move to a quick fix solution without adequately exploring

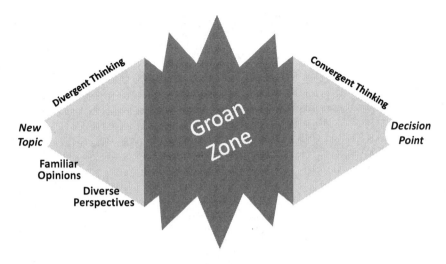

Figure 5.2 The groan zone.
Source: *Dynamics of Group Decision Making* in Kaner, S. (2007) *Facilitators Guide to Participatory Decision Making*, San Francisco: Jossey-Bass, A Wiley Imprint: 19 © Community At Work.

possibly more effective options. Sam Kaner's model of divergent and convergent decision-making in groups helps partnership brokers to explore the value of this approach.

A partnership broker may be able to reassure or support partners by helping them to have courage to: stay the course; try something new and keep them focused on what they are trying to achieve (the big picture). In doing so, there is the possibility of entirely new thinking and innovation to occur.

Courage may also be needed to find new ways to plan and act together beyond conventional, more linear, 'management-by-milestones'. Partners may need to be brave in experimenting with approaches to complex issues, learning together as they go, utilising design methodologies that are agile and iterative and, critically, they must have users at their heart. Such approaches are only feasible where partners have learnt to trust, respect and value each other, and have the backing of their own organisations and systems as well as an enabling environment.

Whose principles?

Who chooses which principles will be adopted and promoted? Is it a partnership broker, based on their global and/or personal experiences? Or the partners themselves? If it is a fundamental precept that every partnership is unique and that no 'one size approach' will fit all, it may be that principles essentially need to be quite partnership-specific.

Accountable, Adaptable, Adventurous, Communicative, Complementary, Courageous,
Diverse, Effective, Equitable, Flexible, Fun, Inclusive, Innovative, Learning,
Mutually Beneficial, Open and Honest, Optimistic, Pragmatic, Outward-Looking, Productive,
Respectful, Responsive, Results-focussed, Risk-taking, Transparent, Trusting

Figure 5.3 Partnership aspirations.

In any event, during the scoping and building phase of the partnering cycle (see Chapter 2, Figure 2.2), it is important to have a discussion between partners to identify the principles that they feel will best govern the partnership and the way they engage with each other. Another way of thinking about this is for partners to consider the 'personality' of the partnership: how would they like others to describe it? What do they want to be known for? Depending on what the partnership is trying to achieve, some examples of the kinds of principled aspirations that may be considered are highlighted in Figure 5.3.

Moving from principles to practice

A key question (all too often forgotten) is how to move beyond aspirational principles to daily practice. How best can principles become part of the very DNA of a partnership? This is not easy, and it cannot be assumed that it will just happen. A partnership broker can play an important role here. When value-laden terms (such as those used as partnering principles which are outlined earlier) are ascribed, they often hold very different meanings for different partners, particularly in cross-sectoral or cross-cultural partnerships.

For example, what does 'respect', a much-cited principle with wide opportunity for discrepancy between theory and practice in partnerships, mean to different partners? Many people can recognise what they consider to be a lack of respect, but this does not automatically lead to them enacting a respectful approach in their daily interactions with others. In one culture, 'respect' may be taken as never contradicting one's elders; in another, it may mean speaking fearlessly. At a more practical level, 'respect' may mean responding to requests quickly and for others, it may be about not clogging up their inboxes with poorly worded and long-winded emails.

These kinds of discrepancies can be a key cause of dissent and ill feeling in partnerships. A partnership broker can assist in avoiding unintended misunderstandings by facilitating a discussion about the types of behaviour that illustrate what respect (or other principles) actually means for each partner. This can be a relatively straightforward conversation opening up debate about different expectations and values. It can be a first step in moving principles from the ideal into reality.

An example of partnering principles, where an effort has been made to better explain each principle, is provided by UNICEF, the UN agency responsible for children. UNICEF has defined 11 guiding principles[11] for its engagement with civil society partners.

Case study 5.2 UNICEF's partnership principles

1 *Mutual focus on delivering results for women and children, especially the most disadvantaged* – Partnerships that directly contribute to the effective and efficient implementation of agreed programmes of cooperation and humanitarian intervention. Such partnerships must contribute clear value to the achievement of UNICEF strategic priorities and internationally agreed conventions and development goals, including the Convention on the Rights of the Child, the Convention of the Elimination of All Forms of Discrimination Against Women and the SDGs.

2 Mutual commitment to the core values of the Convention on the rights of the Child and the principles of good governance, notably transparency, accountability and sound financial management – UNICEF and its partners will each bring specific skills, resources and abilities to the partnership or collaborative relationship based on their respective tolerance for risk and in response to the needs of the relevant programme environment at national, regional and global levels. UNICEF will not partner with organisations found to be in breach of core UN norms or with any other entities that pose a reputation risk to UNICEF.

3 *Equity among all partners* – The objectives and activities pursued throughout the life of a partnership or collaborative relationship should be fully transparent and involve mutual accountabilities and mutual contributions as well as shared risks and benefits among all partners.

4 *Integrity and independence of partners* – Partnerships need to maintain the integrity and independence of both UNICEF and the partner(s).

5 *Cost-effectiveness of the partnership* – Partners should seek to minimise administrative and financial costs without compromising accountability or effectiveness.

6 *Forms of cooperation appropriate to the context and the goals to be pursued* – These arrangements should be formalised through a written, legally enforceable agreement when funds, supplies or other resources are transferred from UNICEF to the partner.

7 *Equality among all partners* – Equality requires mutual respect among all partners, regardless of the size or power of one partner. The participants must respect each other's mandates, obligations, principles and independence.

8 *Transparency in all decision-making processes that affect the partnership* – Transparency is achieved through open and participatory dialogue, with an emphasis on consultation and sharing of information from the earliest stages of the partnership. Communications and transparency, including financial transparency, increase the level of trust among partners.

9 *Responsibility to fulfil all obligations and commitments to the partnership* – Partner organisations have an ethical obligation to fulfil their responsibilities to the partnership in a responsible and context-appropriate manner. They may agree to undertake activities only when they have the means, competencies and skills needed to deliver on those commitments.

10 *Complementarity among partners* – The diversity of the development and humanitarian community is an asset when organisations build on their strengths and advantages and complement each other's contributions.

11 *Capacity development of national partners* – Partnerships with national and international CSOs will actively pursue opportunities to develop the capacities of these organisations at national and community levels. Capacity development initiatives will be undertaken in accordance with the goals and commitments expressed in the Paris Declaration on Aid Effectiveness and Accra Agenda for Action.

It is worth noting that these principles have been developed internally by the agency to inform its wider engagement with all civil society partners, and serve to make its intentions and expectations very clear which can be of great help to the partners. They also assist the agency to filter out unsuitable partners – those who do not subscribe to its approach – and do not necessarily reflect the needs, objectives or expectations of each individual partner which, even if not the same, may be sufficiently aligned for a partnership to be successful. In some ways, while a positive step, it could also be argued that this approach reinforces the power of the larger partner.

The partnering principles from the Australian Government's Business Partnerships Platform initiative among a private sector financial services organisation, a state bank, a government agency and an NGO provide another example of principles in partnership.[12] Here, the principles were de-veloped collaboratively and specific to this particular partnership through a guided discussion facilitated by a partnership broker as part of the Part-nering Agreement negotiations. These principles reflect the partners' shared intent of how they plan to work together going forward and were not used as part of a due-diligence process to select or exclude partners.

Case study 5.3 Australian government's business partnerships platform partnership principles

Principle	For example, this means:
1 Assume good intentions	• Everyone wants the project to achieve • Understand each other's constraints • Keep Partners informed early and equally allow time to reflect
2 Shared, long-term goal	• Can solve short-term problems if we commit to the long-term view
3 Retaining a sense of urgency	• Be responsive to other partner's needs • Be practical – keep an operational perspective • Meet commitments • Be aware of constraints and deadlines
4 Openness and trust	• Work through problems together, proactively • Inform each other as soon as any issues arise: 'early warning' • No surprises • Clear and transparent communications • Do what we say we are going to do • Trust that Partners can and will want to help • Build on existing good relationships and reputations
5 Willingness to adapt and change	• May need to be flexible and change as things evolve • Recognise the diversity of the different Partners
6 Respecting diversity and ensuring mutual benefit	• Respect what each Partner brings to the Partnership • Partners bring different skills, talents and knowledge • Ensure there is some benefit for each Partner

---

Dealing with dilemmas

Brass, Butterfield and Skaggs describe an ethical situation as one in which the 'consequences of an individual's decision affect the interests, welfare or expectations of others'.[13] In no situation is this truer than where a partnership broker is walking the fine line between a range of partners, many of whom may have competing interests and agendas, and he/she is seeking to help partners explore complementarity and arrive at alignment. There is, of course, considerable potential for abuse or misuse of this influential role: partnership brokers are often privy to confidential and sensitive information from a variety of sources within the partnership and must carefully navigate and understand what can and cannot be revealed in the interests of a principled and effective partnership, and what needs to merely inform the work they do with the partners. Partnership brokers can also be at risk of becoming too powerful themselves as players in the partnership, and must be alert to the danger of taking over leadership and direction from the partners, even where this is encouraged by the partners, thereby undermining one of the most fundamental principles of good partnering (as outlined earlier).

For independent partnership brokers, there is always the issue of who they are paid by and what impact this might have on their neutrality and how partners perceive them: in whose interests do they act if paid by one partner? In sensitive partnerships with low levels of trust, partnership brokers may be required to actively demonstrate the principles of openness and equity in all engagements. Partnership brokers may even find it necessary to consider negotiating with partners in advance to ensure that all partners agree to their appointment. To help build a sense of accountability to the entire partnership, they can also suggest a sharing of costs and responsibility relating to their hiring arrangement (for example, one partner paying, another managing the contract, another providing accommodation, etc.).[14] At all times, partnership brokers (whether internal or external to the partnership) need to act in the interests of the *partnership*, not the individual partners, though in our experience, this is ultimately one and the same.[15]

An ethical code for partnership brokers?

In light of these challenges, how can partnership brokers aspire and commit to a professional ethical code of conduct for their work? The answer to this question is likely to help determine the future role and credibility of this emerging profession. The Partnership Brokers Association advocates for (and requires its Accredited Partnership Brokers and Associates to sign up to) ten principles of partnership brokering good practice as a means of embedding/promoting ethical practice (see Table 5.2).[16]

Conclusion

Partnership brokers can play a fundamental role in supporting partners to establish efficient, effective and ethical ways of working collaboratively. Partnership brokering requires a nuanced and sophisticated skill set that

Table 5.2 The ten principles of partnership brokering good practice

1 Keep up to date with new developments in the theory and practice of brokering multi-stakeholder partnerships	Partnership brokering is an emergent and rapidly evolving profession. For this reason, it is important that partnership brokers remain abreast of current practice and thinking, reflecting on current lessons acquired from partnerships worldwide. This can be done in a number of ways: reading of practitioner and academic journals[17] and case studies; peer review and participation in Communities of Practice and other active forums of learning and exchange with other partnership brokers, as well as continuing professional development.
2 Being reflective and striving for diversity, equity, openness, mutual benefit and courageous practice when operating in a partnership brokering role	'Do as I say, not as I do' is anathema to principled partnership brokers, who strive to role model the types of behaviours and approaches they are trying to support partners to embed themselves. This is particularly important for partnership brokers at the start of a partnership process when they are establishing their credentials and trustworthiness as 'neutral brokers' but must be consistently so throughout their engagement with any partnership. A critical aspect of partnership brokering is the individual's ability to cultivate a reflective approach to their practice. This is in the interests of continuous professional development and assists understanding of the impact the decisions they make and how the way the broker has an impact on the outcomes of the partnership. A partnership broker therefore needs to systematically consider in advance of any intervention: What am I planning to do or say? What design choices will I make in running the process? How will I role model and promote the partnering principles in the partnership? And afterwards: What did I do? What happened? How did what I do impact on the partnership? What could I do differently? What patterns or insights do I notice in my own partnership brokering?[18]
3 Being prepared to challenge assumptions and poor partnering behaviour at any stage of the partnering cycle in ways most likely to bring about constructive change	This is frequently described as one of the areas in which the role played by a partnership broker is substantially different to that of a facilitator. It is often a partnership broker's role and responsibility to ask the tough questions; the ones that make partners uncomfortable; to uncover the 'elephants in the room' which no one else is prepared to ask about; to expose poor partnering behaviour which is inhibiting progress – just as much as it is to recognise and acknowledge positive partnering behaviour – when partners go above and beyond the upholding of principles they have committed to. Displaying such courage judiciously, at times when others are not prepared to do so, can often unblock and help partnerships to progress. In this way, a partnership broker can support partners to challenge their own and each other's assumptions and behaviours, in the interests of progressing the partnership. In order to build resilient and sustainable behaviours in partnerships, a partnership broker ideally builds the capacity of partners, over time, to surface and work through tough conversations themselves.

(Continued)

Table 5.2 (Continued)

4 Taking every opportunity to build partnering and partnership brokering capacity in others	For effective partnerships to be sustainable, it is essential that partnership brokers build their own capacity to be internal brokers, acting for and on behalf of the partnership as well as their own organisations. To do this requires a focus on the skills and processes involved in good partnering, as well as both a commitment and an understanding that good partnering takes a little time and attention throughout: it is not just a 'set and forget' process. This is a key role for a partnership broker who, from the outset, can raise this need to build a sustainable approach which is not reliant on external support over time. A good approach is for an external broker to work hand in hand with internal brokers from some, or all of the partner organisations, building their skills and understanding of what the broker is doing and why. For partnerships which have internal brokers from the start, building capacity may mean similar things – raising and acknowledging the partnering component of what they are doing, perhaps conducting short trainings or encouraging other partners to attend partnership training and development, and sharing responsibility for the partnership processes which they may have introduced.
5 Share knowledge generously and not hold onto knowledge for personal aggrandisement or gain	It is important that partnership brokers 'wear their skeleton on the outside', being purposeful and explicit about what they are doing, why and how, and not allowing what they do to become something 'mystical'. This goes hand in hand with the previous principle, where partnership brokers need to be committed to building capacity in others. It also speaks to the need for partnership brokers to be committed to the concept of 'servant' or invisible leadership, understanding that their role is to act in service of the partnership. Jim Collins identifies what he calls Level 5 leaders of consistently high-performing organisations as having both personal humility and professional will, noting that 'their ambition is first and foremost for the institution, not themselves'.[19] The same is true for partnership brokers, who need to be both modest and forthcoming with their knowledge, in the interests of the institution (the partnership) which they serve.
6 Explore any available alternative approaches before promoting a partnering process, in a commitment to achieving the best possible outcomes	With the flourishing of 'all things partnership', there is a risk that the approach itself is being done a disservice. A partnering approach is not always the best or most appropriate paradigm to achieve outcomes: partnerships can be costly in terms of transaction costs compared to alternative approaches, though in successful partnerships, this is usually considered a worthwhile investment. Partnership brokers have a responsibility to *not* promote the approach when they are aware that there is a better alternative model, such as a straight service contract or grant mechanism. It may be a partnership broker's role to identify this disconnect to the potential partners, and to help move the partnership to where it should be.

7 Be open about risks and seeking prior endorsement of those most likely to be affected by them before taking actions that might entail such risks

Partnership brokers are often privy to a great deal of information and also have the benefit of being able to take an overview of the entire partnership. For these reasons, they are often well placed to identify early any potential risks to partners, and also, very importantly, to project users or beneficiaries. The fundamental principle must be to do no harm, and to act with openness and integrity when identifying those risks and ensuring that partners are aware of them and act accordingly.

8 Be an ethical and responsible practitioner by raising concerns about the partnership or the actions of individual partners

Should a partnership broker become aware of any ethical issues which are impacting or have the potential to adversely affect the partnership or the partners, whether due to an external influence or to the actions of an individual partner, they must have the courage to raise them with those concerned. This may be highly sensitive and requires sound judgement and careful consideration of the most appropriate approach, but not to address the situation would be negligent.

9 Acknowledge competence limitations and be open to requesting assistance from others who will bring complementary skills or different approaches to the task

Every partnership broker is unique and different. They each bring different strengths to the partnerships they serve; based on their own experience, skills and training, and each will find their own unique style and approach. It is important for partnership brokers to have an objective understanding of their own capabilities and to know when to call on others for assistance. The test question should always be: What does the partnership need now and am I best placed to provide it?

10 Be willing to let go and hand over the partnership brokering role when the time is right

For partnerships to be successful and sustainable, they need to become self-reliant. This has particularly implications for external partnership brokers who have to avoid partnerships developing a dependency on them to manage the partnership or jump in and resolve conflicts. However, even those acting as internal partnership brokers have to consciously work to build capacity in others and manage the process of partnering in order to help protect against their own eventual departure. This requires a considerable degree of judgement: letting go too early and before partnering capacity has been developed can mean partnerships flounder; holding all the knowledge and expertise for the partnership can collapse them when partnership brokers do withdraw. Such an approach requires a certain amount of detachment and selflessness. Partnership brokering is not a role for those with egos which need constant affirmation, but more for those individuals who can draw satisfaction from seeing the partnership itself succeed.

Source: The Partnership Brokers Association (PBA).

can be adapted to each unique partnership scenario, along with sound judgement and a strong internal moral compass. A principled approach to partnering, as outlined here, requires a partnership broker to role model behaviours and approaches that can help partners to navigate complex challenges and solutions in a mutually beneficial way. While it is indeed a feature of partnership brokers that they seek to 'lead from behind', it is nevertheless important that they do not underestimate the direct impact they can have on improving (or undermining) partnership outcomes through their own behaviours, approaches and choices.

Notes

1 Principles 2–4 were originally identified and written about in Tennyson, R. (1998) *Managing Partnerships: Tools for Mobilising the Public Sector, Business and Civil Society as Partners in Development,* London: IBLF: 63. Principles 1 and 5 were added by the Authorised Practitioner Trainers of the Partnership Brokers Association in 2016.
2 Acland, A. (2011) *Working with Uncertainty.* Working Paper. UK: Andrew Acland & Associates.
3 As noted in Chapter 2, it should be noted that conflict may not always be a bad thing and can sometimes be a force for creativity and the development of innovative/radical solutions to problems.
4 Dixon, I. (2013) Partnering Solutions: How to build effective partnerships between the Business, Government, Community and Education Sectors. *White Paper.* Adelaide: Dixon Partnering Solutions.
5 French, J. & Raven, B. (1959) The bases of social power. In D. Cartwright (Ed.) *Studies in Social Power,* Ann Arbor, MI: Institute for Social Research: 150–167, and Raven, B.H. (1965) Social influence and power. In I.D. Steiner & M. Fishbein (Eds.) *Current Studies in Social Psychology,* New York: Holt, Rinehart, Winston: 371–382.
6 Hall, T. (n/d) Adaptation of French & Raven (1959) Op cit; and Raven, B.H. (2008). The Bases of Power and the Power/Interaction Model of Interpersonal Influence. *Analyses of Social Issues and Public Policy,* 8 (1): 1–22.
7 Adapted from Tennyson, R. (2004) *The Partnering Toolbook,* London & Geneva: IBLF & GAIN: 12.
8 Ibid: 6.
9 For more information about risk management approaches and tools in cross-sector partnerships, see: Mundy, J. (2006) Risky Business: Removing Barriers to Effective Partnerships for Development. Risk Management for the Broker's Toolbox. In *Café Conversations, A compendium of essays on the practice and theory of brokering multi-sector partnerships for sustainable development,* London: Partnership Brokers Association and Overseas Development Institute: 105–118.
10 Kaner, S. (2014) *Facilitator's Guide to Participatory Decision-Making,* 3rd edition. San Francisco: Jossey-Bass.
11 https://www.unicef.org/about/partnerships/index_60074.html August 2016 (accessed 9/2/2018) for a detailed description of UNICEF's civil society partnership principles.
12 See: http://dfat.gov.au/aid/who-we-work-with/private-sector-partnerships/bpp/Pages/business-partnerships-platform.aspx (accessed 9/2/2018).

13 Brass, D.J., Butterfield, K.D. & Skaggs, B.C. (1998) Relationships and Unethical Behavior: A Social Network Perspective. *The Academy of Management Review*, 23 (1): 14–31.

14 These issues are explored in more detail in Dixon, I. (2006) Funding Approaches for External Partnership Brokers. In *Café Conversations: A Compendium of Essays on the Practice and Theory of Brokering Multi-Sector Partnerships for Sustainable Development*, London UK: IBLF and Overseas Development Institute.

15 Sarah Nyanti explores some of these dilemmas further in her paper, Dealing with ethical dilemmas – a partnership brokers personal perspective. *Betwixt and Between, The Journal of Partnership Brokering*, Issue 6, June 2016 which is reproduced in Part 2 of this book.

16 These principles have been developed and refined collaboratively by partnership brokers from PBA's Communities of Practice, led by Ros Tennyson and Bulbul Baksi, and were expanded from the original seven to ten in 2016, reflecting the Communities' experience and lived practice over the preceding 10 years.

17 *Betwixt and Between, The Journal of Partnership Brokering*, is available online and includes articles addressing current practice from partnership brokering practitioners worldwide.

18 Ros Tennyson discusses different reflective approaches for partnership brokers in, 'The Imagined Conversation' in MacManus, S. & Tennyson, R. (2008) *Talking the Walk: A Communication Manual for Partnership Practitioners*, London: IBLF/TPI.

19 Collins, J.C. (2001) *Good to Great*, London: William Collins: 39.

Chapter 6

Partnership brokers as planners, managers and administrators

Surinder Hundal

The administrative and management role of a partnership broker is often seen as a given and receives little special attention. It is, however, critical to the success of the partnering process and outcomes. Much of the importance of planning, management and administration is revealed by a detailed study of the journals ('log books') written by individuals operating as partnership brokers as part of their formal Accreditation.[1] This study has provided the main source of information for this chapter.

A partnership broker with good management and administrative competencies will help put in place the infrastructural foundations for all partnership functions and activities. This will encourage at the outset efficiency, connectivity, interdependency and inclusion in the partnership's way of working and will help to avoid haphazard and piecemeal development of the partnership and its working relationships.

> When it works, it is as if the broker is providing invisible glue to hold the partnership together. And the value of good brokering for partnership effectiveness is such that it makes the struggle to establish good working relationships worth all the effort it can take to get it right.[2]

A partnership manager is more than a project manager

There is often a temptation to view a partnership project or programme from the lens of a project management paradigm. It is important to recognise that managing a partnership is not the same as managing a project. Although a partnership broker may draw on project management methodologies and skills in their work, their primary role is to bring a broader range of relationship-building, people management and engagement skills to the partnership.

The personal attributes of partnership brokers are slanted towards the ability to manage complexity and uncertainty. They may operate in multiple, complex, often matrixed structures and relationships where they have to manage a group with multiple accountabilities and responsibilities not directly under their control. Their own relationship management and people skills will hold primacy over their project management skills – the latter is easier to delegate to a colleague but if the partnership is to work effectively and efficiently, the partnership manager has to own the responsibility for facilitating and managing relationships within a partnership.

Role and tasks in the partnering process

Irrespective of the partnership broker–partner relationship, a partnership broker will be expected to perform and/or support a range of planning, co-ordination, administration and communication management roles during the lifetime of a partnership. These may include some or all of the following tasks:

Partnership management

- Be the primary interface and first-point-of-call for the partnership, acting as a coordinator and hub manager for all communication between the partners and between the partnership's wider stakeholders.
- Support the partners to develop the annual budget for the partnership; if required, manage and track expenditure.
- Facilitate definition and management of the core governance and operational processes and procedures for the partnership.
- Record key decisions and commitments of the partnership.
- Submit monthly and/or quarterly status reports to the partners.
- Support partners to review emerging problems and issues, anticipate and react to operational changes in the partnership.
- Recruit and manage staff to support partnership's projects or operational activities.
- Monitor and measure partnership programme performance using appropriate systems, tools and techniques.

Partnership planning

- Work with partners to identify resources for the partnership, ensure timely availability and access to contributions committed by partners and donors, and assign responsibilities for resource utilisation.
- Co-develop with partners a detailed project plan for the partnership.
- Support partners to manage a regular review process of the partnership and its work plans.

Partnership communications

- Work with partners to develop a communications plan.
- Regular communications with partners and other stakeholder groups.
- Manage the partnership's communications channels and products.

Partnership administration

- Organise and facilitate meetings, producing agendas and minutes.
- Manage the partnership contacts and other databases, keeping them up to date and compliant with privacy policies and national data protection laws.
- Create and maintain comprehensive partnership documentation, ensuring the documents are complete, current and appropriately stored in filing and retrieval systems.

Outcomes of effective management

Ideally, when a partnership broker is appointed, s/he should have a contract of employment, a contract for consultancy services or terms of reference. The agreement should include a clearly defined job description with the main activities required of the partnership broker, a set of associated goals, process of 'line management' and accountability as well as details of performance assessment. These will not only define the mandate for the partnership broker to perform their management role but also provide them with the opportunity to assess and develop that role as their individual contribution to the effectiveness of the partnership.

Typically, partnership brokers are appointed to provide a finite level of support to a particular partnership. Unlike traditional managers, they are not in a permanent position. We would not look for the same breadth and depth of assessment of a partnership broker's managerial ability as we would in a conventional management role. However, assessment has an important role to play in understanding the changing requirements of the partnership broker as the partnership develops and in making any adjustments to their management tasks and the working relationships within the partnership.

There are a number of ways in which management effectiveness can be assessed, ranging from ongoing self-assessment to informal dialogues with a line manager, to formal annual performance reviews involving multiple inputs. Effective partnership brokers are often reflective partnership brokers, familiar with concepts like dialogical reflection and self-evaluation.

The action research undertaken by PBA into logbooks of 250 accredited partnership brokers shows that self-reflection is viewed as an essential skill in improving managerial attributes.[3]

When I started the PBAS programme, my focus was on applying the skills and tools of brokering – scoping, selling, mapping, convening, negotiating, facilitating, reviewing, training, resourcing, institutionalising and more. Then with the deeper reflection (much encouraged by my mentor) I focused on examining how I, as a person, could lead and move partnerships. I wanted to examine and improve how I related to the people in the partnerships through listening, questioning, empathising, speaking, negotiating, proposing, counselling, confronting, preventing, intuiting, and finally giving and receiving.[4]

Assessing the performance of a partnership broker

Partnership brokers are invariably accountable to partners as well as to the employing organisation and may report on a day-to-day basis to an assigned line manager. They will all have a view on how effectively the partnership broker is performing their planning, managing and administrative role.

The views of partners and the employing organisation can be collected on an informal or formal basis. Informal review can be done as part of the normal working relationship, where, for instance, the line manager and the partnership broker may regularly set aside some time to review progress on designated tasks and milestones and any emerging management issues the partnership broker might face.

Formal reviews can take two possible formats: through an assessment interview led by the line manager, which can be done midway through the assignment or through a 360° review involving all the partners, either at the midway point or as part of the overall evaluation of the partnership. Given the complex nature of a partnership broker's role, which may change during the life cycle of the partnership, and their accountability to both a single organisational line management structure and the partners as a group, a 360° review would bring in multiple perspectives on assessing the different aspects of a partnership brokers' performance. These different forms of review are explored further in Chapter 9.

Challenges of managing partnerships

Given the complex nature of multi-stakeholder partnerships, they often present challenges for a partnership broker which managers in a single organisation would not necessarily face. Unlike their organisational counterparts, partnership brokers have a limited tenure, ultimately making themselves redundant. Over-dependency on the partnership broker can become a challenge.

I sometimes felt as if I was Shiva – with many hands – as it seemed that I was managing everything. It was exhausting...[5]

I was seen as the main contact for the partnership – but this seemed to slip very quickly into me doing all the work and partners simply handing everything over. Then at a later stage I got a lot of feedback that the partners resented how much initiative I was taking. It seemed like a bit of a "no-win" situation.[6]

There have also been instances where the partners just refuse to interact with one another and have expected me to do all the work. Although I see my role as helping the partners, it is vital that they also step up and learn how to deal with issues on their own.[7]

A partnership broker has to ensure that the management processes they help put in place for a partnership have to support self-management and assumption of responsibility and accountability amongst the partners. This has implications for a partnership broker's ability to know when to be directional and when to take a supporting/facilitative role. The dependency can also work in the opposite direction where a partnership broker is unwilling to hand over ownership to the partners, risking exhaustion and resentment.

Maybe I became too close to the partners and the whole thing became too personal with social activities – some partners began to resent it.[8]

I knew that once the partners were communicating well, collaborating on the projects and had systems in place for dealing with any future difficulties, I needed to step back. But this was not an easy process – I found it hard to untangle whether my reluctance was out of genuine concern of what might happen without me or whether I just didn't want to let go. I am still working this out.[9]

Challenges may also result from the partnering process and/or from working with individuals. A partnership broker may have to deal with 'non-compliance' where processes and procedures put in place to support management are ignored/dismissed and undermine efficient working. They may have to deal with staff turnover, requiring investment in time to address newcomers who may reveal different priorities, vested interests and prefer different management approaches. Inefficiencies may also be introduced if there is poor or erratic engagement with the partnership's day-to-day activity, causing delays and disruptions to the partnership programme plans.

External developments that have an impact on partnership management include the following:

- Remote and matrix working – a partnership broker may have to work with multiple individuals in partner organisations which are located in multiple locations and/or time zones; they may also have to monitor geographically dispersed and matrixed elements of a project. This can create challenges in collaboration and communication and make it harder to build personal relationships and a partnership culture. As a manager and administrator, the partnership broker will need to become competent in using online collaboration, project management, file sharing and networking tools.

- Technologies – there is a plethora of digital communication, collaboration and networking products as well as planning, modelling, accounting and other 'business' software applications. Each partner organisation or individual may have their own preferred systems and ways of working related to their organisational culture. In such a situation, the partnership broker may have to assess the value of different systems and negotiate the best course of action for a mutually agreed system. It may be counterproductive to introduce unfamiliar or unpopular technologies which may be poorly adopted by the partners.
- Donor requirements – there is a growing emphasis on demonstrating value for money in development and humanitarian financing where many donors now operate complex policies on financial management and reporting. Although the partnership broker is not expected to be a financial expert, they will increasingly need to support partners to demonstrate 'value for money': to set 'goals and outcomes that will capture and account for the value of partnership process and indirect value created through partnership model delivery'.[10]

Conclusion

The nature and content of a partnership broker's role as a manager can be differentiated from our usual understanding of a 'manager' in that first and foremost, it is focused on building and managing complex and dynamic relationships within the partnership, which goes beyond the operational management of a partnership project or programme. As well as an ability to know when to be directional and when to be facilitative, this requires ongoing efforts by a partnership broker to ensure the cultivation of self-management and accountability amongst the partners so that they take ultimate responsibility for the partnership governance and administration.

Notes

1 Offered by the Partnership Brokers Association and, to date, the only formally examined partnership brokering qualification available.
2 Extract from a logbook entry of an external broker provided by PBA.
3 PBA (2012) What do partnership brokers do? An enquiry into practice. http:// partnershipbrokers.org/w/wp-content/uploads/2010/07/What-do-Partnership-Brokers-Do.pdf (accessed 9/2/2018).

4 Ibid: 8.
5 Ibid: 24.
6 Ibid.
7 Ibid: 25.
8 Ibid: 24.
9 Ibid: 27.
10 Poupart, E.C. (2014) Value for money in partnerships – A challenge to partnership brokers. *Betwixt & Between, The Journal of Partnership Brokering*, (4). http://partnershipbrokers.org/w/journal/value-for-money-in-partnerships-a-challenge-to-partnership-brokers (accessed 9/2/2018).

Chapter 7

Follow the leader? Leadership in a collaborative model

Ros Tennyson and Rachel Houghton

The success of any partnership depends fundamentally on the willingness of all those involved to act collaboratively rather than competitively. It also requires accountability, not only vertically (to line managers/decision-makers) but horizontally (to each other). This often necessitates a radical change in both individual and institutional mindsets, cultures, systems and behaviours. Such a change takes commitment, confidence and courage, because it often involves challenging norms and seeking to work in a deep way with others to 'co-create' alternative approaches and practices. In other words, it takes leadership.

Yet what sort of leadership are we talking about? Is it 'business-as-usual' leadership, or is something palpably different needed as we navigate an increasingly complex and multi-polar world?

A wide-ranging review of leadership literature reveals that conventional notions of leadership are essentially grounded in a single-sector or single-organisation paradigm. Leaders in this model are generally those in a specific, named role who head up a team or an organisation, and who have recognised status, authority and relatively unilateral decision-making power. This seems to be the recognised norm when we speak of 'leaders', and there is a tendency to assume that this is de facto what constitutes leadership. There is also the leader who has acquired their status because of her or his charismatic personality and/or personal vision, and as a result has become a figurehead for others and has inspired dedicated followership. Such people become leaders on the strength of their conviction rather than as a result of an allocated hierarchical role, though they may, of course, also become powerful figures at the top of a hierarchy (for example, 'dissidents' who become presidents).

These types of leader are similar in terms of the unilateral nature of their authority and, as such, their role and function could be considered to be at odds with a more collaborative, multi-stakeholder model (i.e. a 'partnership') that seeks, above all, to be equitable and horizontally accountable. We therefore propose that, within any partnership context, ideas and practices of leadership require exploration and understanding, and will be something that both partners and partnership brokers need to address. In this chapter, we consider three things that are fundamental to the issue of leadership in a collaborative model: the impact and influence of leaders on partnerships; new models of leadership emerging from within the partnership paradigm and the role of partnership brokers in helping partners to navigate leadership issues effectively.

A starting premise is that 'leadership in collaboration is more an activity than a role'.[1] This idea is enriched by consideration of what might be described as 'human consciousness literature' on leadership as well as literature that looks at leadership in global networks.[2] Human consciousness literature recognises that '...inner work is [increasingly] a prerequisite for effectiveness',[3] while literature on leadership in networks considers the art of collaborating across boundaries and the need for 'systems intelligence'. These and similar works introduce us to the idea that some leaders are already seeing the need to pay attention both to what lies within human beings and to the systems within which they operate. These two factors are key to developing appropriate forms of leadership that support and build collaboration as a new operational paradigm.[4]

It is worth noting (and declaring our bias) that the Partnership Brokers Association (PBA) has, since its inception, stressed the importance of the 'interior condition'[5] of the partnership broker. Indeed, what follows is as much informed by the authors' affiliation to PBA and their many insights from partnership brokering practice, as it is from reviewing leadership literature. It is very much a starting point for an early exploration of partnership brokering as a leadership issue.

Leaders and partnership

Those involved in partnerships commonly cite 'buy in' from senior management as central to a partnership's capacity to operate. Without this endorsement from those in authority, a partnership is perceived to be at risk of marginalisation and/or of being dropped when other things take organisational priority. While some partnerships are initiated by senior leaders, often to address common challenges that one organisation realises it cannot address alone or for reasons of, for example, increased policy impact, partnerships are more frequently established for reasons of expediency. These may include the need to gain access to funding or as a result of prevailing 'political correctness' rather than an ideological commitment to collaboration and partnering per se. In other instances, it is donors who require a collaborative approach from their 'partners', usually in pursuit of a reduction in their transaction costs.

One of the biggest challenges to partnership comes from the context of conventional organisational structures and approaches, where organisational identity is paramount and where senior leaders can wield considerable explicit or implicit power over partnerships. This can be problematic for many reasons, including the fact that every organisation represented in a partnership will have a leader who may or may not be aligned with the values and priorities of the other partners. This can easily result in a 'positional' approach to partnering, with all the potential for conflict that this implies. In other words, partnerships that are dependent on the approval of senior people in individual partner organisations (who are often quite remote from the actual partnership) may find that they are trapped in a 'business as usual' model with little room for manoeuvre and even less for the change and transformation that many of those promoting a partnership approach hope for.

It is useful at this point to consider a definition of the term 'leader'. The Oxford English Dictionary defines a leader as *the person who leads or commands a group, organisation or country,* while the Oxford Thesaurus presents a long list of synonyms such as: *chief, head, principal, boss, commander, captain, figurehead, controller, chairman/chairwoman, president, premier, governor, ruler, monarch, sovereign, master.* Only towards the end of the list do the terms *guru* and *mentor* appear.[6] This suggests that somewhere, albeit buried in the myriad of conventional definitions, a leader is not only defined in terms of hierarchy and power, but also in terms of wisdom (guru) and guidance (mentor). In this way, and in our experience, a leader can either 'enable' or 'disable' a partnership.

Of course, leaders, even in conventional models, come in all types and styles, and they can exercise their authority in a range of ways that may either help or hinder a partnership's ability to flourish. An enabling leader or decision-maker can enhance partnerships by being someone who is willing to cede control to a more equitable, inclusive and self-directing model; understands and practises effective communication and accountability at all levels of the partnership; knows that they don't know what they don't know; gives space for change to happen and sees the potential of partnering as a mechanism for challenging and changing the status quo when necessary. On the other hand, a disabling leader or decision-maker is someone who exercises too much control; is risk averse; is resistant to change; avoids or shuts down disagreement; sees disruption as insubordination and regards partnering as little different from more conventional approaches that only support the status quo.

Linked to the issue of the impact and influence of leaders on the effectiveness of a partnership comes the question: how many partnerships disappoint (or even fail) because they stay at the level of compliance and fall short of achieving real change or transformation? And how much is the result of leaders that disable rather than enable?

An important driver for all leaders is the need to achieve results. What kinds of leadership will drive the results that partners seek to achieve through partnering? What kinds of leadership will ensure that a partnering approach optimises its potential and achieves bold targets, for example, for the highly ambitious global Sustainable Development Goals?

Newer leadership models

The terms 'guru' and 'mentor' helpfully challenge the idea that leadership is synonymous with authority and power. This is important because, in a complex, multi-polar world, where challenges are not merely technical (which conventional managerial leadership is oriented to resolve) but rather adaptive (which compels flexible, creative and experimental approaches) '...the distinction between exercising leadership and exercising authority is crucial'.[7] In a multi-stakeholder model, leadership involves mobilising a whole range of people to tackle complex challenges, an approach that is, of course, familiar to partnership brokers and at the heart of effective partnership brokering. This brings us back to the notion that leadership in a collaborative context is more a practice, '... a verb, not a job'[8] and an activity, '...that can be done by anybody, independent of their role'.[9]

Within partnership theory and practice, there is a move away from leadership understood as a heroic, senior figure (usually male) in a position of sole and ultimate authority at the top of a hierarchy, generally within a single institution, dispensing instructions and expecting to be followed. The recognition of complexity, and of the need to approach complex challenges from a systems perspective, necessitates very different ideas about leadership from our traditional thinking.

This is evidenced by the plethora of literature that examines leadership from a systems perspective, and that also considers the inner life of leaders, that has grown over the past 20 years to reconsider and reconfigure notions of leadership. 'Systems Leadership',[10] 'Collective Leadership',[11] 'Connective Leadership',[12] 'Distributed Leadership',[13] 'Shared Leadership',[14] 'Servant Leadership',[15] 'Stewardship',[16] 'Universal Leadership',[17] 'Authentic Leadership',[18] 'Adaptive Leadership'[19] and 'Soulful Leadership'[20] are just some of the concepts that are helping to challenge and reframe more traditional views of leadership, and to explore the activity of leadership in networks and collaborative arrangements.[21] While many of these approaches and concepts overlap and are mutually reinforcing, some are worth exploring in more detail in terms of their relevance to partnering and multi-stakeholder collaboration.

Servant leadership

The idea of servant leadership was developed by Robert Greenleaf in the late 1970s and, as such, is one of the oldest alternative notions of leadership that we consider. The premise of 'servant leadership', which has become quite widely used, is that:

> The servant-leader is a servant first... It begins with the natural feeling that one wants to serve, to serve first. Then conscious choice brings

one to aspire to lead. That person is sharply different from one who is leader first, perhaps because of the need to assuage an unusual power drive or to acquire material possessions.[22]

This model of leadership aligns well with the notion of the partnership broker as someone whose primary task is to serve partners in developing and delivering their intended goals. Whilst the concept of 'servant' is somewhat out of favour (perhaps being too easily associated with 'servitude'), the theme of a non-egotistical approach to leadership is still appropriate for the collaborative paradigm we are concerned with here.

Notwithstanding, some concern has been expressed about the universal suitability of the concept of 'servant leadership' as applied in partnerships:

> As attractive as servant leadership is as a guiding framework, it has limitations in practice. Service to others is an important way to develop human potential and build a collaborative community. Yet other leadership approaches may be necessary when the environment for collaboration is constantly changing. For example, where projects are complex, participants leave, new people come on board, deadlines loom, conflicts emerge, stakeholders shift their positions or other priorities require attention. These dynamics are very common in partnering projects. They demand more adaptive and situation-driven approaches than servant leadership tends to offer.[23]

Adaptive leadership

Questions about servant leadership have arisen because, in dynamic, complex partnership contexts, brokers must ensure that they do not just stay in the role of 'servant of what is' but know when to become 'shapers of what might be'.[24] This is borne out by PBA's experience where partnership brokers are encouraged to ask themselves the question 'what is needed now?' and to exercise good judgment about when to step back and support partners' decisions or when to step up to be more intentional and to provide direction for the partnership.

Ideas about adaptive leadership have also developed as challenges, and the partnerships required to address them, have become increasingly complex in terms of their scale, global reach and number of stakeholders. Complex challenges (and the leadership required to address them) sit at the 'transformational' end of the partnering spectrum. This requires: knowing what to build on or what to jettison; willingness to be experimental; learning what works in a particular time and place; maintaining an overarching vision and the necessity of persistence over time. All these are the key leadership competencies encompassed in the notion of adaptive leadership.

Leadership from a systems perspective

Any collaboration can be viewed as a system, defined by the Oxford English Dictionary as '... a set of things working together as parts of a mechanism or an interconnecting network; a complex whole'. Authors such as Lipman-Blumen (2000), Neal (2006), Senge (2008), Waddell (2011), Scharmer and Kaufer (2013) and Western (2013) are useful for us here.[25] In *Global Action Networks*, Waddell[26] presents the competencies captured in Figure 7.1 as central to leadership from a systems or network perspective:

Systems intelligence is at the heart of what it means to be a successful leader in any partnership or network. This reconnects us to the importance of wisdom, mentioned earlier. On this, Peter Senge writes:

> For me, the fundamentals start with a set of deep capacities with which few in leadership positions ... could claim to have developed: systems intelligence, building partnership across boundaries, and openness of mind, heart, and will to develop such capacities requires a lifelong commitment to grow as a human being in ways not well understood in contemporary culture.[27]

The pragmatic leader

Huxham and Vangen use a different lens through which to view adaptive, situation-driven approaches.[28] They argue that leadership in a collaborative model requires a mix of pragmatism and idealism.[29] They find that leaders in collaborative contexts tend to adopt both a facilitative and a directive role at different phases of partnership building.[30] Essentially, what is being expressed is the necessity for some form of 'push', and the authors' premise is that leaders operating in partnerships are likely to require a firm

Leadership skills	Leadership attributes
Connecting Stewarding Handling paradox & uncertainty Inspiring	Systems intelligence Being 'leaderful' Trustworthiness Entrepreneurial flair
Network development skills	**Network development attributes**
Systems thinking Community development / network Strategising Empowering	Empathy Trustworthiness Visionary Entrepreneurial

Figure 7.1 Leadership competencies.
Source: Waddell, S. (2011) Global Action Networks, Creating Our Future Together, London: Palgrave Macmillan.

hand to ensure that things move forward, given their often distributed and complex nature:

> Leaders in a partnership model need to have vision and diplomacy. They need to be someone who can steer where the partnership is going and have a clear picture of what success looks like. As opposed to organisational leadership, which is essentially self-serving, leadership in partnership needs to take account of multiple perspectives. It is more holistic and systemic. Above all, partnerships require leaders with good antennae who can read signals and help partners to adjust the partnership accordingly. This involves patience and persistence.[31]

This reinforces the idea of leadership as a set of activities and approaches rather than a specific role or function. Moreover, as leadership is often distributed within a partnership, it involves a range of individuals stepping up into leadership activities and stepping back when the needs of the partnership change. Leadership thus becomes something fluid, responsive and time-bound.

These new leadership models and approaches could be referred to as 'post-heroic'[32] and take, as their starting point, a concern with shared goals, teamwork and coordination to effectively release the power of the many, not the few.

Different types of leadership within a partnership

A case study of a corporation working in partnership with NGOs provides a useful insight into the issue of leadership in a partnership. Leadership was regarded by those involved in this partnership as a key issue and, interestingly, it took several different forms (see Table 7.1).[33]

Of the five types of partnership leader identified in this study, the researchers concluded from their interviews and observations that the single most important form of leadership in terms of the partnership's success, and interestingly the least visible, was the leadership provided by a small number of individuals tasked with managing the partnering process, described in the study as 'partnership brokers'.

Growing new leadership approaches: the role of partnership brokers

Our experiences of partnership, consortium and network brokering over many years have led us to conclude that partnership brokers are at the cutting edge of promoting (and even shaping) new leadership approaches. Some of these approaches have been highlighted in this chapter, and some are still emerging.

Table 7.1 Types of leadership

Type of Leadership	Leadership Characteristics	Typical Activities
Champions	• Recognised status • Credibility with all key audiences (internal and external) • Authority	• Selling the idea to different stakeholders • Demonstrating commitment by example • Seeking out other people of influence
Specialists	• Subject knowledge • Direct experience of issue • Expertise	• Project development • Explaining options and what is appropriate in different contexts • Ensuring standards
Brokers	• Understanding of different sector perspectives (systems intelligence) • Good verbal and written communication skills • Patience	• Acting as interpreters between different players (within and across partner organisations) • Managing meetings and navigating areas of potential conflict or confusion • Developing appropriate tools and procedures for the project to ensure it is efficient and effective
Coordinators	• Ability to mobilise (people and resources) • Access to people and projects • Enthusiasm	• Engaging staff at local levels • Communicating/reporting upwards • Connecting to key players/stakeholders at local level
Overseers	• Understanding of project's ambition and complexity • Willingness to give their name/backing to the project • Commitment	• Looking at the project as a whole from an objective perspective • Asking challenging questions • Providing quality assurance to external stakeholders/donors

Source: Tariq, H. & Tennyson, R. (2010) *In the Bank's Best Interest – Case Study of an Ambitious Partnership,* London: International Business Leaders Forum.

It is becoming increasingly clear to us, and perhaps to others, that a core activity for those in partnership brokering roles is to encourage all those involved to consider 'the leadership question', and to help all stakeholders work together to decide what leadership activities are required and how leadership and decision-making will be exercised. This is likely to be different in each collaboration since context and culture inevitably influence what is acceptable and, as importantly, what may (and may not) be possible.

Partnership brokers are sometimes a partnership's initiators. In other words, they become its de facto leaders, at least at the beginning. Their role as partnership initiators may be because they generated the idea of a partnership or because they have been chosen (or have opted) to take a leading role. Perhaps they have been appointed as leaders of global networks or consortia where they find that adhering to core partnering principles and new 'horizontal' leadership models can help to guide them in their collaboration-building activities.

In our experience, where partnership brokers have the responsibility for leading complex networks and multi-stakeholder or multi-country programmes of work, they have often had to help their members and other stakeholders understand different operating structures and frameworks and associated models of leadership and decision-making in order to ensure that the desired outcomes are achieved. This suggests that knowledge and expertise in partnership theory and practice is an essential skill for both partnership brokers as leaders and leaders who need to adopt a brokering role in a particular context.

Partnership brokers with leadership responsibilities also need to work hard to juggle their strong sense of intention and direction with suitably non-directive approaches, such as:

- **Holding** space for the group to work through disagreement or even breakdown to breakthrough;
- **Accepting** when compromise is no longer acceptable;
- **Modelling** the behaviours that are at the heart of productive collaboration;
- **Understanding** how to use time optimally and creatively;
- **Judging** when (and when not) to intervene;
- **Integrating** learning and feedback processes into day-to-day working practices;
- **Supporting** exploration, experimentation and a level of risk-taking;
- **Drawing out** the innate (perhaps very different) leadership qualities in others.

Not all partnership brokers are in recognised leadership roles per se, but certainly they all need to think about facilitating and growing the capacity of a range of people to lead on behalf of the group. This helps to build not only the leadership skills of others but, as importantly, their adaptive skills as well. Partnership brokers can provide support to partners (as individuals and as a group) to challenge poor leadership where it holds back the vision, values and operations of partners. Poor leadership can be manifested at the level of: behaviour (whether dogmatic or evasive); decisions (what the decisions are as well as the way they are taken) and/or in the promulgation of strategies and systems that disable rather than enable the partnership.

Continuing in this vein, once an agreement to partner has been reached, the programme of work defined and the management arrangements established, the partnership broker's role is likely to move towards guiding the partners in the direction of an operational model where responsibility is held collaboratively and in which, despite the possible differences in scale and resource contributions of the different partners, leadership is shared.

In some instances, partnership brokers may adopt the role of 'coach' in helping to build the necessary skills and/or confidence of those involved in the partnership. At other times, it may be more a question of acting as a 'mentor' and providing background support by helping individuals to reflect on their emerging leadership role or to make sense of what is (and is not) happening in the partnership and how they can best help to optimise the partnership's potential.

There may be circumstances where the partnership broker sees the need to challenge a pattern of subservience or collusion with unhelpful systems and practices or to call out unacceptable behaviours that inhibit genuine progress. In this instance, the partnership broker may choose, or may be asked to become, a 'challenger' or 'disruptor' either internally (within the partnership) or externally (on behalf of the partners) or both. Being 'disruptive' may require partnership brokers to promote a shift that involves 'not just building inspiring visions but facing difficult truths about the present reality and learning how to use the tension between vision and reality to inspire truly new approaches'.[34]

Partnership brokering and the issue of power

Imbalances in power are often cited as the major challenge for those involved in partnership and collaboration. The inappropriate exercise of power, whether in the form of asserting authority, exercising tight control, demanding linear accountability, making decisions unilaterally, or the bullying effect of a dominating personality, is fundamentally anticollaborative. The misuse of power is often, understandably and correctly, seen as deeply destructive to partnering endeavours.

It is, however, important not to demonise the concept of power but to understand and manage it constructively within a collaborative working arrangement (see Chapter 5). Partnership brokering itself is not a powerless role; far from it. Yet, it requires an exercise of power that is subtle, disciplined, flexible and context-appropriate. It requires partnership brokers and partners to reframe power as taking responsibility rather than as exercising authority, and doing so for the benefit of the whole rather than the one. In this regard, it is important to redefine power away from authority in the same way we have redefined leadership away from authority and traditional concepts of power:

> Power is an instrument, not an end in itself. It must be used only in order to bring about the greater good. Power is different from force. It is most useful when it turns into service.[35]

This returns us to the importance of adaptive capacity and to the idea that the judicious exercise of power in collaborative initiatives is ultimately a question of balance. A partnership broker who seizes power inappropriately, or is unwilling to let go of control when the time is right, acts as a disabler and betrays one of the core principles of effective brokering in that it is essentially about serving the partnership's goals and not the partnership broker's ego.

Breaking new ground: building into the unknown

With their work firmly focused on collaborative initiatives that pursue sustainable outcomes across a variety of issues and contexts, partnership brokers are uniquely placed to support more fluid forms of leadership. These are likely to require the capacities suggested in Quinn's notion of 'fundamental' leadership and in Scharmer's concept of 'presencing', and occur when we become 'results centred, internally directed, other-focused and externally open'.[36]

> When we commit to a vision to do something that has never been done before, there is no way to know how to get there. We simply have to build the bridge as we walk on it.[37]

One of the more common definitions of partnership brokers (see Chapter 1) is that of 'bridge builder'. This implies far more than connecting people, though that is important. It suggests linking across a divide, engineering a fit-for-purpose structure, and saving time and energy. Building the bridge as we walk on it requires us to step into the unknown and, possibly, by doing so becoming 'a distortion to the social system in which we reside'.[38]

Bridge-building is not for the faint-hearted. As they build new bridges, partnership brokers and all those with whom they work require a significant level of courage, a quality that, for many, is also a key characteristic of new leadership.[39] Courage is also a key partnering principle (see Chapter 5) and is at the heart of partnership brokering.

Conclusion

We would like to conclude by drawing attention to what lies within and to ways in which partnership brokers can manifest their best selves in service to their partnership practice. Whatever their relationship to the issue of leadership, and assuming that it changes frequently during the life cycle of a partnership, partnership brokers need to take time to review their role and to reflect on how effectively they are undertaking it. It is a good practice for brokers to seek, and be open to, feedback as part of their commitment to constantly improving their practice. This is a matter of professional discipline. How far a partnership broker is willing to learn and change can make or break a partnership. How a partnership broker acts to promote, support and model new leadership approaches that are fit for partnering purposes can also have a significant impact on how effectively a partnership is able to lead change.

Senge, Hamilton and Kania regard the fostering of reflection as an essential component of being a 'system leader', one of the core partnership and collaboration concepts advocated throughout this chapter:

> Deep, shared reflection is a critical step in enabling groups of organisations and individuals to actually "hear" a point of view different from their own, and to appreciate emotionally as well as cognitively each other's reality. This is an essential doorway for building trust where distrust had prevailed and for fostering collective creativity.[40]

Partnership brokers will find their own ways of becoming more reflective practitioners. An illustration of this is provided below, where partnership brokering as leadership is seen as an 'experimental art' in which 'opportunities for exercising leadership are also learning opportunities'.[41]

Case study 7.1 Extract from partnership broker's log book[42]

On trying my best to become a new kind of partnership broker modelling-distributed leadership by example, I regularly find myself abashed and ashamed at how often I fall short because of my excessive enthusiasm, impatience and quickness to judge. New Year's resolutions to do better:

1 **Be prepared** – be ready for what may be needed from me and attend to my own physical and mental well-being. Be attentive and ready for action, but don't over-plan.
2 **Become a more reflective practitioner** – by making the time to step back and review what has happened in ways that will inform what the next steps should be.
3 **Keep learning** – by using all information (verbal and non-verbal) as data for better understanding and deeper insights – keep this logbook going and make the recording of new ideas, reactions and lessons a matter of habit.
4 **Hear the stories and see the bigger picture** – every individual has a unique story and is part of a bigger and complex context. Every person's story has significance beyond the immediacy of the presenting issue.

5   **Be more self-aware and self-critical** – be determined not be too easily satisfied with my own performance and equally determined to keep reviewing and refining skills, knowledge and experience whilst also remembering that too much introspection is also a form of egotism.

6   **Follow up** – it isn't only a question of preparation but how to support insights that have emerged, confirm agreed action points or to lay the groundwork for what needs to come next.

7   **Let go** – ultimately, the fruits of this work belong to everyone not to me. My role as a leader may be important but it is fundamentally transient. Be ready to let go of the leadership role when the time is right, with warmth and with grace.

I wonder what constitutes 'good enough' in the Bettelheim use of that term[43] and how does one avoid this as a justification for mediocre practice?

The modern-day journey of partnership brokering and of emerging new leadership fit for a collaborative model is about working at the frontiers of self and of system. Time and again, the quality of results produced by any system depends on the quality of awareness from which people in the system operate. The formula for a successful change process is not 'form follows function', but 'form follows consciousness'. As O'Brien says in a conversation with Otto Scharmer: 'The success of any intervention depends on the interior condition of the intervener'.[44]

Partnership brokers who exemplify and/or promote effective leadership have learnt the art of give and take and know when the time is right for them to step up or to step away. They understand that it is not their work but the work of the partners that achieves results. Their reward for good work is that they know that they are no longer necessary. This is an indicator of a competent professional partnership broker and an expression of personal disciple and self-confidence. It is also an act of leadership.

Notes

1 Waddell, S. (2011) *Global Action Networks, Creating Our Future Together*, London: Palgrave Macmillan: 146.

2 For example, the inspiring book by Frederic Laloux (2014) *Reinventing Organisations: A Guide to Creating Organizations Inspired by the Next Stage of Human Consciousness*, Leuven, Belgium: Nelson Parker; Judi Neal (2006) *Edgewalkers: People and Organizations That Take Risks, Build Bridges, and Break New Ground*, Wesport, CT: Praeger Publishers; Steve Waddell (2011) Op.cit. and Peter Senge (2008) *The Necessary Revolution: How Individuals and Organizations Are Working Together to Create a Sustainable World*, New York: Crown Business.

3 Elworthy, S. (2015) The tools for a radical new kind of leadership, *The Guardian*, 7th January.
4 Another important discourse for collaborative leadership is that of eco-leadership. Simon Western (2013) posits: 'Eco-leadership is becoming the most important leadership discourse for our time, although it is not yet the dominant discourse. The prefix 'Eco' signifies how progressive leaders conceptualize organizations as ecosystems and networks, rather than closed systems. Organizations are rethought as "ecosystems within ecosystems" meaning that organizations are webs of connections, networks that operate like ecosystems'. Unfortunately, the authors did not have the time to engage fully with this literature. See Western, S. (2013) *The Eco-leadership discourse: Connectivity and ethics* in S. Western (Ed.) *Leadership; A Critical Text,* London: SAGE Publications Ltd, 2nd edition, 243–280.
5 A phrase taken from Scharmer, O. (2016) *Theory U: Leading from the Future as it Emerges*, Oakland, CA: Berrett-Koehler Publishers, 2nd edition.
6 It is only towards the end of a long list that terms are cited that convey something a little different. These include *guru* and *mentor* suggesting that somewhere, rather deeply buried in conventional definitions, leadership is also about wisdom, not just power.
7 Heifetz, R.A., Linsky, M. & Grashow, A. (2009) *The Practice of Adaptive Leadership: Tools and Tactics for Changing Your Organization and the World*, Boston, MA: Harvard Business Press.
8 Ibid: 24.
9 Waddell (2011) Op.cit: 146.
10 Scharmer, O. & Kaufer, K. (2013) *Leading from the Emerging Future*, Oakland, CA: Berrett-Koehler Publishers; Western, S (2013) 'The Eco-leadership Discourse: Connectivity and Ethics' (pre-publication copy of a book chapter; personal communication), Neal (2008) & Waddell (2011) op.cit.
11 Cullen, K., Willburn, P., Chrobot-Mason, D. & Palus, C. (2014) Networks: *How Collective Leadership Really Works*, University of Cincinnati: Center for Creative Leadership.
12 Lipman-Blumen, J. (2000) *Connective Leadership, Managing in a Changing World*, Oxford University Press.
13 Spillane, J. (2006) *Distributed leadership*. San Francisco: Jossey-Bass
14 Pearce, C.L. & Conger, J.A. (2002) *Shared Leadership – Reframing the Hows and Whys of Leadership*, London: Sage Publications.
15 Greenleaf, R.K. (1998) *The Power of Servant Leadership,* Oakland, CA; Berrett-Koehler Publishers.
16 Block, P. (1996) *Stewardship: Choosing Service over Self-interest,* Oakland, CA: Berrett-Koehler Publishers.
17 Bennis, W. (2007) The Challenges of Leadership in the Modern World. *American Psychologist*, 62 (1): 2–5.
18 Peltier, B. (2009) *The Psychology of Executive Coaching,* UK: Routledge, and Goffee, R. & Jones, G. (2015) *Why Should Anyone be Led by You?* Harvard Business Review Press.
19 Heifetz, Linsky & Grashow (2009) Op.cit.
20 Fry, L. & Altman, Y. (2013) *Spiritual Leadership in Action: Achieving Extraordinary Results through Ordinary People*, Charlotte, NC: Information Age Publishing Inc and Benefiel, M. (2008) *The Soul of a Leader: Finding Your Path to Fulfilment and Success*, New York: The Crossroad Publishing Company.
21 See for example Collective and Connective Leadership (op cit) as well as Network Leadership, see: https://ssir.org/network_entrepreneurs.

22 Greenleaf, R.K. (1977) *The Servant as Leader,* Servant Leadership— A Journey into the Nature of Legitimate Power and Greatness, New York: Paulist Press: 6.

23 Miller, E. (2014) Partnership Brokers as Leaders published in *Betwixt & Between, The Journal of Partnership Brokering* (3) http://partnershipbrokers. org/w/journal/partnership-brokers-as-leaders/ (accessed 9/2/2018).

24 Heifetz, Linsky & Grashow (2009) Op.cit: 52.

25 Lipman-Blumen (2000); Neal (2006); Senge (2008); Waddell (2011); Scharmer & Kaufer (2013); Western (2013) Op.cit.

26 Waddell (2011) Op.cit.

27 Senge (2008) Op.cit.

28 Huxham, C. & Vangen, S. (2004) Doing things collaboratively: Realizing the advantage or succumbing to inertia? *Organizational Dynamics*, 33 (2): 199.

29 Ibid.

30 Ibid.

31 Taken from an interview with Ken Caplan, pioneer partnership practitioner at the forefront of promoting international partnerships for water and sanitation (www.partnershipsinpractice.co.uk).

32 Bradford, A.L. & Cohen, A. R. (1998) *Power Up: Transforming Organizations Through Shared Leadership*, USA: Wiley.

33 Tariq, H. & Tennyson, R. (2010) *In the Bank's Best Interest – Case Study of an Ambitious Partnership*, London: International Business Leaders Forum.

34 Senge, P., Hamilton, H. & Kania, J. (2015) The dawn of system leadership. *Stanford Social Innovation Review*, Winter: 29.

35 Kalungu-Banda, M. (2006) *Leading like Madiba, Leadership Lessons from Nelson Mandela*, Cape Town: Double Story Books: 124.

36 Quinn, R.E. (2004) *Building the Bridge As You Walk On It – A Guide for Leading Change*, San Francisco: Jossey-Bass. Quinn describes the normal life state as a tendency to be *"comfort centred, externally driven, self-focused and internally closed"*

37 Ibid.

38 Ibid.

39 See. Lee, G. (2006) *Courage! The Backbone of Leadership*, San Francisco: Jossey-Bass.

40 Senge, Hamilton & Kania (2015). Op.cit: 28.

41 Heifetz, Linsky & Grashow (2009) Op.cit.

42 This extract is taken from a logbook written by Ros Tennyson in 2011 when she was working with others to establish the Partnership Brokers Association as an independent entity. All those seeking formal Accreditation as partnership brokers are required to keep a logbook about their partnership brokering strategies and reflections for a period of 3 months. The author completed her Accreditation in 2006, but it seems old habits really do 'die hard'!

43 Bruno Bettelheim, author of *A Good Enough Parent, A Book on Child-Rearing*, Vintage,1988 in which he explores how parents put undue pressure on themselves for being less than perfect in their parenting role and argues that most parents do the very best they can in the circumstances in which they find themselves and that this is 'good enough'.

44 Ibid: 18.

Chapter 8

Going local

Partnering with citizens and communities[1]

Leda Stott, Marcia Dwonczyk, and Joanna Pyres

Those involved in building partnerships are increasingly being called upon to engage more deeply with local stakeholders such as communities, citizens and people in general.[2] This call responds to recognition that the achievement of sustainable development requires greater participation of local actors in the delivery of programmes and services.[3] Local involvement in partnering processes, however, is frequently viewed as being too complicated and easiest to address by working with organisations that 'represent' citizens or communities, often with inadequate attention to their legitimacy, their interest in or relevance to the work of a partnership. This chapter explores how a partnership broker might work with local actors in order to promote and support their meaningful engagement in partnerships. In this regard, an important component of partnership brokering involves ensuring that, rather than 'beneficiaries' or 'recipients', local actors are acknowledged as important stakeholders and potential partners, and as co-creators of their own destinies.

Defining local stakeholders

As a distinction is often made in partnership literature between 'partners' and wider 'stakeholders',[4] it is useful to explore where local actors 'sit' in relation to these categories. Distinguishing between internal and external stakeholders is helpful here:

> Internal/primary stakeholders can be classified as recognised signed-up "implementing" partners who have clearly agreed to contribute resources to a partnership, carry out concrete tasks on its behalf, and assume a level of risk in order to obtain benefits through working in this way. External/secondary stakeholders meanwhile are non-partners who, in line with their different priorities and concerns, may either exert an influence upon a partnership, or be influenced by it. They may also bear risks and access partnering benefits but not, we would assume, to the same degree as partners.[5]

While local actors, or more habitually organisations that ostensibly represent them, may assume roles as internal stakeholders or partners, more often than not they are included in the external stakeholder category. Here, as the above quote suggests, we may find influential players, such as funding agencies, whose risks in relation to a partnership arrangements are unlikely to be as great as other actors in this category with less power and influence. These greater risk bearers generally tend to be local community actors. Often classified as a partnership's 'target group' and cited as 'beneficiaries', 'recipients', 'clients' and sometimes as 'customers', local stakeholders can broadly be defined as those whose needs a partnership is designed to address.[6] In reality, local stakeholders are also 'rights holders' whose identity and human rights are inextricably linked to the area in which a partnership is being implemented or to the challenge it seeks to address.[7] They may often include vulnerable or marginalised groups with limited access to goods and services as a result of structural inequalities such as spatial distribution and geographical location; socioeconomic background and educational, racial or gender disparities.

All too often the risks that local actors bear in relationship to partnership arrangements go unrecognised and unacknowledged. They frequently support extra work and activities for a partnership without clear recognition of the possible benefits of collaboration. A central task for partnership brokers is thus to encourage and find appropriate ways of promoting the engagement of different local actors in partnerships, both as potential partners and/or as key stakeholders with an interest in partnership outcomes. Choices regarding these possibilities need to be explored carefully in relation to a partnership's purpose and scope, its operational environment, the phase of development in which it is working and the availability of time and resources to support its activities. Ensuring that chosen options are suited to contextual and cultural circumstances is also crucial to the promotion of effective partnerships.

Why local stakeholder engagement is important

The rationale for local stakeholder engagement in partnership arrangements is clear: as important social actors, community members and citizens bring unique knowledge, skills, resources and experiences to collaborative processes. As end users of the services, products or change processes that a partnership might seek to develop, local actors have a distinct set of resources and perspectives that can be shared in these arrangements. As well as assisting appreciation of multifaceted social, economic and environmental challenges in particular contexts, the insights and experiences of different local players are critical to ensuring partnership relevance and effectiveness. Indeed, it can be argued that without this voice partnership, success and sustainability are unlikely. Muhammad Yunus puts this neatly in relation to partnering with 'poor' communities: 'When policy makers finally realise that the poor are their partners, rather than bystanders or enemies, we will progress much faster than we do today'.[8]

The importance of more fully understanding local needs and views is highlighted in the work of development theorists such as Paolo Freire,[9] Robert Chambers[10] and Amartya Sen.[11] Arguing from an empowerment perspective, they suggest that sustainable livelihoods depend upon the ability of local actors to 'express their reality, to put that reality first and to make it count'.[12] It is only in this way that people may '...lead the lives they have reason to value and... enhance the real choices that they have'.[13] These arguments, which are clearly relevant for wider situations and contexts, suggest that it is critical to build genuine collaborative spaces where people can steer their own development trajectories. This participation can assist in bridging top-down:bottom-up disconnects by improving policy-level accountability to players on the ground where impact is sought, play an important role in ensuring the avoidance of duplication among different initiatives operating in the same space and bring a level of humanity and authenticity to discussions that are often lacking in inter-institutional contexts.

In recent years, social and political activism by local actors has been manifested globally in the growth of the cooperative, commons and de-growth movements, as well as via collaborative initiatives such as the Social Solidarity Economy, Peer Production and the Sharing and Collaborative Economy.[14] These civic engagement processes, supported by advances in information and communication, call for the 'constructing new structures, reforming existing organisations, changing legal structures and reforming economic structures'.[15] As well as suggesting that conventional forms of government leadership may require a radical rethink, these new collaborative forms imply that governments no longer have sole power and responsibility for shaping and managing public goods and services, particularly in the light of global concerns about the stewardship of these commons. They also indicate that deeper public participation in governance decision-making processes is necessary.

In many countries, public authorities are recognising that efforts to bring in the voice of the 'citizen' can enhance inclusion, legitimacy and democratic governance. In the European Union, for example, this thinking is central to the promotion of the 'partnership principle'[16] and Community-led Local Development (CLLD).[17] However, although local community actors and citizens are frequently cited as indispensable partnership players, 'top-down' collaborative initiatives still tend to be composed of established or formally constituted organisations and the diverse interests of local stakeholders are either excluded or represented by others. Some authors have even suggested that 'managerialist' practices assist the ability of these organisations to retain control of collaborative arrangements by marginalising community participation in decision-making processes.[18] Partnering efforts are consequently placed at risk because of a focus among these actors on streamlining and improving rather than seeking genuine change.

The role of partnership brokers in promoting local stakeholder engagement

A central task for partnership brokers is to encourage and find appropriate ways of promoting the engagement of different local actors in partnerships, both as potential partners and as stakeholders with a vested interest in partnership outcomes. This requires close involvement with different community actors in order to identify and design appropriate and contextually relevant formats for partnership interactions. In many cases too, a partnership broker can assist in promoting clarity around the needs and expectations of local stakeholders so that they can play a more effective role in partnership negotiations. The creation of space for building relationships that support diverse groups of stakeholders to understand each other is central to this process and may include work by partnership brokers in the following areas:

Clarifying who local actors are

Partnership brokers can assist partners to define exactly who 'the community', citizens or local stakeholders actually are and which groups or individuals they should be working with. The term 'community,' for example, may encompass people living within a specific geographical setting, as well as those who define themselves (or are defined by others) according to particular beliefs, characteristics and interests. It is also important to recognise that local stakeholders do not comprise a homogenous unit and include a range of divergent voices and alliances. As their composition is often fluid, an understanding of the particular and changing contexts in which community actors operate is important. In a place-based partnership, this will involve meeting people to understand who both formal and non-formal players are, how they represent themselves and what their interests might be.

Making the case for working with local actors

During the scoping phase of a partnership, a partnership broker can endorse the rationale for working with local stakeholders by positioning the importance of the resources and competencies that they might bring to the relationship. In order to raise awareness about local stakeholders and promote ongoing connections with other partners, a partnership broker would ideally be expected to have a good contextual understanding and/

or experience of working with local stakeholders in the area/s in which a partnership operates. As well as sharing information gained through desk research, opportunities for partners to visit and participate in conversations with different community members, individually or collectively, can do much to build understanding and awareness of context. Informal connections such as attending a community event or using local facilities are particularly useful ways of promoting interaction. Such efforts can do much to demonstrate genuine interest in a particular locality and assist in diversifying the range of perspectives that can be gathered to inform the work of a partnership.

Understanding the drivers for participation

A partnership broker can assist partners to examine the reasons why local actors may or may not wish to engage in partnership activities. The premise here is that if the incentives or obligations for individuals and groups to participate in a partnership are clear, they are likely to participate more fully. If there are disincentives, however, they may show little interest in engaging in partnership activities and, in some cases, may even seek to obstruct them. To assess incentives, partnership brokers may find it useful to conduct a regular check on how far a partnership responds to the interests of the local stakeholders it seeks to engage with.

Consideration of why local actors may or may not wish to participate in partnership processes and activities can also assist a partnership broker to find ways of addressing obstacles to the participation of particular individuals and groups. As well as asking questions about who leads an initiative and whether the process is open to all or reserved for pre-selected stakeholders, this may necessitate negotiations with community leaders and/or 'gate-keepers' who speak on behalf of a community and may block the participation of certain members.

Using appropriate forms of participation

Because no partnership is the same as another, and because all partnerships are determined by their particular and dynamic contexts, local stakeholders may be involved in a variety of ways during a partnership's development. Partnership brokers may need to explore which avenues may (or may not) be appropriate for the engagement of different groups or individuals in partnership decision-making processes and activities.

The IAP2 Public Participation Spectrum distinguishes between passive forms of participation, in which participation of stakeholders in decision-making is limited, to active connections in which they exert more control.[19] Progress along this continuum is manifested by more interdependent relationships as stakeholders rely more deeply upon one another. It is also worth noting that the nature of stakeholder involvement in this spectrum changes from the

Informing	Consulting	Cooperating	Collaborating	Co-creating
Providing stakeholders with adequate information to enable them to make decisions and take action.	Obtaining feedback from stakeholders in order to make decisions and take action.	Involving stakeholders in decision-making processes and development of activities.	Working with stakeholders *as partners* to ensure that decisions and activities are appropriate.	Decision-making and activities initiated and undertaken by stakeholders.

Passive ➡ Active

Figure 8.1 Degrees of stakeholder participation.

Source: Adapted from International Association for Public Participation Public Participation (2007) *IAP2 Spectrum* and Stott, L. (2016) Partnership: Exploring the terminology, *Paper for Thematic Network on Partnership*, Brussels: ESF Transnational Platform.

one where participation is encouraged from above (in top-down approaches) to the one where accountabilities are more horizontal in nature as responsibilities are shared among the different actors involved.

The spectrum in Figure 8.1 implies the existence of a power dynamic in stakeholder connections. More passive forms of participation involve decisions being made by those with power who may inform or invite feedback from other stakeholders in a limited or controlled manner. Arnstein[20] notes that genuine forms of participation such as partnership should enable citizens with less power to negotiate and engage in trade-offs with traditional power holders. This suggests a more equitable and long-term connection than other forms of participation and is at its strongest when citizens are able to steer, influence and decide upon a course of action.

While the active engagement and co-creation options outlined in Figure 8.1 may clearly be the ideal, participation may vary and require adjustment according to the nature of different citizens or community members, the specific context in which activities are taking place, and the particular phase of a partnership's development.[21] Overloading local actors or community members with involvement in collaborative activities may not be helpful when they do not have the time or inclination for this and, unlike organisational representatives, are not being paid for their participation. A partnership broker may thus need to give careful consideration to how much risk particular local actors might bear on behalf of a partnership and what form of engagement is appropriate, even if the chosen avenue is construed as 'passive'. In this sense, it is important to highlight that, while every effort should clearly be made to ensure that the form of involvement selected is not contrived as a substitute for genuine participation, passive levels of participation and engagement may be appropriate at certain times for particular groups, contexts or programme phases.[22]

Local stakeholders have often had poor experiences of being involved in processes of 'engagement'. This negatively impacts on their willingness to participate in further collaborations, no matter how well intentioned and planned. In such situations, a partnership broker has an opportunity to learn from the difficulties of the past and encourage partners to work with local stakeholders to address these concerns. For example, some collaborative activities might be specifically designed and agreed early in the scoping and building phase of the partnering process to build trust, understand different perspectives and contributions, and establish areas of mutual benefit prior to a partnership embarking on its change agenda.

In order to provide a useful assessment of where avenues for the involvement of specific local stakeholders can be built into partnership processes and activities, the checklist below (Table 8.1) may be useful for a partnership broker. This table attempts to break down possible engagement categories so that decisions can be made about the best ways to ensure and promote community involvement during different phases of a partnership cycle or programme; in other words, who should be involved, when and how.

In this schema, a partner would clearly expect to participate at the top end of the scale, while external stakeholders might be 'engaged' at different levels depending on their connection to a partnership, their interest in it and

Table 8.1 Checklist for appropriate engagement of local actors during different partnership phases

Level	Forms of Engagement
8	*Steers* Directs/manages activities
7	*Initiates action* Develops/manages particular steps/activities/plans
6	*Participates in decision-making* Is directly involved in decision-making and 'has a vote'
5	*Able to influence* Participates marginally in decision-making processes
4	*Involved in feedback loops* Regularly shares opinions/feedback
3	*Consulted* Able to express opinions and give feedback
2	*Informed* Receives information/messages
1	*Access to basic communication channels* Grievance/complaints mechanisms available
0	*No involvement* No channels available

Source: Adapted from Stott, L. (2009) Stakeholder Engagement in Partnerships. Who are the 'stakeholders' and how do we 'engage' with them? *BPD Research Series*, London: Building Partnerships for Development.

the extent to which their involvement is sought in its work. As noted earlier, to avoid the box-ticking of desired objectives, it is important to ensure that choices around different forms of community participation are authentic. Thus, if a basic communication channel (Level 1) is perceived as suitable during a specific programme phase, the emphasis might be on making it as accessible as possible; if the choice is to 'inform' (Level 2), efforts might focus on guaranteeing a clear information flow. With a consultation exercise (Level 3), it may be useful to ensure availability of information on the process for gathering opinions, sufficient time and communication of the process, as well as feedback on the results of the exercise.[23]

Case study 8.1 Including local stakeholders in ESF programmes

The 'partnership principle' is promoted as a policy instrument for improving employment and social inclusion and supported by Structural Funds such as the European Social Fund (ESF).[24] Within this context, partnership brokers (as individuals and organisations) play a vital role in ensuring that local actors are clearly positioned in partnership frameworks and activities. Some of the methodologies used to promote this engagement at different stages of partnership development in different EU Member States are outlined below.

Design

Campaigns and awareness-raising events
Public consultation forums and open meetings
National SWOT workshops
Opportunities to comment via publicly available web pages
Needs analysis/assessment

Delivery Planning

Co-design of application forms
Country-wide consultations/surveys to make adjustments to programmes
Newsletters, pamphlets, use of media

Implementation

Structures to support partnership processes, e.g. National Thematic Groups
Capacity-building and support
Meetings, seminars, conferences

Monitoring and Evaluation

Participatory evaluation (discussion groups, focus groups, interviews)
Information systems that enable ongoing stakeholder feedback on
    programmes
Story dialogue

Source: Adapted from Stott (2016) Partnership: Exploring the terminology, *Paper for Thematic Network on Partnership*, Brussels: ESF Transnational Platform.

Whatever 'engagement' option is selected, it is clearly important that the involvement of local actors is facilitated in a genuinely participatory manner. This is where the personal and professional skills of a partnership broker can make a big difference. If, for example, those assuming a partnership broker role are attached to a particular outcome and seek to steer local stakeholders towards this, or if they have a set of judgements around a particular group of people, the possibility of promoting genuine participatory practice is likely to be limited. While a clear understanding of participatory leadership is important for a partnership broker in all partnerships, it is critical when partnering with local stakeholders.

Case study 8.2 Developing a shared understanding of the system from different perspectives

It can be difficult for people who are recipients of services to voice their perspectives or to have their views understood. Partners in Recovery[25] is a programme in Australia seeking to reform the services system in respect of complex mental health. In an effort to build a shared understanding of the service system, one region brought together potential partners: those with lived experience of complex mental health needs, funders, government, non-government and for-profit service providers as well as people from more vulnerable communities such as refugees. Here, the partnership broker worked with the group to visually map the service system using a large collection of reused plastic bottle tops of different shapes, sizes and colours. All participants had access to the bottle tops and worked together to create an agreed 'picture' of the service system from their different perspectives. This enabled those who felt less articulate, confident or powerful to participate in the same way as others. The group focused on the shared picture and gained valuable insights negotiating where something was placed in relation to other things. The group were also able to agree where and how the partnership they were seeking to build needed to change the system. It created a 'level playing field' for all to scope the issues.

Addressing assumptions and stereotypes

In order to embed behaviours that dismantle the perpetuation of stereotypes that reinforce discrimination, a partnership broker may need to address partner biases and prejudices in relation to local actors. This may involve drawing out and reflecting on the viewpoints of local stakeholders themselves, who will also have their own assumptions of one another and of different partnership players. Working in partnership with local actors also requires that partnership brokers understand and address their own preconceptions so that they are better prepared to assist others in confronting these. As well as being authentic, consistent and non-patronising in their approach, this often requires the courage to address uncertainty and fear of differences in viewpoints, values and experiences. At times, as the example from rural India below suggests, this may directly challenge cultural norms of behaviour. It may also necessitate dealing with conflict as partners challenge, or are challenged by, local stakeholders.

Case study 8.3 Speaking different languages

In rural India, there is a highly diverse population due to migrant labour and at times no common language. This means that individuals often speak different languages which can also be linked to caste, class and religion. Finding ways to approach people in their own language is important. Similarly, women and youth may need to be consulted separately from men at first to build their confidence and ensure that they will participate with their voice and perspective. The broker may thus need to visit different groups separately in their own spaces for a while and build trust before expecting diverse groups to be happy to meet together. It is important to seek to understand how to invite participation from all and to recognise that there can often be divisions in communities that prevent members meeting together for a gathering or consultation.

Building capacity

In order to encourage 'unheard' voices, it is often necessary to develop capacity-building activities that assist those whose participation in partnership is limited due to lack of resources, skills and confidence or cultural norms around whose voice counts more than others. This can be a challenge where, for example, funders fail to appreciate the length of time required for behaviour change to take place. A partnership broker may often need to work hard to ensure promotion of long-term and holistic capacity-building efforts, investigating what participatory forums exist and how they can be drawn upon to work with local stakeholders. Encouraging reflection on the role of capacity builders so that the power they exert is mitigated through the building of equitable relationships is also an important consideration for partnership brokers. This requires recognition that the promotion of ongoing capacity-building processes should ultimately result in the relinquishing of this role as those they are working with grow in competence and confidence.

Finding the right time and place

The 'right' timing and the use of appropriate venues for engaging with local actors are also important considerations for the partnership broker. Indeed, consideration of where and when meetings with local stakeholders are held is often as important as the selection of engagement approaches. Choosing venues that are considered to be community spaces, or are at least safe, easily accessible and non-partisan, can help redress power imbalances and promote equity. The time of day and day of the week can also act to include or exclude people from full participation. The classic illustration of women's exclusion from decision-making processes because their domestic commitments preclude their attendance at meetings that are timed to suit others is relevant here. Local stakeholders may also be inhibited from participating in meetings if they are held in places that they are unfamiliar with or have to find money to travel to. Partnership brokers may thus need to ensure that discussions take place in a comfortable or 'safe' space within their locality where they feel 'free' to express their ideas.

Case study 8.4 Creating the right space

In Australia, local community elders appeared to feel safe in attending a partnership broker training session because of their familiarity with the local venue where the training was undertaken and the fact that the course was hosted by an agency that had built trusting relationships with them. A local Indigenous Group was also contracted to provide catering services and the training commenced with a welcome from an Elder who had gone to a great deal of trouble to prepare this. These elements set the scene for the establishment of Elders as respected participants and, although senior Government and NGO representatives were also present, no challenges around power imbalances were experienced. Most importantly, all participants were confident in discussing diverse perspectives and experiences.

In Goa in India, meanwhile, community members expressed a preference for holding a meeting at the local authority office rather than in a community hall that was associated with one particular religious group. Similarly, visual materials and musical icebreakers and interludes were found to be helpful in engaging and maintaining participation from community members with minimal education and literacy.

Dealing with resource issues

In some contexts, local stakeholders may expect, demand or require payment or a 'sitting-fee' for their participation, often in terms of money, transport or food. This is particularly important when community members have scarce resources and/or are unable to volunteer their time. Here, a partnership broker may need to explain to partners how community participation is distinguished from that of organisational partner representatives who are usually salaried or cognisant of a clear business case for involvement that can later be related to costs. Additionally, there is often a mandate to be there from their organisation. Community members usually have no mandate as such and their involvement is much more likely to be based upon individual passion, commitment and hoped-for impact.

Promoting reflection and review

Conflicting and changing loyalties and demands, and the contextual issues that cut across these, can exert an enormous influence on both the manner and the depth of participation. The promotion of opportunities for the engagement of particular groups and individuals may also sometimes generate conflict. This may happen because the challenges faced by local stakeholders are often not well addressed. In such cases, it is important for a partnership broker not to shy away from conflict but rather provide space for exploring why such a situation has surfaced and the different perspectives around this. Regular 'health checks' that explore how partners are working together, alongside efforts that deepen engagement beyond individual representatives at the 'partnership table', are also important ways of addressing conflict.

An appreciation of both the positive and negative effects of different levels of local engagement in the partnering process is also a useful exercise for a partnership broker to reflect on. Positive effects may include the growth of capacity, reach and skills, or the increase in confidence and voice of a hitherto marginalised stakeholder group. On the negative side, however, an overemphasis on participation of particular stakeholders may stifle plurality by making 'engagement' a bureaucratic process. It may also allow certain groups to control a partnership or become its prime beneficiaries.[26]

Case study 8.5 Reviewing the context

In Goa, rural India, villages on the coastal belt are composed of diverse communities of Catholics, Hindus, Muslims and include large migrant labour, settler and tourist populations. In village development matters, only voters have the right to sit on official village development committees. This leaves out a large number of migrant labour and other settlers who live in the community but are considered 'outsiders'. As a result, partnership initiatives that target the most marginalised can often result in services being provided to 'outsiders' and not to 'locals' which, in turn, causes problems between community members. Partnership brokers therefore need to manage expectations and communication about who is being invited to participate and who is not.

Applying partnership principles when engaging with local stakeholders

Although the achievement of genuine and sustainable change suggests that relevant local actors should be included as partners rather than external stakeholders, ensuring that this happens can be messy, hard and time-consuming. In this regard, emphasis on ensuring that a partnership broker strives to work with local stakeholders to ensure that what works is consistent with the good practice principles for partnership brokering is a useful rule of thumb (see Table 8.2). This is likely to involve constant reflection by a partnership broker on what forms of local participation may be relevant, at what point, for whom and why.[27]

Conclusion

Partnership brokers have a crucial role to play in promoting the participation of local stakeholders in partnership processes and activities. Their capacity to do this rests upon close familiarity with the partnership context in which they are operating as well as an ability to see the bigger picture and the systems issues that might promote or limit stakeholder engagement.

Table 8.2 Addressing challenges using partnership principles

Common challenges	What the partnership broker can do
Anxiety about difference	*Promote the principle of diversity by:* <ul><li>Assisting different partners and stakeholders to see what they and others bring to a partnership.</li><li>Holding space so that divergent views can be acknowledged as equally valid.</li><li>Using ways for people to introduce themselves that don't reinforce stereotypes, e.g. name, position, organisation. Community members will often say 'I'm just a community member' by way of introduction whereas eliciting connection to a place or issue and why it matters to them can promote more equitable connections.</li><li>Challenging and clarifying assumptions and stereotypes of different stakeholders.</li><li>Creating ways for diverse perspectives to be sought out by partners.</li><li>Exploring perceived conflicts to understand the issues and ideas behind the differences rather than shy away from or smooth over them.</li><li>Supporting partners and other stakeholders to understand patterns of divergence – emergence – convergence and how to weather the discomfort of sharing conflicting viewpoints.</li><li>Gathering a broad range of views from different segments of the community, e.g. age, gender, ethnicity, socio-economic status, occupation or (un)employment status.</li><li>Meeting specific interest/demographic groups separately before bringing them together with others.</li></ul>
Power imbalances	*Promote the principle of equity by:* <ul><li>Working with partners to discuss what equity and respect might look, sound and feel like for them (everyone can say what it looks and feels like when they are not respected).</li><li>Identifying real and perceived power imbalances and looking for opportunities to redress these, e.g. by holding meetings at a community space rather than a funder's office.</li><li>Avoiding systems and processes that might reinforce traditional power imbalances, e.g. who 'chairs' a meeting.</li><li>Practising participatory process with rigour.</li><li>Acknowledging different types of power, e.g. age, personality, position, money, etc.</li><li>Ensuring use of plain language and avoiding jargon that can reinforce educational differences.</li><li>Meeting specific interest/demographic groups separately before bringing everyone (this helps to encourage participation by building confidence and trust that they will be listened to).</li></ul>

(Continued)

Common challenges	What the partnership broker can do

Hidden agendas

Promote the principle of openness by:

- Role modelling the sharing of information, mistakes, problems, etc.
- Helping people be clear about what information can and cannot be shared and why.
- Supporting difficult discussions about why someone might not trust another partner or actor.
- Creating a safe enough space to get beyond just being nice to each other so that people can share hidden agendas and sentiments about what is not working or does not feel right.
- Encouraging the notion of the 'gift of the objection' and the value of contributions perceived as obstructing progress.
- Encouraging the telling of stories to help community members demonstrate their expertise and experience in contexts where others may be positioned as experts.
- Communicating a partnership's purpose, agenda and approach upfront in order to model what openness looks like and to avoid misunderstandings.

Competitiveness

Promote the principle of mutual benefit by:

- Creating images where the group can visually see that individual and conflicting interests can exist along with shared/ mutual interests, e.g. overlapping circles.
- Drawing out individual interests and needs and supporting partners and stakeholders to identify where there is enough alignment to work together for mutual benefit.
- Translating different sector languages so that its easier for others to see where there might be mutual benefit.
- Helping diverse community stakeholders who may not see themselves as one community see and understand the common benefits of working in partnership.

Uncertainty

Promote the principle of courage by:

- Role modelling the taking of risks.
- Holding the space when there is pressure to jump to solutions/actions too quickly.
- Sharing frameworks that might help people understand the role of uncertainty in achieving innovation/change.
- Having conversations to explore what different people are uncertain about and developing contingency plans to address these.
- Recognising that local stakeholders as 'target groups' will need extra time and space for articulating uncertainties and risks.

Senge, Hamilton and Kania[28] describe this as being able to see 'that problems "out there" are "in here" also – and how the two are connected'. This will inevitably take time as, in addition to promoting a clear understanding of the overall rationale and added-value of working with local actors as partners, local actors themselves will need to be convinced that working in this way is worthwhile. This is particularly the case for those who are unfamiliar with partnering or those who have had poor previous experiences with other partnership or engagement processes.

Heeding the slogan 'Nothing about us without us!' is a useful marker for partnership brokers who should ultimately bear in mind that local stakeholders will usually remain long after other partners have moved on and a partnership has completed its work. Working with community actors to put in place the most effective means for participation in the partnering process *in their context* is thus an important step in ensuring sustainable outcomes and demonstrating credible intentions for local empowerment.

Notes

1 Part of this material was developed for the Partnership Thematic Network, a component of the ESF Transnational Platform, with the support of the European Social Fund. See: https://ec.europa.eu/esf/transnationality/ (accessed 9/2/2018).

2 The UN, for example, calls for 'inclusive' and 'transformative' partnerships 'built upon principles and values, a shared vision, and shared goals: placing people and planet at the center' and refers to 'principled and responsible public-private-people partnerships' for achieving sustainable development, see: United Nations (2014) The road to dignity by 2030: ending poverty, transforming all lives and protecting the planet. *Synthesis report of the Secretary-General on the post-2015 sustainable development agenda,* New York: UN.

3 The importance of better anchoring of projects in local communities in order to give life and traction to the Sustainable Development Goals is central to the global sustainable development agenda for 2030. See also: European Commission (2010) *Europe 2020: A Strategy For Smart, Sustainable And Inclusive Growth,* Brussels and (2014b) *Community-Led Local Development, Cohesion Policy 2014–2020,* Factsheet; World Bank (2014) *Strategic Framework for Mainstreaming Citizen Engagement in World Bank Group Operations, Engaging with Citizens for Improved Results,* Washington DC: World Bank.

4 See for example Tennyson (2004) *The Partnering Toolbook,* London & Geneva: IBLF & GAIN: 15 & 26.

5 Stott, L. (2009) Stakeholder Engagement in Partnerships. Who are the 'stakeholders' and how do we 'engage' with them? *BPD Research Series,* London: Building Partnerships for Development: 2.

6 European Structural & Investment Funds Guidance for Member States and Programme Authorities (2014) *Guidance on Community-Led Local Development for Local Actors,* Version 1: 9.

7 See for example: OECD (2015) Due Diligence Guidance for Meaningful Stakeholder Engagement in the Extractives Sector, *Draft for Comment,* April: https://www.oecd.org/daf/inv/mne/OECD-Guidance-Extractives-Sector-Stakeholder-Engagement.pdf (accessed 9/2/2018) and see also: http://socialprotection-

humanrights.org/key-issues/universality-of-protection-and-effective-access/rights-holders (accessed 9/2/2018).

8 Yunus, M. (2007) *Banker to the Poor: Micro-Lending and the Battle against World Poverty*, New York: PublicAffairs:137.
9 Freire, P. (1970) *Pedagogy of the Oppressed*, New York: The Seabury Press.
10 Chambers, R. (1995) Poverty and livelihoods: whose reality counts? *Environment and Urbanization*, 7: 173–204 and Chambers, R. (1997) *Whose Reality Counts? Putting the Last First*, London: IT Publications.
11 Sen, A. (1999) *Development as Freedom*, Oxford: Oxford University Press.
12 Chambers. (1995) Op.cit: 204.
13 Sen. (1999) Op.cit: 293.
14 Bollier, D. & Conaty, P. (2014) A New Alignment of Movements? *A Report on a Commons Strategies Group Workshop*, Meissen, Germany, August 29 – September 1 https://www.boell.de/sites/default/files/report_-_a_new_alignment_of_movements_february_2015.pdf (accessed 9/2/2018).
15 Ibid.
16 European Commission. (2014a) *European Code of conduct on partnership in the framework of the European Structural and Investment Funds*, Directorate-General for Employment, Social Affairs and Inclusion, Brussels: European Commission.
17 European Commission. (2014b) Community-Led Local Development, Cohesion Policy 2014–2020, Factsheet, May 2014.
18 Davies, J.S. (2002) Against 'partnership': Toward a local challenge to global neoliberalism. In: J. Gross & R. Hambleton (Eds.) *Governing Cities in the Global Era*. Basingstoke: Palgrave Macmillan, 199–210.
19 International Association for Public Participation (2007) IAP2 Spectrum http://c.ymcdn.com/sites/www.iap2.org/resource/resmgr/imported/spectrum.pdf
20 Arnstein, S.R. (1969) A Ladder of Citizen Participation, *Journal of the American Institute of Planners*, 35 (4): 216–224.
21 Stott, L. (2016) Partnership: Exploring the terminology, *Paper for Thematic Network on Partnership,* Brussels: ESF Transnational Platform. https://ec.europa.eu/esf/transnationality/filedepot_download/564/24 (accessed 9/2/2018).
22 Ibid.
23 Ibid.
24 See: http://ec.europa.eu/esf/main.jsp?catId=525&langId=en (accessed 9/2/2018).
25 www.health.gov.au/internet/main/publishing.nsf/content/mental-pir-about (accessed 9/2/2018).
26 Stott, L. & Keatman, T. (2005) Tools for measuring community engagement in partnerships, *BPD Practitioner Note,* London: BPD.
27 Stott, L. (2009) Op.cit: 8.
28 Senge, P., Hamilton, H. & Kania, J. (2015) The dawn of system leadership. *Stanford Social Innovation Review*, Winter: 29.

Chapter 9

Improving partnerships

Reflecting, reviewing and revising

Joanne Burke

In recent years, a comprehensive knowledge base has been created on what makes partnerships for development successful, in different contexts and sectors. This evidence base increasingly makes reference to the 'added-value' that partnership brokers or those working as intermediaries play in supporting partnerships to build and manage their relationship in order to meet their expectations and generate value.

The literature suggests that there is a need to better understand the specific benefits and additional value of partnerships in addressing complex social and sustainable development and humanitarian challenges. In what ways do partnerships serve as forces for change and resolve complex issues and challenges? What does successful collaboration involve? Is the collaborative relationship bound up in how well the partnership achieves its results? If yes, in what ways? Many standard monitoring and evaluation (M&E) models are available and can be applied to measure the societal and developmental outcomes (results, scale and cost-efficiency) and the impact of the collaboration.[1] These include goal-based approaches, outcome or results-based evaluation approaches, process-based approaches and expert or accreditation approaches. Yet, traditional evaluation studies and approaches may not necessarily focus on the specific ways that the partnership's relationship and management practices positively contributed to the achievement of the partnership's outcomes. Having a more coherent knowledge base of how and why collaboration works in practice, then, is essential to future decision-making about whether or not to invest in partnering and to be able to determine what it means for a partnership to be 'fit for purpose'.

This chapter explores multiple themes and issues pertaining to the management and maintenance of partnerships, with a particular focus on reviewing and revising. It starts with a discussion on the importance of reviewing and revising partnerships and the need for such processes to be integrated into the partnering mechanism. It looks at how reviewing and revising processes support the well-being of the partnership and its ability to generate value, and how the two are linked. It identifies options for integrating the reviewing[2] and revising function across the different phases of the partnering cycle.

The second part of this chapter explores the role that partnership brokers play in fostering systematic review and revising practices. It explores the partnership broker's role in helping partners strengthen their collaborative mindsets and skills towards enabling them to self-manage their own review processes. It discusses some of the common barriers to reviewing and revising partnerships and the negative consequences such challenges can have on the partnership and on a successful review.

Four approaches are put forward as being focus areas which can underpin partnership brokers' reviewing and revising work and practice: reflection, self-assessment, co-creation and learning. This chapter also identifies ways in which partnership brokers can underpin these four principles in their review work.

Reviewing and revising in the context of the partnership cycle and process

The reviewing and revising phase of the partnering cycle offers partners the opportunity to reflect on their relationship management priorities and practices – *how they collaborate* – and to take stock of whether their interaction supports them to achieve their hoped-for goals and targets – *what they achieve.*

> The ultimate effectiveness of an alliance is a function of how well the partners manage their interaction. It is important that a partnership be viewed as a relationship. Like any valued relationship, a collaborative alliance prospers to the degree that the partners invest in it. The key areas of concern in relationship management are organisation, trust, communication, accountability and learning.[3]

Reviewing and revising are well recognised as being important to the success of the management and maintenance of partnerships.[4] The two functions are anchored in the idea that partnerships are dynamic, not static, relationships that will evolve and change over time and need to be well managed. Consequently, partnerships need to have processes and provisions that support them to assess their relationship and to stay flexible and adaptive, in light of changing internal circumstances as well as changing external contexts.

PBA's partnership model calls for having a distinct reviewing and revising phase in the partnering cycle.[5] In the interest of supporting partners to make reflection and adaptation integral elements of their collaborative work, review provisions and measures should be seen as ongoing, with provisions reflected in the partnering structure and its arrangements.

Partnership reviews are primarily concerned with:

- generating evidence of the benefits and added-value of collaboration and how it is contributing to the partners' ability to meet expectations, create value and produce results;

- assessing the efficiency and contextual relevance of the relationship for the partners;
- creating a collaborative mindset and skills on the part of the partners;[6]
- instilling a culture of continuous improvement and learning within the partnership;
- assessing the role and added-value of the partnership broker.

Reviews can take a wide variety of shapes and forms and be both formal and informal in nature.[7] Review methodologies may include SWOT[8] analysis exercises, individual and group conversations, group workshops and reflection meetings, using 'critical friends', validating findings meetings, partner and stakeholder interviews, surveys and case studies. Areas for assessment can range from the efficacy of the governance arrangements for the partnership, to reviewing the perceived added-value of the collaboration or the partnership broker, or an 'accountability' check in relation to the partnership's work plan and partner performance.[9]

According to the literature, the frequency and type of partnership review will depend on a number of factors. These may include, for example, the nature of the partners' shared purpose and agenda, the stage of the partnership, the status of the project or programme, the number of actors involved in the collaboration and their background, the tenure of the partnership or whether the partnership is brokered or un-brokered.

Partnership reviews should be based on a well-conceived purpose and expected use of the findings. The availability of timely, high-quality data that support reflection and inform decision-making is also important. Participatory approaches can help create conditions for partner engagement during reviews and help partners to accept critical as well as positive findings from the review. This is important if partners are to agree on appropriate revisions and adjustments to their working practices to be more effective. Revisions may include taking decisions to set or modify their performance indicators and how they should be monitored and achieved, or taking decisions on whether it is time for the partnership to change or move on, which may involve taking on new challenges, redefining partner roles and responsibilities or bringing in new partners.

Common barriers to partnership reviewing and revising

Partners need to be in agreement that reviewing and revising supports them to learn from practice, to stay robust and not slip or lose their momentum. Partners may assume that there is a shared understanding on reviewing and revising. However, this may not be the case. When assumptions are not checked, it can lead to barriers and challenges for partnership reviews.

One type of barrier is when partners fail to consider the relationship management dimension of their collaboration as being core to their work. They may not include review provisions in their partnering agreement or work plans or may consider reviewing and revising as being too time-consuming or view it as a tick-the-box exercise.

Other barriers may result from the fact that the types of relationship and process issues that reviews tend to focus on may be sensitive to partners. For example, if partners feel that their respective drivers for engagement are not being met, they may be reluctant to commit to reviewing the added-value of the partnership out of concern that it may turn into an exercise that does not speak to the real issues at hand. There is also the matter of partners having concerns about the prospect of being held responsible for decisions or actions that other partners may or may not have taken in addition to one's own areas of direct accountability.[10]

Challenges can also arise when partners resist changes that emerge out of the review processes and seek instead to contain the partnership in a fixed format, despite the fact that this may undermine the partnership's effectiveness or its ability to manage change. Or, challenges can arise when partners may fail to follow through on their commitments or may over-commit but under-deliver. In instances when the partnership brokering or intermediary function has not been well addressed, partners may tend to skip over undertaking any specific review of the collaboration or may overly rely on certain individuals to provide leadership and make any revisions or changes. This can complicate partners' ability to hold each other accountable for their roles and responsibilities.

The way that partners manage their interaction and invest in their relationship – *how they collaborate* – is inextricably linked to the overall effectiveness of the partnership and *what* it achieves. Having capabilities in reviewing and revising, then, is central to partners' ability to achieve results and to ensure that the partnership operates as effectively and efficiently as possible.

How do partnership brokers foster successful review, revision, reflection and renewal processes? What role and tasks do partnership brokers perform?

In Chapter 2, Tennyson describes the different roles and tasks that partnership brokers can assume in the reviewing and revising phase of the partnering cycle and the key attributes and skills they will need. Partnership brokering tasks can range from promoting a culture of reflection and review at all stages of the partnership, to fostering co-creation for the design of reviews, facilitating review exercises or helping partners to find common ground on the actions that they need to undertake to sustain outcomes and move on. Table 9.1 outlines some specific ways that partnership brokers can support reviewing and revising processes at different stages of the partnering cycle.

Table 9.1 Partnership brokering role for reviewing and revising within the partnering cycle

Scoping and building	Help partners undertake baseline context analysis exercises (socio-economic, cultural and political and related drivers and triggers) towards having a shared picture of the external operating environment and how it may enable or undermine the proposed partnership. Help partners identify how they will monitor the changing environment during the course of the partnership. Elicit partners' assumptions and expectations about the value and role of review in collaboration and how to consider the link between their interaction and their ability to produce results. Incorporate reflection, review and revising provisions into the scoping and building phase of the partnership to help instil reflection and reflective practice into the partnership, at its inception stage. Help partners undertake a partnering capacity self-assessment exercise focused on being ready to partner and on what being 'fit for purpose' means to the partners. The results of the capacity assessment can serve as the basis for identifying existing capacities and to see if there is attention needed for some elements. Help partners formulate outcomes and develop metrics (targets and indicators) for their collaboration as well as their performance (results). Help/remind partners to create an open atmosphere in which reflective practice, giving and receiving feedback and continuous learning, becomes common practice.
Review in the context of managing and maintaining partnerships	Encourage partners to incorporate reflection as a regular practice of their work. Assist partners to work together to have a clear and common purpose for their review, along with its intended use and dissemination. Help partners to select and use participatory tools and approaches to suit their specific review and to incorporate a reflective practice component into their review process. Provide capacity development services (advising, training, coaching and mentoring) to partners to enhance capabilities for reflection, co-creation, self-assessment and continuous learning and to help them integrate these capabilities and approaches into their partnership structure and processes. Design and facilitate review exercises that strike a balance between having a focus on the relationship and the partnership's effectiveness. Tasks may include, for example, data collection, designing and facilitating participatory meetings with partners to interpret/make sense of the data results, supporting partners to draw out and apply lessons and to identify a mix of action priorities (small wins and longer-term) they can undertake, record keeping and documentation. Help partners determine how to celebrate the positive outcomes and successful factors that have emerged from their review in relation to what is working and where they are seeing progress.

(Continued)

Table 9.1 (Continued)

Revision, renewal and moving on	Help partners implement specific actions that emerged from the review and identify how they will monitor progress in implementing those changes.
	Help partners distil good practices and useful lessons about partnering practice and disseminate and share those insights within the partnership and with external actors.
	Guide partners to plan for sustaining outcomes and moving on, e.g. an exit or transition strategy.
	Conduct a 'futures workshop' or a 'scenario planning exercise' with partners to review how external factors may influence the future of the partnership and how they can best adapt to changing circumstances and contexts.
	Help partners develop a termination or moving on strategy for the partnership, based on review outcomes.

As noted, partnership review processes can be sensitive and various pitfalls and barriers can arise along the way. On the one hand, partnership review processes offer the opportunity for partners to test their assumptions and check their perceptions with regard to the well-being of the partnership. Yet, reviews may also surface issues related to power differentials and dynamics, lack of ownership, frustration, disengagement and resentment – all of which can significantly undermine partner trust and transparency and working effectiveness. In such circumstances, partnership brokers may find themselves having to navigate sensitive and contentious issues. Consistent with PBA principle of good practice,[11] a partnership broker may be called upon to challenge mindsets and the status quo or demonstrate confidence to hold the space to enable partners to work through differences of opinion and to deal with uncertainties and areas of disagreement.

Partnership brokers can help partners strike a good balance in their reviews between assessing how they are doing in relation to their task and creating value, and how they are doing in relation to their interaction and their relationship. As noted, partnership brokers may find, however, that this interface between the task –*'the what'* – and process –*'the how'*– dimension of collaboration is not well understood on the part of partners or they may hold different ideas on what it means or requires. For revising the partnership, partnership brokers can help partners to access and use data for improvement and adaptive purposes, including how they will monitor their results.

Typical partnership brokering tasks may range from helping partners to make necessary changes to a project, revising the partnering agreement to brainstorming skill sets that new partners need to bring on board. When the energy or commitment to acting on review outcomes by the partners appears to be in question or at risk, partnership brokers may need to challenge 'blind spots'[12] and assist partners in exploring what lies behind their reluctance or failure to take action.

As for who is best suited to assume a partnership brokering review role, there are advantages and disadvantages of using an internal or external partnership broker or a combination of the two in a review and revising activity. Internal partnership brokers have the advantage of knowing the internal culture and are likely to have high credibility with the partners. They are also familiar with their organisation and the sector and will be familiar with the overarching strategic interest and intent of the partnership. Furthermore, they are likely to have a high investment in the partnership and to see their role through the lens of shaping, influencing and advocacy.

External partnership brokers, on the other hand, bring an outsider's perspective, may have authority and credibility due to their outsider status, and bring in broader expertise and experience with respect to facilitating review processes. They may also be able to confront challenging situations more easily and take risks that an internal partnership broker may find difficult to do.

Depending on the purpose and complexity of the proposed review, a co-facilitation relationship can be an effective solution, drawing on the resources and experience of both an internal and external partnership broker. In such instances, it is important that the external partnership broker is well briefed on the partnership and is actively supported by the internal partnership broker. Using the services of two external partnership brokers can also be considered.[13]

Four partnership brokering approaches to support effective reviewing and revising processes

Principle four of PBA's Partnership Brokering Good Practice (see Chapter 5) speaks to the role of the partnership broker in 'taking every opportunity to build partnering and partnership brokering capacity in others'. Since partnerships depend on the ownership and engagement of diverse players, review processes and activities need to align with principles and approaches that foster active partner participation undertaken 'by the partners for the partners'.

In addition to offering partners the opportunity to review their relationship and results, reviews offer a promising opportunity to enhance partners' ability to work as partnership managers and change makers. Partnership brokers can help partners adopt a structured approach to reviews and do so in a way that seeks to enhance partners' collaborative mindset and skills and their capability to self-manage their own reviews. Partners and partnership brokers may need to negotiate how these aims can best be integrated into a review activity.

> Careful consideration of the design and conduct of a review process is critical to the well-being of the partnership. A partnership review process which is consciously designed and managed, can become not

only a positive experience, but one which, over time, has the potential to contribute to trust building and strengthening relationships between partners. In all stages it is recommended that highly participatory, utilisation focused approaches are employed when reviewing partnerships.[14]

As partnership brokers consider how they can best foster partners' ownership for the review and incorporate a capability enhancement component into their reviewing and revising work, four approaches, in particular, can help to frame and structure their work: reflection, co-creation, self-assessment and continuous learning. Each approach has its own distinct purpose, focus and methods. The approaches complement each other in that, collectively, they can help to structure a sound review in ways that enhance partners' ability to collaborate and self-manage their relationship.

Reflection allows partners to recapture their experience, think about it, mull it over, share it with other partners, evaluate it and reframe it. Reflection can support partners to better understand different motives and drivers for actions, gain new insights into the self and to work together in a spirit of inquiry and openness. It can be a highly useful way for partners to deepen and strengthen their relationship, enabling them to better understand what has been done well by individuals and the partnership and what needs to be improved.

It involves creating a 'safe space' for partners, one that can support the partners individually and collectively to become more aware of their underlying thinking and perceptions. It can help to raise partners' awareness on how they are interacting, show the work is getting done and how they can work together in different ways to be more effective. Reflection can also contribute to more open communication between the partners.

> Reflection-on-action occurs after a situation and focuses on spending time to explore why partners acted as they did, what was happening or not happening, and so on. In so doing, partners develop a set of questions and ideas about their activities and practice as well as build up a collection or repertoire of images, notes, examples, metaphors, theories and actions they can draw upon.[15]

By seeking to make reflection a core feature of their reviewing, partnership brokers can start to sensitise the partners to how they can adopt reflection as a core element of their overall partnership practice.

Partnership brokers will first want to understand the extent to which reflection and reflective practice is part of the partners' ongoing work and relationship management. Partnership brokers can then determine how to best advise partners on how to incorporate reflection into their reviewing and revising process. They can identify entry points for reflective practice – before, during and after the review is undertaken and suggest suitable tools and methods to be used. When designing reviews, partnership brokers can hold conversations with partners to encourage critical reflection by asking probing and reflective questions.[16] Or, during a review partnership brokers may encourage partners to set aside time in the agenda to stop work and use reflective practice to discuss a specific issue or problem or something that just happened. At the end of the review, partnership brokers can ask the partners to share their overall reflections on the review process and discuss how they can integrate reflection in their future work.

Co-creation[17] is an organisational management and leadership approach designed to foster employee commitment and self-organisation. It is based on the premise that new approaches to organisation and management are required in order to meet the type of complex challenges that groups and organisations are likely to face in the future. Co-creation and self-organisation are deemed to be useful approaches to apply when the issue involves a diversity of stakeholders to solve it, if there is no best solution at hand, and if the acceptance of change plans is a criterion for success.[18] Incorporating co-creation and self-organisation principles and approaches into review processes can support the active engagement of partners and the idea of 'by the partners for the partners'.

The design or planning phase for a review exercise can serve as a good starting point for partnership brokers to identify both opportunities and challenges within the partnership for introducing co-creation principles and methods. Partnership brokers need to decide what is 'possible' in relation to how much they can expect partners to actively engage in defining the review's purpose and outcomes and in conducting the review. Depending on what is feasible, partnership brokers can then identify specific co-creation and self-organisation approaches and methods to underpin the review process.

Some partners may hold the view that a partnership broker should take the leadership for planning the review. Others may expect a partnership broker to only work with the partners who have a designated leadership role, before, during and after a review. In such circumstances, partnership brokers may want to propose the idea of forming a small planning group, representing the diversity of the partners, to help flesh out the design, structure and preparation of the review. The role of the planning group can include making decisions on role allocation (discussion leaders, timekeepers, recorders, presenters and facilitators) for review preparation and implementation, and identifying ways that partners can assume these roles. Partnership brokers may want to organise a 'tasting session' for the planning group to orient them to self-organisation and co-creation approaches and explore how they can support their partnership process overall, including their review processes.

During review processes, partnership brokers can support partners to assume leadership roles for facilitating and running review sessions. This may require partnership brokers to coach partners to prepare for their assigned roles, e.g. to facilitate sessions to work on different issues to resolve or to build partner consensus and decision-making. Other approaches that partnership brokers can apply to foster co-creation include structuring the agenda in a way that helps partners refrain from problem-solving too soon, structuring conversations so that everyone has a chance to speak, ensuring that discussions create space to elicit and bridge differences of opinion, synthesising discussions and helping partners find common ground to base decisions and actions upon.[19] By seeking to embed co-creation and self-organisation principles and practices into review exercises, partnership brokers can help partners take and share responsibility for managing and renewing their work and relationship.

Self-assessment relates to the types of methods, tools and interventions that partners utilise for the information and assessment aspects of their review. In keeping with the aim of ensuring that review activities are by the partners for the partners and they incorporate a partner capability element, partnership brokers can advocate for using participatory and experiential methods that call for self-assessment. Self-assessment methods are useful ways to help foster a spirit of open inquiry in which the partners can systematically take stock of the present situation towards identifying the desired change(s) needed to strengthen the partnership.

Partnership brokers can avail themselves of a wide range of participatory data collection tools and resources which can be used before, during and after a review exercise. In addition to individual and group reflection, other common self-assessment methods include peer-to-peer or group conversations, surveys and questionnaires, exercises designed for giving and receiving feedback, timeline and trend-mapping creation, stakeholder mapping and using 'critical friends'. Such methods engage the partners in generating or collecting information which they then analyse and interpret, as a way to bring value and ownership to the information that they have generated.[20] Experiential learning methods in the form of storytelling, imagery, future visioning exercises and role-plays can also be used in reviews for self-assessment purposes. As needed, participatory methods can be complemented by collecting information from other sources including documentation review, observations, bringing in data from prior reviews, etc.

The selection of data collection approaches will depend on the review purpose, focus and intended use. Partnership brokers can help partners to identify and select the most relevant data collection approaches. Partnership brokers can also provide support to structure the data collection process in a systematic manner. This may involve determining what data collection will take place before and during the review process, how it will best be interpreted and clarifying what skills partners will need to use the selected data collection.

Once the data are collected, partnership brokers can help structure and facilitate the interpretation of the data with the partners. The analysis and sense making of the data by the partners may involve surfacing differences of opinion and challenging assumptions and mental models. Using a theoretical model or framework can be a useful way for partnership brokers to present the data and to help partners analyse and make sense of the information that has been collected. The choice of model or framework will very much depend on the review purpose and focus.[21]

Alternatively, partnership brokers may be asked by the partners to summarise the data collected in the form of a report that can then be circulated to the partners for further discussion on the findings or in the form of a presentation.[22] Having analysed the data on their performance and relationship and arrived at areas of agreement, partners can then move to identify improvements and other action measures to be taken to strengthen the partnership. Partnership brokers can also help partners to identify areas of progress and how to best celebrate and capitalise on a 'job' well done and 'what works'. In all aspects of this work, partnership brokers will want to demonstrate their impartiality and neutrality in relation to the selected methods as well as the analysis and interpretation of the data.

Continuous learning emerges as a result of the partners reflecting and self-assessing on how they are performing and better understanding their strengths and weaknesses. Reviewing and revising offers a systematic way for partners to learn from practice and to help them internalise that partnering is a dynamic process that takes place within a broader evolving and often complex external environment. With this clarity and insight, partners can then determine how to revise and adapt their approach to their work and their interaction. Being able to adapt and evolve is part of the partnering process and this occurs when partners can apply the learning from their reviews to improve their practice.

As this chapter notes, an important role of a partnership broker is to help partners to structure reviews in a way that builds a common understanding about the link between how their alliance is managed and their ability to progress together and achieve their desired outcomes. By encouraging partners to focus on their relationship – 'the how' – and their performance effectiveness – 'the what' – in their review processes and to reflect on what they are learning from their practice, partnership brokers can practically demonstrate to partners how they can be more intentional about learning. Partnership brokers can help partners to adopt specific measures they can take to make learning an ongoing part of their work, not an isolated event and to make reviews more central to their thinking and partnering.

The four approaches will have relevance and applicability, in varying degrees, depending on the individual partnering context and typology and the review purpose and outcomes. In more conventional or transactional-oriented alliances, partnership brokers can seek to incorporate aspects of the principles, particularly with respect to reflection and learning. However, as collaboration contexts, drivers and relationships become more complex, successful partnerships will increasingly need to rely on reviewing approaches that cultivate mindsets and partner competency in all four areas: reflection, co-creation, self-assessment and continuous learning.[23]

Personal and professional implications for partnership brokers in relation to their reviewing and revising role and work

With respect to personal mastery and partnership broker capability for reviewing and revising, some specific content areas and types of personal mastery can be identified. In relation to knowledge, the expansive body of resources on partnering includes guidance and reference to maintaining and managing partnerships. It is useful for partnership brokers to be conversant with the current thinking on partnering overall, including how the reviewing and revising function is understood and practised. This includes familiarity with the different types of drivers for partnering engagement and what effective partnership maintenance involves and the role that reviewing and revising plays in partnership management

The literature on M&E of projects and programmes is quite extensive. Having a good understanding of how reviewing and revising fits within the overall M&E discipline is useful. Partnership brokers need to be clear about how reviewing complements, but is distinct from, evaluating the outcomes and impact of a partnership. As part of their review role and work, they may also need to be able to assess the extent to which the partnership mechanism has clearly defined results that are monitored. Familiarity with different results management frameworks and processes for setting and monitoring targets and indicators can help partnership brokers in this regard.

Increasingly, the M&E literature focuses on the importance of stakeholder engagement in M&E activities, and the importance of emergence and adaptation, and of knowledge and continuous learning as integral elements of M&E strategies and outcomes. These are also important focus areas for a partnership broker's attention.

When working with partners in reviewing and revising, partnership brokers will want to check whether there is a clear and shared understanding on the part of partners of different M&E terms, approaches and methodologies and assess the extent to which the M&E function, including reviewing and revising, has been integrated into the partnership's structure and operational arrangements.

Partnership brokers also want to become familiar with the information and guidance of PBA and other partnering resources on the different roles, tasks and personal attributes that brokers may be expected to assume in reviewing and revising processes. Familiarity with these different resources can help brokers to self-assess their own personal attributes and capabilities in reviewing and revising, and identify areas for further development.

In keeping with the idea that building partnering capability for review is a critical role of the broker, exercises need to be highly participatory. Partnership brokers need to be familiar with and confident to use experiential and participatory frameworks, conceptual models, methods and tools to support reviewing and revising processes.[24] This may include, for example, familiarity with organisational management and change approaches, to having expertise in survey design and feedback, being able to use different models related to group performance and dynamics or responsibility and accountability management. Partnership brokers need to be able to match what is in their 'tool kit' with the type of support that partners will need to successfully engage in and benefit from reviewing and revising their partnership.

Most importantly, partnership brokers need to understand their own self and have a clear sense of how they aim to act as 'instruments of change' in relation to partnering.[25] This relates to how they approach becoming a reflective practitioner, being more self-aware, being clear about their beliefs and values and being seen as trustworthy and credible. All these factors figure prominently in partnership broker–partner relationships for reviewing and revising. Partnership brokers also need to be able to test and, if needed, challenge their own assumptions, unhelpful behaviours and emotional reactions. This may mean that they will need to adapt their approach or style, based on the reviewing and revising work that they may be doing. Partnership brokers can also learn a great deal from how other partnership brokers use their 'self' as a vehicle for change. Co-facilitation is a good way to test out different approaches to facilitating reviews and getting practice in trying different approaches, becoming more self-aware and developing proficiency and confidence in specific skills, i.e. negotiation, facilitation, enabling partners to work through complex issues, etc.

Additionally, partnership brokers can also learn a great deal from partners. Partnership brokers can encourage partners to review the partnership broker's role, key tasks and to assess their perceived added-value.

> It is important to access the views of the partner and partner organisations about how effectively the broker is undertaking their role. This can be done on a formal basis (for example by asking each partner/partner organisation to complete a questionnaire) or an informal basis (for example having a discussion with partners as a group at

the end of a business meeting). The review process itself may play a significant part in partners recognising their responsibilities and lessening their reliance on the broker as the partnership moves through the partnering cycle.[26]

Conclusion

Partnerships that are 'fit for purpose' have reviewing and revising as a core element of their work. Review exercises can take a wide range of shapes and forms. Some may be more formal in nature, e.g. an annual progress review, while other activities may be more informal, e.g. a reflective conversation at the end of a meeting. Reviews can be problematic if the function is not well embedded in the partnership mechanism, they are undertaken as a tick-the-box exercise or do not result in change or improvement.

Partnership brokers have a critical role to play in supporting partnerships to embed reviews into their thinking and work. They can help partners ensure that their reviewing and revising processes strike a good balance between the well-being of the relationship – *how they interact* – and their ability to create value and meet their expectations – *the what* of the relationship. Partnership brokers can also help partners ensure that the outcomes of their review and revising processes serve to enhance the partnership's ability to learn, improve, stay flexible and dynamic. Partnership brokers should seek to include a partnering capability development component into their reviewing and revising work, towards building partner capacity to self-manage and to collaborate. Partnership brokers and partners should consider how they can both learn from reviews of the partnership broker's role, performance and added-value.

Notes

1 Stott, L. & Van Kampen, H. (2015) Reviewing, Revising and Reflecting on Partnerships, the Partnership Broker's Role. *Level 1 Training: Reviewing and Revising Session' Slides 3, 5.* London: PBA.
2 The *Partnership Brokers Training Workbook* defines review as an assessment of how things are going. In this context used to describe the process of reflecting on the effectiveness, efficiency and value of the partnership: 90.
3 Austen, J. E. (2000) *The Collaboration Challenge: How Non-profits and Businesses Succeed Through Strategic Alliances,* San Francisco: Jossey Bass: 121.
4 World Economic Forum and Deloitte Consulting (2016) *Building Partnerships for Sustainable Agriculture and Food Security: A Guide for Country Led Action.* Geneva: World Economic Forum. Positions review as one of 8 steps in the partnering. cycle.http://www3.weforum.org/docs/IP/2016/NVA/NVAGuidetoCountryLevelAction.pdf (accessed 9/2/2018) and see: *Putting Partnering to Work.* Business Partners for Development: 1998–2001: Tri-Sector Partnership Results and Recommendations: 26–27
5 *Partnership Brokers Training Workbook*: 36–38.

6   *Partnership Brokers Training*: Reviewing revising and reflecting on partnerships, the role of the broker (2015). Slide 8.

7   These may include health checks, see: Caplan, K., Gomme, J., Mugabi, J. & Stott, L. (2007) *Assessing Partnership Performance: Understanding the Drivers for Success*, London: Building Partnerships for Development or looking at: drivers, interests and the added-value of the partnership; partnership effectiveness, and efficiency; review of context (the external environment (as reflected in financial, legal, economic, environmental and social considerations) that influence the context and shape of the partnership, see: Caplan et al. (2007) (Op.cit: 5) and its influence on the partnership; learning reviews and a review of the partnership broker's role.

8   SWOT: Strengths, Weaknesses, Opportunities and Threats.

9   See for example: Guide to evaluating the collective impact: http://www.fsg.org/publications/guide-evaluating-collective-impact#download-area (accessed 9/2/2018) and the Partnership Learning Loop: http://www.learningloop.nl/ (accessed 9/2/2018).

10 See Mundy, J. (2013) Progressive review and evaluation as a trust building mechanism in partnerships. *Betwixt and Between, The Journal of Partnership Brokering*, (2). http://partnershipbrokers.org/w/journal/progressive-review-and-evaluation-as-a-trust-building-mechanism-in-partnerships/ (accessed 9/2/2018).

11 PBA Principle 3: Being prepared to challenge assumptions and poor partnering behaviour at any stage of the partnering cycle in ways most likely to bring about constructive change.

12 A blind spot is a tendency to ignore something especially because it is difficult or complex.

13 See McCahon, M. & Mitchelmore, N. (2013) Using a review process to strengthen partnerships: A heritage partnership in Newfoundland, Canada. *Betwixt and Between, The Journal of Partnership Brokering,* (2). (Reproduced in Part 2 of this book). http://partnershipbrokers.org/w/journal/using-a-review-process-to-strengthen-partnerships-a-heritage-partnership-in-newfoundland-canada/ (accessed 9/2/2018).

14 See Mundy (2013) Op.cit.

15 See Hundal, S. (2016) The value of reflective practice for partnership brokers. *Betwixt and Between, The Journal of Partnership Brokering*, (6).

16 *PBA Imagined Conversation* offers a set of questions that can be used to foster reflective thinking and conversations: Why –did x happen, What if –x had not been there of x decision had been taken, What –would be the best possible outcome, What next –needs to change/happen to make a difference/how do we do this better?

17 Laloux, F. (2015) *Reinventing Organisations: A Guide to Creating Organisations Inspired by the Next Stage in Human Consciousness*, Leuven, Belgium. Nelson Parker Publisher.

18 Beeger, H. (2017) *Self-Management Blogs about Self-Leadership and Co-Creation*, Belgium: BMC Consultancy. https://bmc-consultancy.be/wp-content/uploads/Hans-BegeerCreating-stakeholders-value-through-commitment-blogs-May-2017-1.pdf (accessed 9/2/2018).

19 See Weisbord, M. & Janoff, S. (2007) *Don't Just Do Something, Stand There!* San Francisco: Berrett Koehler Publisher: 67–78.

20 See Tennyson, R. & McManus, S. (2007) *Talking the Walk, A Communication Manual for Partnership Practitioners*, London: International Business Leaders Forum: 18–30.

21 See, for example, PBA Partnership Cycle, Kolb's Experiential Learning Cycle, The Cynefin Framework-Performance Monitoring: www.complexability.com. au (accessed 9/2/2018).

22 FSG: Collective Impact. *Living Cities Cross-Sector Partnership Assessment: Group Planning and Discussion Guide.* www.fsg.org/publications (accessed 9/2/2018).

23 See Preskill, H., Parkhurst, M. & Juster, J.S. (2013) *Guide to Evaluating Collective Impact: Learning and Evaluation in the Collective Impact Context.* Boston: FSG, Collective Impact Forum: 8.

24 See Minahan, M., Vogel, J., Butler, L. &Taylor H.B. (2007) Facilitation 101: The Basics to Get You on Your Feet. Chicago: Organization Development Network, *The OD Practitioner*, 39 (3): 53–59.

25 Ibid.

26 PBA (2011) *Appointing a partnership broker, Guidance for those involved in making the appointment & assessing the performance*, London: Partnership Brokers Association. http://partnershipbrokers.org/w/wp-content/uploads/2010/09/Appointing-a-Partnership-Broker3.pdf (accessed 9/2/2018).

Part II

Partnership brokering in practice

Chapter 10

Dealing with ethical dilemmas

A partnership broker's personal perspective[1]

Sara Nyanti

The Government of Nepal requested the UN system (all UN agencies in Nepal) to support implementation of their Global Fund to Fight Aids, Tuberculosis and Malaria (GFATM) grant between 2006 and 2009. The UN system established a Management Support Agency (MSA) to partner with the Government and GFATM to accelerate implementation and achieve at least 80% of the indicators within a 7-month period.

The partnership was established with a very clear agreement that was signed between the Government and the UN. It spelled out the role of the UN and basically summarised that the UN was to implement the Government's agreement with the GFATM on its (the Government's) behalf. The Government had a major bottleneck at that time which was its inability (legally/administratively) to subcontract NGOs or community-based organisations (CBOs). Partners were therefore needed to fully implement the GFATM Phase I grant. Since the implementation plan was delayed by almost 2 years, an accelerated implementation plan was required. The GFATM Secretariat needed to see results within 4 months, but required achievement of 80% of the results within 8 months. This would qualify the country to receive the Phase II component (funds).

The major strategy of the accelerated implementation plan was to recruit NGOs and CBOs that could quickly provide us with the deliverables on behalf of the Government. A request for proposals was sent out and over 100 NGOs and CBOs were recruited. The projects were broken down into smaller proportions of the deliverables around the country, and the results reported were managed in a database designed solely for project monitoring and evaluation. All funds were transferred directly to the UN to ensure smooth implementation.

Coordination was essential and this was done at various layers within the UN and between the UN and the Government. The highest coordination mechanism was the GFATM CCM (Country Coordinating Mechanism) which was chaired by the Government and all stakeholders were represented. There were technical committees that functioned around various aspects of HIV prevention, treatment and control, and they were also relied upon for technical leadership.

At the end of the 8-month implementation period, around 80% of the results were achieved and Nepal qualified for Phase II of the grant. Beyond the fact that the results were achieved, the project had great strengths:

- The comparative advantage of the United Nations was to support the Government in the creation of the UN MSA. It emphasised the UN's role in the field as a system versus individual agencies.
- At the political level, the UN was well positioned in leading the rescue of the GFATM grant.
- There was also transparency between the UN and the Government – all strategies were shared and agreed such as the subcontracting of over 100 NGOs/CBOs.
- The Government was committed and supportive.

Unfortunately, however, there were many weaknesses:

- There were too many bosses, too many committees and too little time.
- There was limited capacity of the implementing partners and although at the political level the UN had cohesion and harmonisation, at the technical level, technical officers of the UN wanted to ensure that the funds were divided amongst the agencies in line with their comparative advantages – everybody wanted control over the portion of the funds that had to do with their area of expertise.
- Almost all of the projects were ad hoc. Hardly any were sustained after GFATM.

Looking back at the implementation, I recall several complaints and issues that were raised with the partnership:

1   The UN MSA was accused of a lack of monitoring to ensure quality implementation.
2   It was accused of undermining the Government's leadership role.
3   Many UN agencies and other external technical partners felt as if the MSA did not do enough to ensure that the required technical capacity was in place.
4   The capacity of the NGOs/CBOs was questioned.

As all of the concerns and issues raised centred around the ethics of how the agreement was implemented, the ethics of the whole arrangement came into question.

As a partnership broker, the first thing that I have learned in looking back at this experience is that the UN MSA itself was actually playing the role of a broker. As a partnership broker, were the actions of the MSA (which I headed) as ethical as they could be?

1   We were acting on behalf of the Government, but the Government had no input into the selection of the NGOs and CBOs.

2   Due to time constraints, limited monitoring was conducted. Data were collected and a very strong M&E system was in place, but it was reliant on reports from the partners.

3   We missed the opportunity to bring in others with greater technical capacities to fill the skills gaps.

The MSA was created to broker the implementation, and was specifically (in line with the agreement) focusing on scoping, building, managing and maintaining the partnership (see Partnering Cycle, Chapter 2, Figure 2.2). When one looks at the concerns and criticisms, one sees that basically the MSA (although not specified in its agreement) was expected to review and revise, and also sustain outcomes. Given the large investments, that would make sense. However:

- Where do we draw the line on contractual agreements versus doing what is required? We fulfilled the contract, but couldn't we have done things better?

- How do we use other brokering skills such as negotiating when we know that existing agreements do not address all possible issues that could be addressed within the same envelope of resources? Is it binding on a broker? Is it unethical not to do so?

- Could selection of the NGOs/CBOs have been more inclusive? Since the Government reviewed the terms of reference, did they need to be a part of the selection of the partners? Would it have helped to boost their role and relevance?

- Would it have been better if we had enabled the Government or others to monitor and provide feedback? Could the review and revise role have been highlighted as a gap and then delegated? We did know during implementation that this area was a gap. The agreement did not require it, but we knew that it was needed.

- Can we be unethical in our partnership when we have done exactly as the agreement articulated?

Needless to say, these questions are not likely to be unique to my own experience. Peers in partnership brokering will have faced similar dilemmas – and no doubt we will continue to do so. The reality is that we deal with complex and established ways of working where it is often difficult to bring about more than a degree of change at a time. The important thing is that collectively we need to keep challenging and catalysing through those small degrees to bring about change.

Also, the aid infrastructure has changed significantly and remains dynamic. This results in evolving partnerships that are sometimes unpredictable. The

Sustainable Development Goals present all development stakeholders with a chance to reduce the huge disparities that exist in wealth, power structures and opportunities. Strengthened partnerships will be central to maximising the effectiveness of the limited resources available in aid, and ethics around partnerships will be central in determining access to funds.

Note

1 Originally published as Nyanti, S. (2016) Dealing with ethical dilemmas – a partnership brokers personal perspective, in *Betwixt and Between*, *The Journal of Partnership Brokering*, (6), June. http://partnershipbrokers.org/w/journal/dealing-with-ethical-dilemmas-a-partnership-brokers-personal-perspective/ (accessed 9/2/2018).

Chapter 11

Internal partnership brokering within the private sector

Gillian Pearl

As private sector organisations engage more and more in multi-actor partnerships, those that are responsible for managing the partnerships (internal partnership brokers) are largely expected to possess project management skills. The role of an internal partnership broker is often not recognised as a distinct role with its own skill set, and even if it is acknowledged, it is often de-prioritised in the context of the project management responsibilities that come with the same role.

As an internal partnership broker within the private sector, my view is that brokers must play the dual role of project manager and internal partnership broker and move fluidly between the roles in the context of the partnership while at the same time increase awareness and perceived value of the internal brokering role to achieve the greatest outcome for the partnership.

To address the duality of the internal partnership broker and project manager role as well as the low levels of awareness and adoption of internal brokers as an essential component in multi-actor partnerships, this chapter will examine the three components in more detail. Firstly, we will identify and analyse the skill sets and fluid application of the skills that one person must possess to deliver on internal partnership brokering responsibilities, as well as the project management responsibilities associated with the partnership. Secondly, we will examine the lack of awareness and perceived value of partnership brokering and how to approach the issue. A major barrier will be removed by addressing perceptions (or lack thereof) of partnership brokering as an essential discipline and skill set required to facilitate a successful multi-actor partnership. Thirdly, we will look at ways in which partnership brokering principles and skills can be better understood in a private sector context, which will lead to increased recognition and socialisation of the role within private sector organisations that want to engage in multi-actor partnerships.

Internal partnership broker and project management skill sets and fluid application

There are similarities in the skill sets of partnership brokers and project managers, and yet there are also many differences and even different variations of the same skill that seem to overlap. Secondly, the priority of the skills of each role differs. Particularly with partnership brokering, there are skills that underscore the guiding principles of the practice and hold a different level of priority in partnership brokering activities. However, the most important difference in the two roles comes down to the core principles of partnership brokering: equity, transparency, mutual benefit and building on diversity.

Table 11.1 presents an indicative list of the skills of the two disciplines:

There is consistency in the common understanding of project management phases and partnership cycle phases:

- Partnering Cycle[1]: (1) Scoping and Building; (2) Managing and Maintaining; (3) Reviewing and Revising; (4) Sustaining Outcomes
- Project Management Phases[2]: (1) Planning; (2) Build-up; (3) Implementation; (4) Closeout

To help facilitate a comparative analysis on how the dual role works in application, please see the chart detailing common activities from multi-actor partnerships. The dual role of internal partnership broker and project manager works fluidly, but the application of the skills differs in emphasis and approach in and around the activity.

Using the partnership cycle stages as the paradigm, I have included examples from project and partnership activities in which I have been involved, so that we can see the real application of the dual roles of internal partnership broker and project manager and how the skills of both roles are applied in the context of the same activity (Tables 11.2–11.5).

Table 11.1 Partnership brokering and project management skills

Partnership brokering skills*:	Project management skills*:
• Confidence to hold space	• Leadership
• Articulation and presentation	• Communication
• Empathy	• Emotional intelligence
• Coaching and capacity building	• Coaching
• Negotiation	• Intelligence
• Institution building	• Calmness
• Facilitation	• Critical thinking
• Reviewing and revising	• Impact analysis
• Synthesising	• Budget management
• Information and record keeping	• Time management

*These lists are not exhaustive and are meant to be demonstrative.

Comparative analysis using the lens of partnering cycle stages

Table 11.2 Skills for scoping and building

Stage 1: scoping and building		
Project activity	Internal broker	Project management
A/ Discussing shared project objectives amongst (potential) project partners	An internal broker would take time to understand the drivers and underlying interests of not only their own organisation, but also of the partner organisations. With the core principle of transparency and mutual benefit, the internal broker would work towards ensuring there is agreement on shared objectives.	A project manager would focus on agreement of the shared objectives and the clear documentation thereof, but would not emphasise the principles of mutual benefit or transparency throughout the discussion.
B/ Establishing equity during the project's scoping of deliverables and assigning roles and responsibilities to project team members	The internal broker would be concerned with equity as roles and responsibilities were assigned to project team members. The broker would also be very mindful of the power dynamic that can play out between funding partners and implementation partners, and would explicitly highlight the core competencies of ALL partners to create an environment of mutual respect and understanding.	Maintaining a respectful project team environment would be the responsibility of a project manager, but the project manager would not focus on explicitly establishing a deeper understanding of core competencies amongst partners to dispel attitudes of inequity.

Table 11.3 Skills for managing and maintaining

Stage 2: managing and maintaining		
Project activity	*Internal broker*	*Project Management*
A/ A challenging situation has arisen with one of the partners not being able to deliver on a specific commitment	An internal broker would not look to ascribe blame but would aim to work through alternative solutions or approaches to the issue. Being driven by the principle of mutual benefit, the broker would recognise that the partnership should work towards the stated objectives, regardless of responsibility.	A project manager may be more concerned with the root cause analysis and clinical assessment of the problem and may not be as concerned about resolving the issue if the responsibility was with another partner rather than their own organisation.
B/ Creation of a work plan	Discussing the impact of the activities in the work plan, based on the principle of transparency, hold an open discussion related to challenges the partners might face during implementation.	Listing of tactical activities that will take place, and document the timeline associated with each activity.
C/ Managing the budget	Budget management would be outside of scope.	Budget management is high on the priority list of the project manager who must pay close attention to the budget spend, comparing the budgeted versus actual amounts spent on various activities and reporting regularly.
D/ Partner contributions at meetings	Acknowledging the differences in partners and ensuring both introverts and extroverts have ways that best suit them in terms of how they represent their thoughts. Equally, considering those that are non-native English speakers or English speakers who are limited in contributing in the local language of the project and how the meeting environment will affect their ability to contribute equally, and proposing ways in which to address that difference.	Providing each partner with a chance to share updates at meetings and managing the process associated with the meetings.

Table 11.4 Skills for reviewing and revising

Stage 3: reviewing and revising

Project activity	Internal broker	Project management
A/ Reviewing deliverables, roles and responsibilities	Explicitly naming the added value of the partner's contributions and recognising the same in other partner's contributions.	Reviewing project commitments as per agreed work plan.
B/ Identifying and capturing lessons learned	Openly discussing lessons learned from the partnership experience.	Documenting and sharing lessons learned only from the project, and not focusing on lessons learned from the partnership as distinct from the project.

Table 11.5 Skills for sustaining outcomes

Stage 4: sustaining outcomes

Project activity	Internal broker	Project manager
A/ Holding discussions about sustainability of project	The sustainability of a project would naturally be something that an internal partnership broker would consider at the outset of a project, using the topic also to examine how and when the internal broker could remove herself/himself from the partnership.	The concept of sustainability may or may not be something that a project manager is familiar with and the role of a project manager could continue to be required in the context of a partnership even if it is well established and sustainable given the requirements of the project on an on-going basis. The need for a project manager is not an indication of the sustainability of the project, per se.
B/ Helping partners celebrate and learn from their partnership story	The internal broker would focus on identifying and capturing the partnership-specific benefits from the project that would be above and beyond the project objectives themselves. Often there would be unintended outcomes that are worthwhile documenting and sharing that fall outside of the project agreement.	The project manager may be responsible for working on the case study of the project and documenting the objectives, process and outcomes.

Lack of awareness and lack of perceived value of partnership brokering

A lack of awareness and perceived value about partnership brokering is a major hurdle in the acknowledgement of the partnership brokering role and added value in a multi-actor partnership. A strategy built around influential people and processes is an impactful way to raise awareness and change perceptions.

The first step is to conduct stakeholder mapping. This activity entails the identification of the most important and influential stakeholders who can change perceptions and become spokespeople or ambassadors for the value of partnership brokers and their skill set. A typical list of stakeholders would include: (1) Senior leadership within the partnership; (2) Internal brokers from the organisations within the partnership; (3) People responsible for external and internal communication about the partnership; (4) Roles responsible for funding the partnership.

Once the stakeholder mapping is conducted, a list of tactics that could be used with each stakeholder or stakeholder group can be prepared. The tactics could be applied at various stages throughout the partnership, given that the opportunity to engage with the stakeholders may only present itself at different times, and not necessarily at the outset of the partnership:

- *Senior leadership within the partnership*: Hold sensitisation sessions with senior leadership within partnerships through a round table or conference call as the initial partnership discussions take place. Discuss the attributes of partnership brokering and how they differ from or complement project management, and the benefits of using a partnership broker in the partnership.
- *Internal brokers from the organisations within the partnership*: Discuss internal brokering principles with internal brokers from the organisations and work towards agreement and commitment to abide by them throughout the partnership. Regardless of whether the others identify as 'internal partnership brokers', the principles of partnership brokering are easy to understand and having an open discussion about the commitment to the principles upfront will enable the same individuals to be mindful of their application throughout the partnership and enable them to raise concerns if they feel the principles are not being upheld.
- *Roles responsible for external and internal communication about the partnership*: Document the outputs, outcomes and benefits of internal brokering activities, specifically differentiating them from project management skills and outcomes. Discuss the most effective way to share the insights within the partnership and within partner organisations as appropriate. Discuss how to share the same insights and examples with external stakeholder organisations, like the UN and multilateral or bilateral funding agencies that invest in multi-actor partnerships.
- *Roles responsible for funding the partnership*: Encourage multi-actor partnership funders to insist that those in management positions

within the partnership possess partnership brokering certification or minimum experience in managing multi-actor partnerships and familiarity with the concept of internal partnership brokers. Embedding the requirement of a certification or minimum years of experience raises awareness and integrates the requirement within the partnership process at the outset of the partnership.

Making partnership brokering principles and skills understood

Of all three sectors – government, civil society and the private sector – the private sector has the lowest involvement and experience in addressing development issues other than purely through philanthropic or CSR efforts, or through the delivery of products and services that might address a deeply felt, poorly met need of an underserved or underprivileged community.

As a private sector organisation evaluates a multi-actor partnership, the 'business benefits' must always be very clear. Whether this is articulated as return on investment (ROI), or other key performance indicators, it is important to articulate the value of partnership brokering principles and skills and how they support the achievement of the business objectives of the private sector. The more effectively we can do this, the more support there will be from the private sector for the requirement of partnership brokering principles and skills.

As such, the communication of the principles and skills should be framed in a format that is relevant for the private sector.

The reasons for private sector engagement in multi-actor partnerships can broadly be grouped into three categories: (1) Support for communities and causes; (2) Engagement with key stakeholders; (3) Incubating shared value. Using the categories as the framework through which to communicate the benefits of partnership brokering principles positions their value from a private sector perspective.

Business rationale for private sector engagement in partnerships[3]

Reason 1: support communities and causes

The private sector organisation wishes to positively affect relevant issues in locations where it operates and is interested in being considered a 'good corporate citizen'. The private sector organisation would contribute time, funding or in-kind resources to address issues that are relevant to the community, and would expect to build a positive public reputation through the partnership. It would also expect to be depicted as a trusted partner within the partnership, especially with respect to civil society or government organisations.

Partnership Brokering Principle: The brokering principle of mutual benefit ensures that the partnership is established to deliver benefit for all in the partnership and commits to working towards a partnership where all partners benefit. This would assure the private sector that the structure of the partnership was not one-sided in their favour and that the value of the partnership to all partners could withstand public scrutiny.

Reason 2: engage key stakeholders

The private sector develops an understanding of what employees, customers, regulators, key business relationships and civil society value, and then designs programmes and partnerships to address those priorities.

Partnership Brokering Principle: The brokering principle of equity supports the development of partnerships that ensure balance between the private sector organisation and the other partners. Whether the partnership is based on employee values, or those of customers, it is imperative that the key stakeholders feel the partnership achieves equity for all involved.

Reason 3: incubate shared value

The private sector invests in a shared value model, supporting the conditions for long-term growth and profitability, including risk reduction.

Partnership Brokering Principle: The brokering principle of openness is of value in a shared value model where the private sector organisation is developing a product or service for the bottom of the pyramid. There can be sensitivities when the private sector targets this demographic because of their vulnerability, so the principle of openness is particularly valuable in partnerships with a shared value business objective.

Conclusion

As a discipline, my view is that partnership brokering is not yet widely recognised by the private sector. Raising awareness about the unique skills that an internal partnership broker brings to a multi-actor partnership, and how the skills can coexist fluidly with those of a project manager, will help to establish partnership brokering as a recognised practice. By demonstrating how partnership brokering directly contributes to achieving business objectives, the private sector will come to see partnership brokering as an important contributor to the success of the private sector in multi-actor partnerships.

Notes

1 Partnership Brokers Association: http://partnershipbrokers.org/w/wp-content/uploads/2010/07/Partnership-Brokering-roles-and-tasks-March-2016.pdf (accessed 9/2/2018).
2 Harvard Business Review (2016) The four phases of project management: https://hbr.org/2016/11/the-four-phases-of-project-management.
3 The list is demonstrative but not comprehensive.

Chapter 12

Partnership brokering in a university environment
The case of itdUPM[1]

Carlos Mataix, Jaime Moreno Serna and Sara Romero

Because of their potential for offering spaces that encourage interdisciplinary and multi-actor collaboration, universities and research centres appear well-suited to the role of partnership broker. However, many of these institutions face enormous challenges in assuming this function. The experience of the Innovation and Technology for Development Centre at the Technical University of Madrid (itdUPM) suggests that the assumption of a successful partnership brokering role in a university environment rests upon the promotion of two complementary change processes: a move away from a conventional silo structure to an interdisciplinary environment, and a shift towards open and diverse 'communities' that can co-produce and transfer new kinds of practical knowledge. The possibility of accomplishing these is dependent upon a range of organisational and cultural factors within universities such as purpose-driven leadership from at least a few faculty members, an open-minded culture, organisational flexibility and individual cooperation skills.

itdUPM has successfully managed to create a multidisciplinary collaborative network of internal and external professionals that promotes action research and education for sustainable development. Founded in 2012, the Centre now has over 250 affiliates from both inside the University (faculty and researchers) and outside (practitioners and policymakers). itdUPM has also developed an inter-university Master's programme on development strategies alongside a range of innovative technological research and trans-disciplinary projects focused on sustainable development.

The partnership broker role played by itdUPM has been that of providing the 'connecting tissue' for provoking, accelerating and sustaining transformative collaboration among different disciplines and actors. Using a distributed leadership and governance model, the Centre:

- promotes multi-actor collaboration among UPM faculty members and students, as well as external professionals and entities;

- encourages participation in a university-based ecosystem work-ing for sustainable development by exploring intrinsic incentives for collaboration;
- uses trans-disciplinary research oriented towards problem-solving by using local resources to create new conceptual, methodological and transnational innovations that integrate and move beyond discipline-specific approaches to address challenges;
- insists upon the co-creative use of available capacities and scarce resources.

itdUPM's business model has a strong client focus that is based upon reci-procity rather than simply looking for grants. The Centre's strategic agree-ments thus seek to promote long-term collaboration with public and private institutions able to offer financial support for its activities. This has meant the inclusion of 'external' people willing to interact with itdUPM members in co-working research and training processes.

To carry out its partnership brokering work effectively, the organisa-tional design of itdUPM has undergone an evolutionary and learning pro-cess in which special attention has been given to brokering an effective collaborative environment. The core elements adopted by the Centre for this work are outlined below.

The development of a network structure

itdUPM functions as a horizontal networked structure with the inclu-sion of clear and regulated decision-making bodies that are connected to UPM authorities. The network's 'nodes' are built upon pre-existing uni-versity Cooperation Groups by inviting individual researchers, faculty members and non-academic experts to join the initiative. Meanwhile, a Technical Team has assumed the functions of external representation; communication and administration (see Figure 12.1). Technical Team expenses are covered by a fee from contracts signed with public and private institutions.

A network is very likely to become a 'foreign body' in an academic envi-ronment. Indeed, for many, the word 'network' is synonymous with 'messi-ness' and a risk of loss of control. For this reason, a 'sense-making' process through which people could understand and experience the advantages of collaborative processes was devised. The Technical Team at itdUPM set up a series of awareness-raising, training and targeted communication activ-ities that focused on how relationships might evolve in an open network environment. Conducted as workshops, these activities were designed to enable participants to experience the dynamic interactions between depart-ments and research groups, and external organisations.

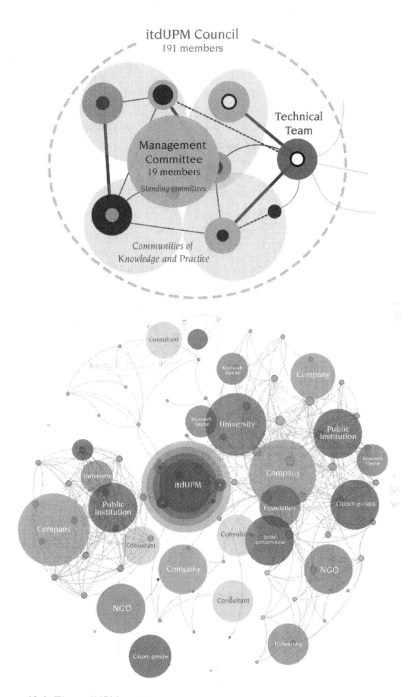

Figure 12.1 The itdUPM environment.

Source: Mataix et al. (2017) Working for Sustainability Transformation in an Academic Environment: The Case of itdUPM, in Leal Filho W., Mifsud M., Shiel C., Pretorius R. (eds) *Handbook of Theory and Practice of Sustainable Development in Higher Education*, World Sustainability Series. Springer, Cham.

Decentralised leadership and governance

Although leadership in itdUPM is distributed, focused decisions are taken by formal bodies such as:

- the itdUPM Council which is composed of 250 itdUPM affiliates and chaired by the President of UPM;
- a Management Committee composed of 19 Research Group coordinators and elected by the itdUPM Council;
- Communities of Knowledge and Practice such as the Commission for Experimental Spaces which manages itdUPM's Research Programme, and the Quality Commission for the Master's programme;
- the Technical Team of six full-time staff who support the network;
- ad hoc teams for specific projects.

The governance model seeks to move 'from ego-systems to eco-systems'[2] by ensuring the encouragement of increased personal autonomy and decentralised leadership; creating a sense of community and purpose; promoting far-reaching transparency and accountability processes and the promotion of self-criticism, rather than sanctions, as the most appropriate way of ensuring continuous improvement. Within the Centre, a range of individuals have played an important role in engaging with University authorities to position itdUPM as an integral and valuable part of the university system. As well as guaranteeing institutional support for the Centre, these efforts have also created a positive enabling environment for its work.

Attention to incentives

Open affiliation was a critical element in itdUPM's design. Membership of the Centre for UPM faculty members is secured on an individual, personal basis and affiliation is fully compatible with other School, Department, Research or Cooperation Group linkages. Acceptance of new members is agreed upon by the itdUPM Council which is held twice a year. Because affiliation is voluntary, a given member may leave by presenting their formal resignation or simply ceasing to participate in itdUPM's activities.

Membership of itdUPM has not been without personal risk. The success of the Centre has at times been insecure due to spending reductions for research and limited financial support from UPM. However, on the more positive side, many members have stated that the chance to interact and collaborate with members of different disciplines and external professionals in action research projects has been a great incentive for joining itdUPM. Other motivations for joining the Centre are more emotional in character and include trust, a shared passion for a theme of interest and a warm atmosphere. As the Centre expands and gains in recognition, it is hoped that long-term participation will be reinforced by incentives that are more directly related to the professional careers of researchers. The growing number of scientific papers published in relation to itdUPM projects suggests that this is beginning to happen and should be built upon.

Managing different identities

Collective identity stems from the interpersonal interactions that make up an organisational culture. The development of itdUPM as a horizontal network with its own culture *within* the UPM was enabled by the official acknowledgement by UPM authorities of its status as an 'innovation centre'. UPM faculty members are used to belonging to a diverse range of organisational units, including Schools, which are their most traditional, permanent homes; Departments, for teaching purposes, and Research Groups, for disciplinary research activities. Against this background, itdUPM has positioned itself as having a different aim: to develop innovations using a multidisciplinary, multi-actor action research approach so that a faculty member is able to engage in disciplinary research in their Research Groups and collaborate with members of other disciplines and external professionals through itdUPM. The development of both an itdUPM culture and a new membership identity has been carefully managed by the Technical Team via network communications and workshops. Through this process, a shared itdUPM culture has taken form and the Centre's identity has become interiorised by its members.

Finding common spaces

Since its inception, itdUPM's activities have encouraged members to act as a community of researchers and practitioners with a trans-disciplinary approach to addressing sustainability challenges through technology-based social innovations. The renovation of itdUPM's main building involved public agencies, private actors, members of the educational community and society working together. The resulting itdUPM space (see Figure 12.2) has attracted a vibrant community of voluntary UPM faculty and students, as well as external professionals and entities, engaged in developing multidisciplinary technological research and sustainability projects.

The building not only serves as the headquarters for itdUPM, it is also an open demonstration space devoted to sharing technologies and innovations for sustainability. Concepts and prototypes for urban agriculture, decentralised energy systems and the circular economy, among others, are being tested there and scientific and dissemination activities take place inside the building. The facility also encourages multi-actor relationships and the exchange of

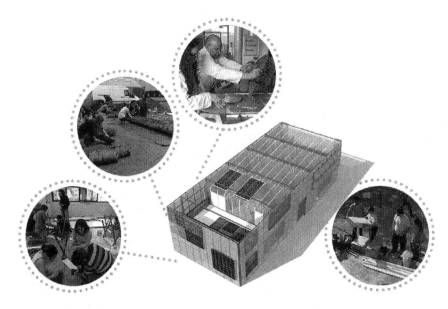

Figure 12.2 itdUPM's main building.

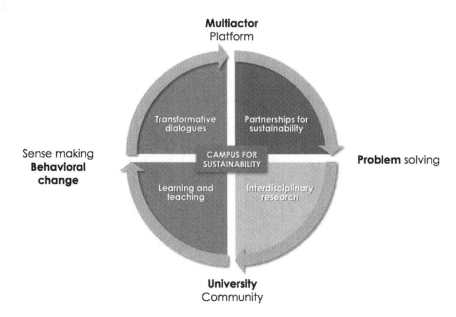

Figure 12.3 itdUPM framework.

experiences among the large number of social innovation spaces promoting citizen's involvement that are currently emerging in Spain and elsewhere.

itdUPM's research, training and advocacy activities are designed and implemented through co-creation and co-production methodologies. These activities are fostering a more open and collaborative culture among researchers that has enabled itdUPM to develop a working model that aligns its sustainability goals across four quadrants: i) a campus that provides space for multi-stakeholder collaboration; ii) the promotion of solutions to sustainability problems; iii) the encouragement of sense-making and behavioural changes that support sustainability and iv) the engagement of the wider UPM community in activities for sustainability (see Figure 12.3).

Conclusion

The creation of collaborative interdisciplinary and multi-actor spaces in the UPM has not been a simple task. It has involved a complex design process and careful decision-making with regard to organisational and human factors such as leadership style, culture and values. Particular capacities were needed to pilot the launch of the Centre, not just in terms of financial resources but, above all, in terms of human resources and institutional support. A dedicated team has been crucial to the development of the internal and external networks and the nurturing of the ecosystem for this. The change management process that has seen behaviours, relationships and practices move away from those typical of a conventional university environment to those that are appropriate in a more collaborative and diverse environment has also required an important investment of time.

Five years after its establishment, itdUPM is now in a phase of consolidation. The Centre continues to operate without a centralised control structure and has responded well to the growing expectations that have resulted from its increasing visibility. Funding from diverse sources for several large long-term projects has provided itdUPM with a degree of financial security. Meanwhile, the Masters course continues to go from strength to strength with an increasing number of students each year from Spain and further afield. The Centre has also received accolades for its work in the sustainability field.[3] itdUPM's success appears to demonstrate that when transformation for sustainability is both urgent and desirable, universities can broker better development pathways through collaboration.

Notes

1 This chapter draws extensively from: Mataix, C., Romero, S., Mazorra, J., Moreno, J., Ramil, X., Stott, L. Carrasco, J., Lumbreras, J. & Borrella, I. (2017)

Working for sustainability transformation in an academic environment: The case of itdUPM, In W. Leal Filho, M. Mifsud, C. Shiel & R. Pretorius (Eds.), *Handbook of Theory and Practice of Sustainable Development in Higher Education*, World Sustainability Series. Cham: Springer: 391–428.
2 Scharmer, O. & Kaufer, K. (2013). *Leading from the Emerging Future: From Ego-System to Eco-System Economics*, San Francisco: Berret Koehler Publishers.
3 The itdUPM building was awarded second prize for its bioclimatic and experimental design in the design category at the World Green Infrastructure Congress 2016 held in Bogotá, Colombia, and presented as a best practice for its work in 'Collaborations to Address Global Challenges' by the ISCN Secretariat (2017) *Educating for Sustainability 2017. Sustainable Campus Best Practices,* Boston: International Sustainable Campus Network (ISCN).

Chapter 13

Partnership brokering for local food systems in Poland

Rafal Serafin

In 2011, the Polish Environmental Partnership Foundation, an NGO committed to grassroots, community-based sustainable development, initiated the 'Local Products from Malopolska' (LPM)[1] initiative using a partnership approach. The motivation for the initiative was to revitalise rural development by building a functioning and self-sustaining local food system that connected small-scale producers and consumers with each other as directly as possible. Such food systems are referred to as short-chain food systems and are growing in popularity in the policy arena.[2] This is because, in line with the UN's Sustainable Development Goals,[3] they are seen increasingly as practical opportunities for engaging smallholder farmers as partners in reconfiguring our food system away from its agri-industrial focus so that it is once again beneficial to people and planet.

In Poland, the challenge was to work out how a local food system might be established in a country in which hygiene and tax rules discouraged small farmers from processing and selling products. At the same time, consumers were expressing a preference for cheap and convenient food in their purchase habits. Industrial forms of agriculture were favoured in public policy, whereas the market was dominated and shaped increasingly by supermarkets and international food retailers. Functioning in this way, the food system was excluding over a million small farmers and subsistence landholders by limiting market access, and so leading to rural impoverishment. With its emphasis on industrially produced food, the food system was also contributing to health problems, especially amongst children and youth, including obesity, diabetes and other related issues.

The LPM project was initiated as a response to the challenges outlined above by aiming to turn the many small farms and landholders, who were seen as a problem by many politicians, into a resource for creating a new type of food system that put a premium on healthy eating and locally produced chemical-free food. The response focused on Malopolska, one of Poland's 16 provinces, which is located in south Poland. The distinguishing feature of this region is its potential for small-scale farming and food processing with approximately 140,000 small farms, averaging between four to five hectares in size, but operating largely for subsistence. This situation, while not typical of many parts of Europe, has much in common with food systems in other parts of the world which are dominated by small-scale farming and food processing. Thus, the LPM partnering experience should be of interest to those seeking to increase the contribution of small-scale farming and food processing to the political, economic, social and cultural regeneration of rural areas and to food systems that provide for better nutrition and healthier lifestyles.

Using various organisational, technical and IT solutions to connect geographically dispersed producers and consumers, the LPM project has developed a local food system that now involves some 175 farmers and producers and more than 3,000 consumers. Those concerned with ensuring sustainability of the LPM system in ways that maximise social, environmental and economic benefits are looking to scale up the numbers of producers and consumers involved, the range and diversity of products offered for sale and the volume of sales.

Partnership brokering has been important to the development of the LPM system and lies at the heart of efforts to scale up and achieve greater impact. In this regard, the Polish Environmental Partnership Foundation has acted not just as the initiator and organiser of the LPM initiative, but also as a partnership broker seeking to form and develop it as a self-organising and self-sustaining cross-sector partnership arrangement. This focus has necessitated awareness-raising, support and reinforcement in four key areas: partnership brokering for partnership impact, reinforcement of partnering as a journey, partnership brokering as learning and partnership brokering for transformation.

Partnership brokering for partnership impact

An explicit effort was made by the Polish Environmental Partnership Foundation to develop and implement a local food system as a partnership involving farmers and food producers, community groups, local and regional governments, businesses and other stakeholders. Funding support for a project was secured from the Swiss–Polish Cooperation Programme for the period 2011–2017. During this period, the Foundation succeeded in establishing a functioning LPM system involving in excess of 25 organisational partners, including public agencies, and more than 175 food producers. The Foundation focused from the outset on trying to develop an organisational ecosystem with the various partners, playing different roles, but with no single organisation in charge. This was to ensure that the organisational ecosystem would continue to function and evolve once the start-up funding ended, adapting and responding to changing needs, opportunities and constraints.

The project represented an investment of nearly €2 million over an 8-year period, which helped the Foundation initiate a network of seven Buyers' Clubs enabled by a customised IT platform for organising weekly transactions, farmers' markets, a kitchen incubator for enabling food processing with the latest equipment, advice and training, a food centre organising catering, restaurant and other gastronomic services, and a quality-assurance scheme with branding verifying traceability, as well as ongoing technical and training assistance to participating farmers/producers.

In addition, the project involved financial support for 23 NGO projects to help ground the whole system in local communities and a campaign that changed sanitary and tax legislation at the national level to enable farmers to process and sell what they grow on their farms directly to consumers. All these elements have combined to form a living 'organisational ecosystem' with the Foundation as the animator and broker. The project has contributed to the emergence of a countrywide movement focused on locally sourced food which is gathering momentum across Poland. As a result of these efforts, government policy has also changed in the direction of support for small-scale farming and food processing, local markets and short-chain food systems that connect producers and consumers. Whether such a local food system can grow to provide a real alternative to the industrial food model, however, remains to be seen.

The partnership brokering journey

The LPM project was conceived and implemented as a prescribed undertaking on account of the funding mechanism involved. The Foundation prepared a grant proposal containing a detailed description of how the local food system would be developed, what activities would take place and what would be financed. In short, the proposal articulated a goal and mapped out a journey that the Foundation and its local and regional partners tried to implement to achieve that goal. The journey turned out to be much more complicated than initially anticipated due to the need to constantly modify and adapt the initial map to changing needs and circumstances. The project team at the Foundation sought to find ways of engaging farmers and producers in joint work on upgrading their production capabilities, and developing distribution channels and markets for locally produced food. Thus, farmers, community groups, consumer groups and local and regional governments were encouraged to take collective or joint action wherever possible. But the goals and objectives, activities and funding allocations were all prescribed in the project proposal and so were not easy to change.

The limitation of the approach was the lack of flexibility in adapting to changing needs and circumstances, which became apparent as the project unfolded. As the grant holder playing the role of the manager, guide and leader, the Foundation was also constrained in the sharing of risks and costs with partners. In addition, the nature of the grant funding meant that, by definition, the benefits accrued mostly to partners and beneficiary NGOs and producers, whereas the Foundation was left to deal with paperwork, cash-flow issues and organising own contributions to draw down the grant funding. Limitations notwithstanding, the advantage of this grant-aid approach was that significant funds could be deployed over several years in a systemic and sustained way.

Partnership brokering as learning

In the LPM project, it soon became apparent that the key to establishing a local food system lay in nurturing personalised relationships between those involved. Project activities brought dividends where the Foundation was able to work with those involved to better understand how the food system functioned in Poland. In this regard, it became apparent that collective undertakings were essential, such as establishing Krakow's first farmers' market or the organising of a nationwide campaign to change sanitary legislation and policy in favour of small-scale production. These were areas which had not been prescribed at the outset but had to be realised if the local food system was to become a reality, such as regulatory changes in hygiene and tax rules.

As the project unfolded, farmers, producers, specialists, public agencies, NGOs and other actors became part of an effort to better understand the opportunities and constraints of public policies, regulations, markets and consumer preferences, as well as agricultural and food processing practices. This meant that, in addition to working to change regulations, advances could be made in articulating what needed to be included in them.

The LPM project thus became a framework for learning, experience exchange and a promoter of good practice. Study visits, exchanges, meetings with specialists and opportunities for discussion with peers all contributed to building an LPM identity, solidarity and a sense of joint ownership. These human interactions and interrelationships helped to build a sense and recognition that the benefits from collective action could never be achieved by acting alone. In its role as a partnership broker, the Foundation team sought to facilitate, nurture and create as many opportunities for interaction as possible among those involved. The farmers' markets established through the project came to play a crucial role in this regard, serving to forge personal relationships with consumers that became crucial to expanding and sustaining sales volumes.

Partnership brokering as emerging opportunities

The LPM project succeeded in building a constituency of interest in food among producers; consumers and other public, private and community actors, which generated opportunities for further development that could not have been envisaged or anticipated at the start. These opportunities, included, for example, the development of a Malopolska Cold Meat Plate and a Malopolska Cheese Plate, grouping together traditional cheeses and cold meats into a single product offering, which had not previously been available. In both cases, local organisations have taken on these initiatives. Another example is the development of a logistical system for the LPM system based not on third-party service providers but on making use of the unused logistical resources of the producers and consumers involved in the LPM system (i.e. transport, storage and travel itineraries/routes). A further example is the opportunity for developing a Diaspora Financing[4] scheme for LPM development which involves tapping into the remittance transfers from families and friends of producers and local community groups living in other countries. Yet another scheme seeks to provide schools with locally sourced food.

The important point here is that these schemes were generated or brokered through interaction and learning, and their different stages of development are a function of the interest, relevance and enthusiasm of those involved in them. They are collective initiatives which, by definition, are intended to benefit both individuals involved in the LPM system and the system as a whole. In this sense, the opportunities for new ventures should be seen as opportunities 'emerging' from the myriad of interactions and interrelations. The task of a partnership broker is to keep a watchful eye out for 'emerging opportunities' and to explore the possible added-value or benefits that might result together with those participating in the partnership.

In its partnership brokering role, the Foundation has been working with those involved in the LPM system to scan for new opportunities that can potentially generate individual and collective benefits for all those participating, building cohesiveness, identity and interdependence in the process. These new opportunities emerge from the interactions of those involved and the reality of a living, functioning ecosystem of individuals and organisations, in which no single organisation is in charge. The role of the Foundation is to facilitate, share and reflect back new ideas and opportunities to those involved, to push for increased competitiveness in the market place and to underscore how the social and environmental benefits generated are vital to the current and future economic benefits for individuals. The opportunities that generate an interest and traction among those participating in the LPM system will be the ones that will go forward, not just those which secure funding.

Partnership brokering as transformation

In the LPM project, the transformational dimension has become increasingly important as those participating have come to recognise that Poland's food system as currently constituted is failing both farmers and consumers while also doing a disservice to rural development and heritage conservation. The emphasis on large-scale industrial farming and a food sector geared to export has not just neglected small-scale farming and food processing but discriminated small food producers and consumers seeking access to locally produced food. Individually and collectively, many of those involved in the LPM system have come to identify with the wider transformational role of the LPM system and other local food initiatives across Poland. The partnership brokering role of the Foundation in this regard is that of a focus for campaigning for further changes in policy and planning, regulations and seeking to engage with others working explicitly to create alternatives to the industrial farming approaches that still dominate.

An important role for the Foundation also relates to assisting those functioning in the informal economy to join the formal economy, to help work out ways of establishing and growing business ventures that can contribute to and prosper within the LPM framework. The role is that of empowering and giving voice to those who have hitherto been ignored or left out of the economic, social and political mainstream. This transformational role is less about enabling a sharing economy of the type favoured in the partnership-as-emergence model, which generates values through networking and networks. It is more about a social economy that keeps farmers and food producers in control of their destinies and their share in the surpluses and value-added that they are helping to create. The consequence of this role can be illustrated in relation to dealings with potential investors.

Commercial or conventional investors seek to maximise commercial returns by taking control of their investments, whereas socially oriented impact investors seek to maximise not just economic returns, but also social and environmental benefits. Attracting and negotiating with impact investors is thus an important priority and opportunity. In this situation, the key role of the partnership broker is to develop relationships that allow local producers to retain control of the LPM system that they are co-creating and sustaining. This is not about acting for and on behalf of those involved in the LPM project but about playing an assigned role in an organisational ecosystem that has taken on a life of its own.

Lessons learned

The LPM project suggests that partnerships are often established as part of the conception and delivery of a predefined set of actions, which are supposed to lead to a predefined result. Partnering is the tool or method that is used to ensure that the actions are undertaken in a way that leads to the anticipated result. Funding is allocated in accordance with a schedule (usually called a log-frame), ensuring that progress towards the result can be monitored. Yet, the reality of partnering is that, irrespective of what may be contained in a project document, log-frame or partnership agreement, partnerships are about individuals and organisations seeking to achieve their own objectives and goals. Most, by nature, will be seeking to extract benefits while shifting costs and risks to others. The extent to which these can be achieved through group or collective action will determine partnership performance and impact.

In the case of the LPM initiative, the focus was on encouraging and enabling collaboration among farmers, consumers, food processors, regulators, civic groups, public agencies and other stakeholders in the food economy. Their collaboration was and continues to be central to the performance of the LPM food system as a collective social, economic and environmental initiative. The practical implication for partnership brokering is that it is has little to do with log-frames, but everything to do with using the partnership to reconcile and deal with the different motivations, objectives and goals of the numerous individuals and organisations involved by trying to align them with a shared LPM mission. It is about creating individual, as well as group benefit. Partnership brokering is fundamentally a social process characterised by a never-ending negotiation, emergence of new opportunities and transformation. Inevitably, the process is always unfinished. The partnership broker, in this case the Foundation, was really the only stakeholder focused primarily on the collective benefit of the partnership.

Working with others is not easy, especially when goals and objectives are not shared. Too often, those involved give only lip service to the collective or partnership goals as they remain focused primarily on the benefits accruing to them. This was very much reality in the LPM project. Partnership brokering was thus about giving primacy to operations in the food system where collective action was an essential basis for extracting individual benefit. In the LPM system, the Buyers' Clubs are an example of how collective action generates individual benefit (not the other way around). The Club (the collective) enables producers to sell directly, while providing consumers with access to quality food of known origin. The collective serves, for example, to eliminate food fraud (the practice of selling industrial food as 'organic' or 'local' to secure a higher selling price) through a system of informal, mutual policing and so gives consumers confidence in the authenticity of what is being offered to them. In this case, the benefits are individual in terms of products sold or purchased but they cannot be generated without collective action.

Conclusion

Partnership brokering is about drawing attention to the benefits of collective action by increasing an appreciation for the limitations on what individuals and organisations can achieve when acting alone. In this sense, partnership brokering is not about rules, procedures, technologies and formulaic solutions but about human interactions and interrelationships in a locale or around a theme such as local food systems in Malopolska. Partnership brokering is also about intervening responsibly in both informal (potential partnership arrangements) and formal partnership situations where a document or agreement of some kind is already in place to deploy partnership action. In both situations, the task for the partnership broker is to try to understand not just the social nature of the partnership involved and the context within which it operates, but also how such an intervention (or non-intervention) might affect the social dynamic.

Notes

1 For more information about the Local Food from Malopolska food system, see: www.local-food.pl (accessed 9/2/2018)
2 See Report of the EIP-Agri focus group on Innovative Management of Short-Food Chain Systems, https://ec.europa.eu/eip/agriculture/sites/agri-eip/files/eip-agri_fg_innovative_food_supply_chain_management_final_report_2015_en.pdf (accessed 9/2/2018).
3 17 Sustainable Development Goals underpin the UN's 2030 Agenda for Sustainable Development. All of them relate in some way to patterns of food production and consumption. Two are especially relevant: Goal 2.3: "By 2030, double the agricultural productivity and incomes of small-scale food producers, in particular women, indigenous peoples, family farmers, pastoralists and fishers, including through secure and equal access to land, other productive resources and inputs, knowledge, financial services, markets and opportunities for value addition and non-farm employment" and Goal 2.4 "By 2030, ensure sustainable food production systems and implement resilient agricultural practices that increase productivity and production, that help maintain ecosystems, that strengthen capacity for adaptation to climate change, extreme weather, drought, flooding and other disasters and that progressively improve land and soil quality." See: https://sustainabledevelopment.un.org/sdgs (accessed 9/2/2018).
4 See: http://www.undp.org/content/sdfinance/en/home/solutions/remittances.html (accessed 9/2/2018)

Chapter 14

Learning from Luangeni
Partnership brokering by accident[1]

Martin Kalungu-Banda

I became a partnership broker by accident. Twenty years ago, I was part of a research team working in Zambia's Eastern Province to learn about what sort of governance systems existed in isolated areas of the country. During our travels, we camped for about 10 days in a village called Luangeni. In the evenings, the elders would sit in the centre of the village and tell stories while the children sang, danced and played around them.

One evening, as we watched the children dance, I asked the Village Headman a question: 'How many of these children go to school?'

He answered, 'About four'.

I counted the children. There were 86 of them.

I followed up with another question. 'Why don't people send their children to school?'

'They used to send their children to school until something happened', the Headman responded.

'What happened?' I asked.

'Things changed when the supermarket, Shoprite, came', he replied.

'I don't understand', I said. 'Could you explain?'

The Headman nodded,

> Before the supermarket came here we used to grow vegetables of various types in an area near the village that has water throughout the year. Every weekend we put those vegetables on our bicycles and went and sold them in the centre of our provincial capital. Since the supermarket came to the capital nobody buys our vegetables. We have lost our income. This is the reason why parents in this village cannot afford to send their children to school.

After a long pause, he concluded, 'Our only salvation may be a riot in the city that burns down the supermarket'.

At that point, I had nothing else to say to him.

The Headman's story kept me awake throughout the night, so the following day I went to the local Shoprite branch to meet the supermarket manager. I asked him what prevented his shop from buying from local farmers. He explained that all procurements were managed via the company's headquarters in the nation's capital, Lusaka. He suggested that I discuss the matter with the General Manager responsible for Zambia.

In Lusaka, I made an appointment to meet the General Manager of Shoprite.

'Your business has caused a lot of problems for the people of Luangeni in Eastern Province. They seem to be worse off now than they were before you established your business there', I said to him.

The General Manager asked me to see the bigger picture,

> A few households here and there may not be doing well but look at how many people's lives have changed for the better because of our presence in the area. People are now able to access quality foods, utensils and many other products. People used to line up for bread; now they can have bread at any time they wish. People could not predict when they were going to have fresh vegetables and foodstuffs. Now they know that they can find them in the supermarket. Besides, our prices are unbeatable. Isn't that what service to the community means?

'I understand the benefits you have brought to the area', I replied. 'But is there a way in which we can ensure that villagers in Luangeni are not worse off?'

The General Manager leaned forward and said,

> A supermarket of this quality only works when everything is predictable. We need to know that there will be tomatoes and onions, for example, and not just that; we need to know that the tomatoes and onions will be of a certain size and of a certain quality. And that has to be constant.

When I told him that someone had expressed the view that it would be good if the supermarket was burnt down, the General Manager was shocked, 'Do you know how much money we have invested in that store? Do you remember the small state shop that was there before we arrived?' he said.

I said, 'People are very angry about the loss of their livelihoods. May be you could meet them half-way'.

The General Manager hesitated and then said, 'What would half-way look like?'

I had to think fast to respond to this. I said, 'If you can commit to buying from local farmers, my University colleagues and I will see if we can find ways to ensure that the farmers are properly trained to produce vegetables that meet the standards of your supermarket'. I also told him that this would reduce the costs of transporting vegetables over long distances to Eastern Province. I then asked him if he would allow me to come back to him with a comprehensive proposal for addressing this situation. The General Manager agreed.

After the meeting, I contacted some of the people I knew who might be able to contribute towards resolving what I called 'the Luangeni challenge'. We became the Zambia Partnership Forum[2] and together set out to identify and enrol individuals and organisations that could play different roles in enabling Shoprite to purchase produce from local farmers. This constellation of helpers and collaborators included:

- civil society organisations specialised in training farmers;
- agriculture extension officers who provided technical support to farmers;
- a manufacturing company that designed bicycles that could comfortably and safely carry large quantities of farm produce;
- University of Zambia staff who designed affordable irrigation pumps that farmers could use at a very low cost;
- auditors who gave financial advice to the venture.

A few months later, in the presence of the country's Vice-President and the Traditional Chief in whose jurisdiction Luangeni community falls, a partnership agreement was signed between Shoprite and the people of Luangeni Village. Two years later, research conducted in Luangeni Village found that household income had grown by over 300% as a result of the partnership with the supermarket, and important social advances had been made. According to Kavwanga Yambayamba, one of my University colleagues at the time, and a member of the Partnership Forum:

> The results of this partnership were overwhelming. Local farmers were soon producing high quality vegetables which Shoprite could buy and sell. Their average monthly earnings increased to about US$ 48.55 in less than a year and they were able to pay for family use of social services such as health and education. Furthermore, a woman was chosen as chairperson for the farmer's cooperative society because she demonstrated strong leadership qualities when working in the partnership and a deliberate move was made to ensure that couples participated in the project together. The involvement of widows, a group often marginalised in Zambian society, was also encouraged. The project thus began to address cultural barriers by empowering both men and women equally.[3]

After the Luangeni Partnership was established, I attended a formal partnership broker training programme at the United Nations System Staff

College in Turin, Italy.[4] During the training, I became aware of why and how the process of brokering partnerships encompasses a set of skills that one can acquire and develop. I learnt about how to reveal the underlying assumptions that potential partners hold about one another; how to help potential partners identify which areas of their core work they may be able to partner on and which they could not; how to draw up an effective partnership agreement; how to maintain a partnership once it has started and the qualities a good partnership broker should seek to nurture.

Reflecting back on the Luangeni experience as an accredited partnership broker, I was able to identify the following key pointers for future work in this field:

- *Being perceived as 'neutral' matters*: Both the community and the leadership of the supermarket chain trusted my colleagues and me in our brokering role and saw us as having the interests of both parties at heart. Our commitment was to have a particular problem resolved: restoring the livelihoods of Luangeni Village community members following Shoprite's unintentional disruption of their market.

- *Building capacity by selecting the right partners*: Obvious potential partners are often not the most important ones needed to resolve a particular challenge or to seize a given opportunity. The partnership between Luangeni Village and Shoprite worked well because we were able to identify other crucial parts of the partnership and include partners such as the Ministry of Agriculture, who offered the technical skills support required for the production of good quality vegetables; the Zambia Seed Company, who agreed to supply local farmers with appropriate seeds; the University of Zambia for specialist advice; the bicycle manufacturing company for transport and NGOs that provided community education. An international NGO also provided financial support to implement the pilot phase of the project and provided funding for further community capacity-building.

- *Appreciation of what is at stake:* A partnership broker needs to know what is at stake for potential or actual partners. In my work, I found that there was high correlation between what was at stake for each of the partners and their level of commitment. The higher the stake, the higher the level of commitment. In the Luangeni case, a number of things were at stake for the key players in the partnership; for the community, it was community livelihoods and the education of children; for Shoprite, two things were critical: the company's physical assets (such as fear of arson) and the loss of business that could arise from stocking products which did not meet the company's minimum standards.

- *The importance of relevant data:* Convincing data help partners see the reasons for collaboration. When Shoprite had evidence in facts and figures of the gains that they could make through partnering with local framers, they were ready to take action.
- *Keeping one's word:* Those who present themselves as 'go-betweens' between different actors must keep their word. My colleagues and I were the go-betweens in the Luangeni case. We made sure that we honoured whatever commitment we made with both individual partners and the collective. Sometimes, these commitments were as basic as keeping to agreed dates when reporting back. At other times, it was something more serious, such as honouring the request by the local community of Luangeni that their own representatives would be directly involved in making decisions on the steps to be taken in the process of forging the partnership.
- *Even the partnership broker needs help:* When you are a partnership broker, particularly a formally trained one, you may be tempted to think you are the one who will make things shift or the one through whom things must happen. I learned that even helpers need help. My colleagues and I needed the help of others to make certain aspects of the partnership to work. For example, there were moments when we had challenges in shifting the position of the country General Manager of Shoprite on a given issue. At such times, we drew upon the connections and skills of the Shoprite Regional Manager who was able to communicate effectively with the General Manager and encourage him to listen more closely to our arguments. To enlist the participation of NGOs specialising in agriculture, we also sought the help of a respected faith leader who was trusted by different parties and supportive of the emerging partnership.
- *Working on oneself:* A partnership broker needs to develop ways of doing inner personal work. Assuming this role can give one a sense of self-importance that distracts from the main purpose of the work at hand. My deepest intention was to ensure that the strongest driving motive for me was to promote the interests of the Luangeni community and I needed to remember that. Before each major stage in the negotiation of the partnership, I therefore took time to be on my own and reflect on why I was involved in this work. I sought to centre and be in tune with myself, with the environment around me and the needs/aspirations of the people or organisations that I was going to be working with. This process of reflection allowed me to ensure that I was not being driven by pride, status or a need for recognition. The work eventually gave my colleagues and me national and international recognition,[5] but I was clear that this was not the main reason why I was involved in brokering the partnership.

Notes

1 Some of the information contained in this chapter comes from an interview I had with Kate Raworth in 2005 when Oxfam GB wanted to learn about the successes and challenges of the Luangeni partnership. See: Raworth, K. & Wren-Lewis, L. (2008) *How Change Happens in The Private Sector. From Poverty to Power Case Study*, Oxford: Oxfam International.
2 The Forum for Business Leaders and Social Partners (Partnership Forum) was established in 1999 to promote corporate social responsibility and sustainable development in Zambia.
3 Yambayamba, K.E. (2006) "Do it for us?" The challenges of replicating a partnership. *Partnership Matters, Current Issues in Cross-Sector Collaboration*, 4: 69–70, London: The Partnering Initiative.
4 *Partners in Action: Partnering Skills for Strategic Engagement* was a training programme developed by The Partnering Initiative and the United Nations System Staff College (UNSSC).
5 As well as becoming widely known in Zambia and replicated in other parts of the country, the Luangeni Partnership was showcased at the 2002 World Summit on Sustainable Development (WSSD).

Chapter 15

Using a review process to strengthen partnerships

A heritage partnership in Newfoundland, Canada[1]

Marion McCahon and Nina Mitchelmore

The Northern Peninsula Heritage Cluster is a network of local heritage organisations[2] located on Newfoundland's Great Northern Peninsula. In 2010, these groups began working together to provide a coordinated approach to the delivery of visitor heritage experiences and interpretation in the region. In April 2012, on hearing about the Partnership Brokering model and approach,[3] the Heritage Cluster Coordinator and Advisory Group invited the authors of this chapter to assist with strengthening the partnership and sustainability of the organisation, as it prepared to move into a new phase of its development. Using a combination of brokering techniques, review tools and community development approaches, the authors worked as external brokers[4] with the group to carry out an assessment of the existing partnership.[5] Based on the findings, they designed and delivered (with partner support) a series of workshops and planning sessions to help strengthen and build the partnership and the Heritage Cluster network as a whole. This chapter provides an overview of the review and community development techniques that were used, as well as key lessons learned from our approach.

Background and context

The Northern Peninsula of Newfoundland and Labrador has a vast geography, encompassing approximately 17,500 kilometres[2]. There are approximately 17,000 people living in 69 communities along the coast. These communities were built on the fishery and forestry sectors but have since diversified and have begun to showcase their history, culture and geography through a developing tourism industry. Through numerous initiatives, many heritage sites have started to develop museums and interpretive products that highlight the history of the fishery, medical influences on the peninsula, unique flora and fauna and other features.

Due to the scattered location of the heritage sites throughout the peninsula as well as the number of visitors they are attracting, the need for a Heritage Cluster emerged. This initiative was developed through a partnership between the Red Ochre Regional Board and the Nordic Economic Development Corporation, with both groups supporting heritage sites in the region. The Department of Tourism, Culture and Recreation of the Government of Newfoundland and Labrador supported the initiative through the provision of funding to assist in creating the Cluster. In addition, other government departments have also been active partners. This Cluster has and continues to endeavour to give strength in numbers to these groups, to create more promotion potential and to provide the members with the opportunity to learn from each other.

Review tools and techniques

When designing our partnership review, we utilised a variety of different tools and techniques to give the authors and the group as broad an understanding as possible of the current state of the partnership. The components of the assessment included:

- **Advisory Group Meeting** – We met with this group to gather a history of the Cluster and its work to date, along with information on key players, processes and structures in place.
- **Individual interviews** – We organised a series of interviews, one with each organisational member of the heritage network. Wherever possible, we tried to arrange a meeting with several members of the local heritage organisation, but sometimes (due to lower volunteer numbers) it was only possible to connect with the lead contact of the group.

We felt that these individual interviews were important to get a realistic view of the current state of the partnership and we used the questions to ascertain if members were seeing benefits and felt engaged, and to understand their objectives and priority focus areas. When we designed the questions, we referenced many of the tools in the Partnership Brokering Toolbook,[6] such as the coherence assessment questionnaire and partner assessment tool. The questions asked during the interviews are outlined in Table 15.1.

The **Wilder Collaboration Factors Inventory**[7] – This inventory explores the factors necessary for successful partnerships. During this process, we selected a number of factors (including history of collaboration, respect and trust, compromise, communication, vision and others) and asked the group to assess the Heritage Cluster with regard to particular factors. The assessment was carried out using audience response technology, which allows participants to provide answers and vote on their priorities using handheld keypads, with the results viewed by the Cluster as a whole. This process identified a few key areas where the

Table 15.1 Interview questions

1	What were your reasons for being involved with the Northern Peninsula Heritage Cluster (both personal and organisational)?
2	What do you see as the main outcome(s) of the Heritage Cluster to date and longer term?
3	Do you agree with the Heritage Cluster objectives? Why or why not?
4	What benefits do you see arising from the Heritage Cluster (both personal and organisational)?
5	Are you currently seeing benefits? If yes, please describe. If not, what would you like to see and what needs to change to deliver these benefits?
6	Do you feel engaged with the project?
7	What actions/activities are a priority for you and your organisation?
8	Are there particular focus/activity areas for the Cluster, where you would like to become more involved?
9	Do you have skills or experience in a particular area which you could pass on to the group?
10	Other comments?

group was working well and also a few areas where the partnership could be improved. This focused our agenda for the next steps of the partnership-building process. We summarised the interview results into a presentation (ensuring individual site comments remained anonymous) and delivered this to the Advisory Group, before presenting it to the Cluster members at the first workshop.

Engagement tools and technologies – Wherever possible, we tried to use tools which made the sessions, reviews and discussions as engaging as possible. These included:

- **Polling**– During the process of identifying areas to improve upon and actions and next steps, *Turning Point*, an audience response system from Turning Technology was used. This technology allowed individuals to contribute their opinions anonymously. For instance, when deciding on items for their constitution (executive structure, decision-making policies), voter response keypads were used.
- **Deliberative dialogue techniques** – As a part of this process, we endeavoured as much as possible to have deliberative dialogue opportunities so that the partnership could evolve through idea exchange and debate. Through this process, an issue or idea of importance to the group was selected for discussion in small groups. The groups were facilitated so that everyone had a chance to speak and so that conversations would stay on topic. The ideas from the groups were collected, themed and put into slides to report to the group. From those slides, voter response keypads were again used to prioritise the ideas to move forward.

Partnership-building

As we began the partnership-building process, we had several goals in mind, many of which also aligned with community development objectives. These included:

- *Group sustainability* including resource sustainability as well as building the ability and interest of partners to manage and take forward the actions and projects of the network.
- *Building empowerment and capacity* among group members to lead and deliver projects for the network.
- *Creating ownership and commitment* by group members. Our goal was to see tangible commitments by members to supporting and taking forward the work of the partnership. We also hoped that this contribution would become an expectation for all partners in the network.

In order to work towards these objectives, we held a series of workshops with the group (at several of their regular group meetings). Each workshop took between half a day and a full day to deliver as they focused both on a combination of partnership-building and ensuring the correct structures and processes were in place to sustain the group as an entity over the long term.

Initially, the planning of the workshops took place with resource people and the Cluster Advisory Group and (once the Heritage Cluster had identified its new structure and executive) with both resource people and the chair of the Cluster. This aimed to address the critique (heard in the interviews) that there was no or little involvement from heritage group members in the Advisory Group for the project. This had meant that members were not involved in planning out the direction of the network and there was a sense that this was leading to a lack of ownership of the Cluster. This ownership was critical where the group needed to move to a more self-sustaining structure. The workshop planning also utilised the skills of a wide variety of support organisations, i.e. the authors had skills in partnership-building, whereas staff in other organisations had experience in group governance, structure and processes.

Delivering the workshops

The first workshop began by presenting the results of the interviews and asking the group to vote on the Wilder Review Questions, using the voter response keypads. The results of this polling were reviewed that evening by the authors and given back to the group the following morning. After this, and as the workshop continued, we started to address some of the issues raised by the review and moved into the partnership-building phase. In terms of workshop structure, for day 2 of the first workshop, participants were asked to discuss the questions outlined in Table 15.2.

Table 15.2 Workshop questions

---

1 Going forward, what should be the main purpose for the Heritage Cluster?
2 What are some of the key goals for future work of the Cluster?
3 What are some of the ways in which we can improve collaboration in the Cluster?

The second workshop focused on developing a vision and finalising goals for the Cluster, along with moving forward on action planning items. During the collaboration discussion, a presentation was made on the Partnership Brokering approach and group members were asked what they thought about this and whether the Cluster should be run as a partnership model. Some formal collaboration structures were also discussed as the group was interested in exploring these further.

The final workshop focused on confirming group structure, membership, processes and resource mapping. We used this workshop to get agreement on many of the items that would be incorporated into a group MOU or Partnership Agreement.

Lessons learned

As part of the project, we feel that there are some key areas which are important to highlight or where we had significant learning. These include: building ownership of the Heritage Cluster by its members, action planning, resource mapping and the review process.

Building ownership – We asked a representative of the group to take a lead on a section of the workshop (i.e. for the first workshop, this was around the vision) and as the workshops progressed, we worked to increase the role of group representatives in the meetings. We also asked the Cluster coordinators to take a step back in order to begin reducing the group's reliance upon them.

We asked resource people not to vote on any of the group decision-making, but to leave this as the responsibility of the Cluster members.

We also worked to highlight the positive items that came forward from the review – for example, in the interviews, we asked participants to identify skills and expertise that their individual heritage groups possessed and which could be shared with the wider network. We were impressed and excited by the diversity of experience and practical skills that they identified.

Action planning – Throughout each of the workshops, we allocated time to action planning for the network. Four key themes were identified and we asked people to work in small groups based on their interest in a particular theme and to identify actions, tasks and timelines related to these.

This worked well for several themes, but for others, there was not the level of interest from group members or the projects identified were large and required significant time and resource commitments. Learning from this process is to focus initially on a small number of easily achievable projects and small wins, until greater ownership of the network has been achieved. These smaller wins help to build momentum and a sense of group achievement which can lead to greater willingness and drive to take on larger projects. The delivery of cluster-wide action items by group members was a move away from the previous approach where the network coordinator (a paid position) had been working to deliver projects for the group.

Resource mapping – We used this technique to build on the positive finding in the review of the variety of skills and expertise which group members were willing to share. We initially identified all the resources which were needed for the network to move forward as a sustainable organisation and then asked the partners to highlight what they could contribute. Every single resource needed was found within the group, many from multiple partners. This helped significantly to empower and build the confidence of the group members. One of the challenges we anticipate is keeping these shared resources in group members' minds as an option, as it is tempting to go back to previous models where government funding provided many of the resources.

Review process – We found that it is important to share widely the review findings with the group and their support organisations, even though some of these findings may be difficult to hear. While the results may be critical of particular partners, we found it helpful to present the results in advance to them.

Role of the partnership broker – Both authors acted in an external broker role with this review. Although known to many members of the Cluster through our work in supporting community and regional development, we had not previously been a part of the Heritage Cluster project. We had both been trained as partnership brokers and were able to use many of the tools and techniques provided in the Partnership Brokers Association training and resource materials. Based on our experience of this review process, we found that it was much easier to do the review as an external, rather than internal broker. If we had been internal brokers we feel it could have been very challenging to get the 'full story' from partners, particularly during the individual interview stage. As external brokers with no previous attachment to the project, we feel that Cluster members were honest and open with us in providing their comments and critiques.

Conclusion

While undertaking this initiative we used a combination of brokering techniques, review tools and community development approaches. Through this process and with the support of many partner organisations, we have seen the partnership grow and move forward with positive signs of increased ownership, commitment and sustainability.

This chapter has provided an overview of the review, partnership-building and lessons learned, and is a summary of how we developed and implemented this multifaceted process. We hope we have provided a detailed experience and rationale for using a number of approaches and tools to build strong and sustainable partnerships. This building process is a crucial next step for implementing changes identified through a partnership review.

The authors believe that enhancing ownership, commitment, empowerment and capacity of members is a key to success in the partnership and that individual organisations need to become active members of the partnership, if the project and the Northern Peninsula Heritage Cluster are to become sustainable over the long term.

Notes

1 Originally published as McCahon. M. & Mitchelmore, N. (2013) Using a Review Process to Strengthen Partnerships: A Heritage Partnership in Newfoundland, Canada. *Betwixt and Between, The Journal of Partnership Brokering*, London: Partnership Broker's Association (2). http://partnershipbrokers. org/w/journal/using-a-review-process-to-strengthen-partnerships-a-heritage-partnership-in-newfoundland-canada/ (accessed 9/2/2018).

2 A heritage organisation in this context is a community heritage group whose members work to develop and promote a local natural or cultural heritage site. Examples of sites include: cottage hospitals, fishing premises, museums, natural heritage interpretation centres and archaeological sites.

3 The Partnership Brokering model and approach is presented in Partnership Brokers Training Course run by the Partnership Brokers Association.

4 An external broker is typically an independent consultant or external organisation appointed by the partnership to implement decisions on its behalf. He/she may have also seeded the idea or may even have initiated the partnership.

5 The collaboration was between sites who were members of the Cluster and aimed to move forward the goals and objectives of the Cluster.

6 Tennyson, R. (2004) *The Partnering Toolbook*, London & Geneva: International Business Leaders Forum & GAIN.

7 https://www.wilder.org/Wilder-Research/Research-Services/Pages/Wilder-Collaboration-Factors-Inventory.aspx (accessed 9/2/2018).

Chapter 16

Managing complexity

Challenges for international development partnerships

Donna Leigh Holden

Over the past decade, partnership has become an increasingly common term used within the discourse and literature of the international development sector to describe the working relationships between a range of development actors – bilateral and multilateral donors, governments of aid recipient countries, international non-government organisations (NGOs), local civil society organisations (CSOs), academic intuitions, etc. The language and logic of partnerships for development have been driven by the aid-effectiveness agenda, enshrined initially within the Paris Declaration on Aid Effectiveness (2005)[1] and later the Accra Agenda for Action (2008)[2] and the Busan Partnership for Effective Development Cooperation (2012)[3] which established frameworks for ensuring that development actors held each other accountable for their commitments through a set of shared principles and common goals, namely:

- **Ownership of development priorities by developing countries**: Countries defining the development model they want to implement;
- **A focus on results**: Sustainable impact as the driving force behind investments and policymaking;
- **Partnerships for development**: The participation of all actors, and the recognition of the diversity and complementarity of their functions;
- **Transparency and shared responsibility**: Development cooperation must be transparent and accountable to all citizens.[4]

The critical importance of partnerships in achieving development outcomes has more recently been underlined by the inclusion of Partnerships as Goal 17 of the Sustainable Development Goals (SDGs), a set of 17 global goals set by the United Nations and which aim to 'transform our world by 2030'.[5]

Overlaying these approaches is recognition of the complexity of development in the current geo-political/geo-economic climate. In working on social development issues, we experience complexity in two ways: (i) by addressing complex problems; and (ii) by working within complex adaptive systems, and this has important implications for practice.[6]

Partnerships for development

Partnerships for development are a response to these trends in development thinking, and are now both one of and a part of these complex and adaptive systems within which we practice. At the core of partnership theory is the recognition that it is unreasonable to consider that any one actor can bring about achievement of high-level development outcomes alone, but rather, that various actors play a role in contributing to these through the mobilisation of different resources – skills, capabilities, relationships, networks, reputation, financial resources, etc.

The development sector itself is a complex system. Key to understanding the benefits and challenges of working in partnership is recognising the range of development actors; the different skills, mandates, resources and attributes that they bring to the table and their limitations. Donors, for example, may bring high-level relationships (e.g. with government) through which political pressure can be brought to bear. They are often able to mobilise at scale and address policy change in line with the implementation of national programmes through the mobilisation of government resources (people, institutions, programmes and funds). They are, however, bureaucratic organisations, overly focused on procedure rather than efficiency, and governed by policies mostly outside of the control of the workforce and which can change suddenly. NGOs tend to stronger relationships at the grassroots and with marginal groups who fall through the gaps of national programmes. They can bring evidence of what works, what does not and contribute to understanding why. International NGOs often face operational and financial constraints in implementing independent programmes in developing countries, while local CSOs may be exposed to significant political risks, or experience capacity gaps due to uncertain financial arrangements and poor governance. Academic institutions can lead research, draw on an international body of knowledge and assist in creating linkages between knowledge and policy by connecting theory with practice, but may be slow to respond, depend on specific funding interests and have limited multi-sectoral linkages and relationships. Within these stereotypes, there are, of course, significant differences between organisations and the way they perceive, conceive and operationalise programmes.

Partnership theory suggests two exciting possibilities for development in a complex world, namely:

1 where people and organisations work together, they are likely to achieve more than they can alone; and, importantly,
2 that systems cannot be understood only by understanding the smaller parts that make them up, and that, indeed, once connected, the outcomes may be greater (and most certainly different) than the individual parts.[7]

So how does this promise play out for the different types of development actors working on complex social issues in complex and complicated working environments?

The following discussion draws on my observations and experiences in working as a partnership broker with civil society partnerships for development in Asia and the Pacific. It is by no means an academic exercise.

Challenges and ways forward

Putting the core partnership **principles** of equity, transparency and mutual benefit into practice in a complex industry populated by competing interests, shifting contexts and complex problems presents significant challenges for establishing and delivering effective partnerships.

Challenge 1 Equity: The way in which overseas development assistance (ODA) is dispersed reinforces significant power imbalances between key delivery partners and presents further challenges to equity at several levels. ODA to civil society is generally delivered through grant funding, and international donors are in the large part unable and under-resourced to directly administer these funds. As such, most ODA to local CSOs is delivered through intermediary organisations such as international NGOs, multilateral agencies or private sector aid contractors who accept, by nature of their contract, accountability and liability for the use of these resources. The implications of this in terms of relationship and power dynamics are significant. In its purest form, it places local organisations as subcontractors to external intermediaries. In the context of decreasing ODA spends, value for money and responsible use of public funds, it places financial and asset management at the centre of performance, which, in turn, places a higher value and focus (in terms of effort and accountability) on the financial resources that are on the table. Funding becomes king and partners become accountable to the people and systems that govern it.

Partnership brokers and partners have a range of tools at their disposal to assist with rebalancing this situation and striving for equity, for example:

- Ensuring a clear separation between the Partnership and any specific projects that the Partnership may undertake. Creating umbrella Collaboration or Partnering Agreements which focus on articulating the unique attributes of each partner, their expectations and goals for the relationship, and the potential areas and mechanisms of collaboration should stand alone but provide a framework through which contracts for discrete pieces of work with specific financial obligations can be developed where necessary.
- Resource mapping to outline the range of contributions (financial, knowledge, networks, social and political capital, infrastructure, time, legitimacy and authority) of each partner to a specific activity or

outcome. This can help to illustrate and acknowledge a shared contribution, articulating these within Partnering Agreements, and measuring how resource mobilisation is tracking at implementation.

- Establishing collaborative business processes which seek to affirmatively address power imbalances, e.g. rotating meeting chairs, locations and roles and responsibilities for key administrative tasks such as documentation, reporting, etc.

While these are practical tools, they are insufficient to address the fundamental and indeed complex realities that impact upon the independence of local CSOs, and which work against achieving equity, transparency and mutual benefit within partnerships which include:

- A lack of access to an independent financial base which enables CSOs to take concrete and independent action to implement their own mandates and programmes outside those funded through ODA. CSOs are challenged to access funding outside of working as subcontractors for predesigned interventions. The issue of core funding to CSOs has long been contentious in the development world. Donors work to specific risks or regional or global development trends and priorities. They prioritise the funding of tangible activities as opposed to institutional reforms and priorities that could potentially be construed as management costs. In the current geopolitical climate, they are often averse to risks of association, especially where their partners have a strong mandate and advocacy agenda. Access to core funding for CSOs, however, can be the key to enabling them to invest in their institutional sustainability and independent mandate.
- Limited engagement of partners in creation and design which means that engagement with local partners often commences with performance management processes in which local partners are subjects of M&E activities.
- A lack of space to engage in dialogue with policy decision-makers and service providers which undermines their ability to use programmatic evidence to improve governance, service delivery and development impact. I have seen few partnerships do this in an effective way. A key criticism by local partners is the fact that lead partners most often control meeting and dialogue agendas and rarely bring their CSO partners into government and donor meetings. As such, they become the face and voice of the partnership efforts.

So, can partnership be a tool which helps different stakeholders to address these types of structural challenges? Are there ways that partnership brokers can work with partners to try and rebalance these inherent inequities when brokering partnerships? Is this not our mandate and role as partnership brokers? The following strategies may help to plant equity more firmly into our partnering practice:

- **Sharing the public sphere.** Partnership brokering can explore the potential of supporting the legitimacy of civil society by providing equitable opportunities for them not only to represent the partnership externally, but to engage with government and policy decision-makers on key issues. This can engage them in social change and development processes in a meaningful and equitable way. It requires negotiating with NGO and other lead partners to share the inherent power and opportunity that these spaces offer. It requires external communication strategies which uphold the rights and responsibility of partners to engage in these spaces to be articulated within Partnering Agreements.
- **Ensuring that review processes clearly distinguish between reflection on the partnership and the performance management of specific activities or programmes.** Good or poor performance is brought about by a range of factors and conditions generally beyond the capability of a single actor. Effective partnerships may deliver poor programmes and conversely effective programmes might be delivered despite poor partnerships. M&E systems must clearly define how they will assess the performance of the Partnership and the activities which the Partnership delivers and how the tensions between relationship management and programme performance will be managed to ensure fairness to all parties. Partnership and programme review analyses should also take care to separate these two facets while concurrently seeking to understand how they interact and influence each other!
- **Addressing resource requirements to enable all partners to fulfil their respective and shared responsibilities and commitments.** Partnership financing arrangements need to consider factors beyond the financing of specific activities and include: core funding to CSOs, to enable them to undertake independent actions to achieve their own institutional objectives beyond any specific project objective; resources to support joint advocacy efforts; the costs of engaging in design (monitoring and evaluation and sense-making) processes in order that CSOs have sufficient resources to participate actively in the co-creation of development interventions and the costs of partnering processes to keep partners engaged and mutually accountable.

This means placing a transaction cost on the relationship and partnering processes and ensuring that sufficient staff and resources are allocated to these processes so that they are mobilised in a meaningful way. In the same way that we set aside budgets for monitoring and evaluation, so should we set aside budgets for partnering.

Challenge 2 Transparency: The way in which donors engage intermediary organisations in managing the perceived risks and high transaction costs of working with local civil society places the onus for collaboration upon the intermediary but fails to incentivise good partnership performance.

International and national organisations and donors have very different perceptions of transparency. Donors and intermediary organisations tend to define transparency in practical terms linked to financial accountability and certain programming ethics, e.g. child protection, gender equality, etc. In my experience, this is most often expressed as a one-way relationship where local partners are required to demonstrate upward accountability but there is less clarity on what this means in terms of the obligations of the intermediary to its donor partners. Arguably, there are limited incentives created to encourage intermediary organisations to deliver on good partnering practices.

It is interesting in that when discussing transparency, intermediary organisations and donors are generally positive about transparency within their partnerships. Local CSOs, however, are considerably less so, claiming poor access to financial and planning information outside of their own budgets and most importantly, limited engagement in decision-making processes around programme strategy and resource allocation. They appear to have a significantly broader definition of transparency which takes into account relationships and wider work practices.

As a partnership broker, I am consistently struck by the poor attention paid by donors to ensuring that intermediary organisations have the required capabilities and are incentivised to work in ways which support partnerships that will deliver on development effectiveness. The selection of intermediaries is commonly based on their ability to manage donor funds, i.e. compliant grant management, audit and reporting systems. It is rare that approaches to market require intermediary organisations to identify their approach to partnership, and even rarer for these to be integrated within performance criteria and M&E systems. As such, intermediary organisations, like donors themselves, are poorly incentivised to deliver on partnering outcomes, and this becomes a greater challenge in resource and time poor contexts.

So, what can we as partnership brokers do to assist donors and implementing partners to take a wider view of transparency, beyond financial management, to include greater attention to transparent work practices and decision-making processes? How can we ensure that intermediary partners are incentivised to deliver on good partnering practice? Some possibilities include:

- **Holding grant-making/contract-holding partners to account for partnership practices.** When designing and procuring civil society partnership programmes, donors need to be supported to set clear and measurable performance targets around good partnering behaviours of the lead or grant-making organisations. These, in turn, need to be part of the performance management processes.

- **Defining good business practices from the outset.** Words can have different meanings to different people, and especially in cross-cultural contexts. Partnership Agreements need to move beyond an articulation of good ideas and good will to include clear agreements about the work practices that are expected of each partner. These must provide practical examples of what these processes might mean in practice, and the ways in which partners will come together to reflect on how these are working.

- **Integrating partnering processes within the programme cycle.** Current approaches to partnership brokering in the development sector tend to focus on establishing Partnership Agreements and Partnership Principles at the outset and undertaking 'health checks'. The partnership broker is rarely engaged in critical programming functions such as design and M&E and as such partnership principles are poorly integrated into programming and business processes and the living narrative of the programme.

Challenge 3 Mutual Benefit: The tendency for civil society partnerships in developing countries to engage 'like' organisations undermines the potential power of mobilising comparative advantages.

Let's face it; donors tend to subcontract the outcomes that they want to see based on domestic and regional priorities and trends. Civil society partnerships, in turn, focus on the implementation of sectoral programmes based on these priorities through subcontracting arrangements which are, in their purest form, pragmatic responses to the operational constraints for lead partners of working in another country. As such, what we tend to see in the development space are implementation partnerships between 'like' organisations, with whom the key points of difference are less likely to be interest and mandate and more about access to (donor) resources, power and capabilities. This scenario offers little space to work towards the specific interests on individual organisations.

When dealing with complex social development issues, is simply working with a local organisation enough? Rather than shifting resources from one partner to another, how can we engage new resources and worldviews to address complex problems? Some possibilities include:

- **Engaging with non-traditional actors.** If we return to the notion that partnerships hold the promise of creating greater impact through mobilising the comparative advantages of different actors, then it stands to pass that we, as partnership brokers, need to support wider cross-sectoral partnerships and encourage those with whom we work to expand their engagements with non-traditional actors who can bring alternate world views, wider resources and different capabilities and approaches.

- **Facilitating capacity-building exchange.** Development of the individual partners as well as the partnership itself is a key expression of mutuality. Capacity-building efforts in partnerships however tend to be one-way and often focus on institutional strengthening of CSOs to meet donor reporting and accountability requirements. In brokering partnerships, there is space to identify the specific skills and capabilities of each partner and seek to plan ways in which each partner can gain from these differences. Building in two-way learning processes is critical to this.

Conclusion

The development effectiveness agenda has provided the industry with a key message and focus for strengthening our efforts by seeking to engage in more meaningful partnerships with a range of stakeholders in order to deliver on development outcomes.

We are moving forward. Some organisations are making institutional commitments to strengthening their partnering capabilities by investing in capacity-building and the development of policies and guidelines to support better partnering practice. Some donors are using funding to invest in multi-stakeholder partnerships, including those with non-traditional development actors, and diverse actors are seeking to find ways to mobilise their complementary skills and resources.

However, there are perverse incentives at play within the industry that make this challenging. Large bureaucratic organisations are most often governed by processes and rules meant to maintain order but which work against the flexibility required to partner effectively and implement complex social change programmes in a shifting landscape. Donor organisations are vulnerable to domestic political shifts which place long-term investments at risk and result in rapid and unexplained change that undermines transparency. Development organisations work in complex and often unstable environments that tend to experience regular shocks (e.g. political instability and/or unrest, natural disaster) that place additional burdens on already stretched workforces and resources. Resources are limited and focused on tangible deliverables and there is little to incentivise organisations to deliver on internal quality processes.

Good partnerships rely on a combination of adaptive and flexible processes. They are not only an end, but an important means for working with complexity. They rely, however, on a wide-ranging set of reforms which shift the way that different development actors do business. These reforms move well beyond a philosophical comment expressed through language and rhetoric. To address the complexity, they need to be structural. They need to be behavioural. They need to be institutionalised. And, they need to be resourced.

Notes

1 http://www.oecd.org/dac/effectiveness/parisdeclarationandaccraagendafor action.htm (accessed 9/2/2018).
2 Ibid.
3 http://www.oecd.org/dac/effectiveness/busanpartnership.htm (accessed 9/2/2018).
4 Ibid.
5 http://www.un.org/sustainabledevelopment (accessed 9/2/2018).
6 Cabaj, M. & Auspos, P. (2014) *Complexity and Community Change: Managing Adaptively to Improve Effectiveness*, Washington DC: The Aspen Institute.
7 The saying 'the whole is greater than the sum of its parts' (attributed to Aristotle) is commonly used to communicate the potential of partnering.

Chapter 17

Using partnership-based approaches to improve aid effectiveness

A case study of trilateral cooperation[1]

Sarah MacCana, Moses Laman, Ning Xiao, and Leanne Robinson

In our increasingly globalised world, the case for using multi-actor partnerships to address our most pressing challenges is undeniable. Working separately, different actors develop activities in isolation, leading to competition, duplication and wastage.[2] In the realm of foreign aid, international actors have now recognised the link between building inclusive partnerships and effective aid practices through various global fora.[3]

Trilateral cooperation, a relatively new form of aid, is founded on this partnership-based approach. Defined as a type of south–south cooperation,[4] trilateral cooperation has been adopted by governments and multilateral agencies as a way to engage traditional donors, rapidly developing economies and host countries in addressing a shared development challenge or regional priority. It usually involves the transfer of hardware (infrastructure, goods and services) and/or software (knowledge and expertise) between partners, with each party contributing finance and/or technical assistance and/or in-kind support.[5]

Given the relative newness of this model, there are limited data available on the effectiveness of this form of aid, though there is a general agreement that the model's advantages include leveraging of additional resources and harnessing the comparative advantage of different actors.[6] However, commentators frequently cite the complicated three-way coordination processes associated with the presence of multiple stakeholders in a trilateral cooperation project as a major challenge, which can hamper harmonisation, delay progress and lead to 'higher than normal' transaction costs.[7]

The following case study, authored by the partnership broker and partners directly involved in managing and delivering a trilateral cooperation project, shows this assumption to be specious (and not least because all complex development programmes, irrespective of their form of aid – bilateral, trilateral or multilateral – require effective coordination across multiple stakeholders). The Australia–China–Papua New Guinea (PNG)

Pilot Cooperation on Malaria Control Project (Trilateral Malaria Project), now in its third year, is a small yet innovative partnership that utilises project funding from a traditional donor (Australia) to mobilise in-kind contributions from all three countries (predominantly in the form of technical experts such as laboratory specialists, scientists, researchers and health workers) to tackle a shared regional priority (promoting health security in the Asia-Pacific region).

Nearly 95% of PNG's population lives in areas of high risk for malaria transmission, and PNG contributes over 75% of malaria cases in the Western Pacific Region.[8] China has extensive experience in defeating malaria and is now on track for indigenous malaria elimination by 2020 (an exceptional achievement given that China treated 24 million cases every year in the early 1970s). Australia is a long-term supporter of health sector improvements in PNG. Given this context, the Trilateral Malaria Project aims to reduce the burden of malaria in PNG through supporting Australian, Chinese and PNG experts to work together in strengthening PNG's laboratory network, and establish operational research studies to inform relevant malaria control policy and programme decision-making. It enables China to share relevant knowledge and lessons learned in health policy and malaria control strategies with other partners, with the aim of both strengthening existing interventions and developing new ideas for reducing malaria in PNG. Importantly, the model provides an opportunity for institutions who may otherwise not naturally partner in this way to learn from each other while working towards a shared goal.

The three governments have established a Project Management Unit, led by an accredited partnership broker,[9] to support partners in establishing and implementing this project. Early experiences generated through this Project suggest that trilateral cooperation models, when established using a partnership-based approach[10] supported by a dedicated partnership broker, can in fact *reduce* transaction costs. This is because, returning to the theme of Part 1 of this book, investing in a well-designed partnership-based approach offers an opportunity to 'do development better', increasing efficiency and reducing resource wastage and time delays through overcoming or avoiding many of the limitations of traditional foreign aid models.

Over the past 2 years, we have been able to build ownership and sustain momentum through fostering equitable decision-making; enhance relevance and sustainability through ensuring local actors are in the driving seat; maximise collaboration potential through harnessing multiple perspectives and promoting flexibility in work planning and increase value-for-money through leveraging in-kind contributions and additional resources. We readily share the following observations which we hope will be of interest not only to those engaged in delivering south–south or trilateral cooperation projects, but anyone contemplating the question 'what added value does a partnerships broker actually provide?'

Unfortunately, despite the commitments espoused in Paris Declaration and Accra Agenda to promoting greater partnerships in aid delivery, it is our experience[11] that much of foreign aid still falls into the traditional donor–recipient binary, where aid agencies adopt a highly directive approach in subcontracting activities to implementing 'partners'[12] who, in reality, have limited influence over project decision-making. In contrast, under the Trilateral Malaria Project, the partnership broker worked with partners to develop a consensus model for decision-making where, irrespective of the fact that the Australian Government is the sole provider of project financing, activities and business procedures had to be jointly discussed and endorsed by representatives from each government at the appropriate level.

This three-way consultation process is where one might think the concern of excessive coordination/transaction costs associated with trilateral cooperation holds most water. Figure 17.1 illustrates the governance and management arrangements for the Trilateral Malaria Project, and depicts the agencies involved in planning, implementation and review at the strategic, technical and administrative levels within the partnership.

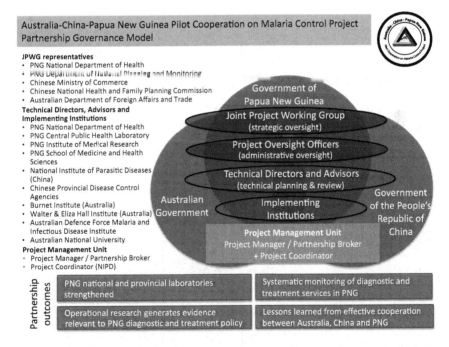

Figure 17.1 Australia–China–Papua New Guinea pilot cooperation on Malaria Control Project – partnership governance model.

Clearly, this model requires an active investment in good communication, but promoting shared decision-making means that all partners have a genuine stake in the outcomes of the work, and are committed to ensuring the success of each activity. Because of this ownership, partners actively seek to resolve any differences or disputes arising, to ensure that momentum is not lost. It is true that fostering ownership takes time, and only occurs once partners have confidence that the partnership broker manages the interests and priorities of all partners in a neutral and genuine manner.[13] However, in our experience, the time and resources invested in supporting joint decision-making are *much less* than the time that is frequently wasted in other collaborations where a neutral partnership broker has not been able to ensure that the views of each partner are heard, for example, in cases in which one partner feels excluded and delays or blocks an activity.[14]

This joint decision-making approach also means that we are better able to harness multiple perspectives to address a particular challenge, thereby improving the effectiveness of project activities and maximising the opportunities that can be generated. At the technical level within our project, the partnership broker supports joint planning by technical specialists nominated by each partner government through quarterly meetings where work plan activities are designed or reviewed in accordance with a common set of agreed criteria. The work plans are flexible and partners are able to propose new activities, or adjust existing approaches, based on an analysis of which activities offer the best chance of meeting these agreed criteria. Through this process, natural areas of mutually beneficial collaboration emerged and expanded in a manner that could not have been envisaged in the initial project design. Furthermore, this approach enhances the project's ability to achieve longer-term outcomes, as it allows partners to prioritise activities that are needed, rather than being tied to implement what has been 'funded' in an original project design or grant agreement.

At all project meetings, space is created for PNG, as the host government, to occupy the driving seat for these decisions. PNG experts use their local knowledge and expertise to identify key priorities for support and reach out to Chinese and Australian counterparts to contribute to work plan activities in specific areas according to their comparative advantage. Activities are relevant and impactful because the right people (those who best understand the prevailing contextual conditions such as politics and culture, and who possess the relationships and perspectives required for effective delivery of activities) have been involved in their design. An unexpected – but valuable – benefit of this approach has been the strengthening of partnerships between local PNG institutions, which will endure beyond the Project end date.

In supporting a partnership approach, partnership brokers help partners to imagine a world in which money is 'off the table'. They support conversations that allow partners to recognise the value of non-monetary contributions to achieving success within a partnership. This approach has both built equity between partners and promoted sustainability for the Trilateral Malaria Project, as we deliberately support activities that can be delivered by the partners themselves, rather than externally contracted. Furthermore, by unlocking the potential of relevant experience within the partners themselves, such as the provision of technical experts, laboratory space, diagnostics equipment, access to in-house training programmes and sharing specimens for referral, the partnership delivers excellent value-for-money as funding can stretch further and partners reach out to their professional networks to obtain additional (in-kind) expertise where gaps exist.

This pilot project has also thrown light on a specific issue worthy of further reflection within the scientific and medical research communities. This type of research typically comprises interdisciplinary partnerships or consortia between multiple institutions who collectively implement a funding grant secured by a 'lead' institution or individual researcher. We believe that the value of investing in a neutral partnership broker may be underestimated in this setting, where the lead actor typically identifies an employee or postdoctoral candidate within their own institution to act as a project manager on behalf of the broader group of partners. Whilst internally appointing a project manager can promote ownership (as the project manager's own academic and professional advancement is bound up with the success of the project), conflicts of interest concerning personal affiliations and career aspirations can lead to disunity and competition amongst partners, delaying progress and hindering genuine collaboration. Supporting the professional development of key partnership brokering skills in individuals appointed to a project manager position, or agreeing for such positions to be filled by an external partnership broker who does not have a pre-existing affiliation to consortium partners, can assist in overcoming these all-too-familiar roadblocks.

We started this chapter noting the relative infancy of the trilateral cooperation model, and the limited data available to assess its effectiveness (or otherwise). Building this evidence base rightly remains a priority for each of us concerned with aid effectiveness, but we also believe that our case study demonstrates the need to move the discussion from 'whether trilateral cooperation works?' to looking at when it works and how it can work better.

The Trilateral Malaria Project is still being implemented,[15] but early indications are that, with the support of well-designed partnership approaches and dedicated partnership brokering support, common challenges (such as high transaction costs) associated with trilateral cooperation models can be mitigated and reduced. It is our hope that other international actors (not just those involved in south–south cooperation, but also traditional bilateral and multilateral initiatives, and any form of scientific or medical research collaboration) might consider the potential that investing in a partnership-based approach can achieve. By using partnerships to build an 'effective framework in which good development can occur',[16] we *can* improve aid effectiveness and advance shared solutions to our world's most critical development challenges.

Notes

1 The opinions expressed in this article are the authors' own and do not necessarily reflect those of the authors' institutions, nor the Governments of Australia, China and Papua New Guinea.

2 Tennyson, R. (2011). *The Partnering Toolbook: An Essential Guide to Cross-Sector Partnering*. The Partnering Initiative, International Business Leaders Forum: 5.

3 Notably the Paris Declaration on Aid Effectiveness (2005) and the Accra Agenda for Action (2008).

4 The exchange of resources, technology and knowledge between developing countries that are also known as the 'global south'. Stahl, A.K. (2012). *Trilateral Development Cooperation Between the European Union, China and Africa: What Prospects for South Africa?* Stellenbosch: Centre for Chinese Studies, Stellenbosch University: 11.

5 Han, C. (2017) *Trilateral Cooperation with China: Sharing China's Development Experience through Innovative Partnerships*. Beijing: UNDP China: 3.

6 Other advantages frequently cited include (a) greater relevance of contributions (given similar development challenges between new donors and host countries); (b) cost efficiencies as hardware and software are provided at a lower cost and (c) role modelling of effective aid practice to new donors. For further reading, refer to Fordelone, T.Y. (2009) *Triangular Co-operation and Aid Effectiveness: Can Triangular Co operation Make Aid More Effective?* Paris: OECD; Fordelone, T.Y. (2013). *Triangular cooperation: What's the literature telling us?* Paris: OECD. Han (2017) Op.cit; Zhang, D. (2015) *In-Brief: China-Australia-Papua New Guinea Trilateral Aid Cooperation on Malaria Control*. Canberra: Australian National University. See: http://bell school.anu.edu.au/sites/default/files/publications/attachments/2016-05/ib-2015-14-zhang-online.pdf (accessed 9/2/2018) and Zhang, D. (2017). Why cooperate with others? Demystifying China's trilateral aid cooperation. *The Pacific Review*, 30 (5), 750–768. See: http://www.tandfonline.com/eprint/EZv8eYceC6HHvi3iZ9Z4/full (accessed 9/2/2018).

7 Fordelone (2009) Op.cit: 5; Han (2017) Op.cit: 11.

8 World Health Organisation (2016). *World Malaria Report 2016*. Geneva: World Health Organisation http://www.who.int/malaria/publications/world-malaria-report-2016/report/en/ (accessed 9/2/2018).

9 The Partnerships Brokers Association is a registered not-for-profit which sets an international benchmark for partnership brokers and awards formal accreditation to those who reach the required standard and promotes partnership brokering good practice principle. For further information, refer to http://www.partnershipbrokers.org (accessed 9/2/2018).

10 We understand this approach to comprise the following elements: common purpose; recognition of shared and individual interests; co-creation of activities, business processes and solutions; sharing of risks and benefits; a commitment to mutual accountability and a principled approach to working together (Partnership Brokers Training Materials).

11 Collectively, the authors have almost 60 years experience in working on international collaborations with foreign donors.

12 Be they host governments, non-government organisations, private entities or community-based groups.

13 In our experience, when a broker demonstrates fairness in facilitating conversations between partners over a period of time, individuals within each partner institution begin to 'trust' the partnership and are increasingly willing to invest their time and expertise in joint activities.

14 Zhang observes that other trilateral cooperation projects have stalled or failed due to a lack of ownership and consultation with host governments, and cites the European Union (EU) Council's experimentation in trilateral aid cooperation with China in Africa in 2008, which China was reluctant to support given complaints by African countries of insufficient consultation (Zhang, 2017. Op.cit: 763).

15 The independent midterm review of the Trilateral Malaria Project is planned for early 2018, and this will assess the effectiveness of technical, cooperation and management aspects of the project.

16 Nixon, N. & Mundy, J. (2017) *Partnering Agreements: Effective Relationship Management in Complex Development Programs.* Development Policy Centre, Australian National University. http://devpolicy.org/partnering-agreements-effective-relationship-management-in-complex-development-programs-20170523/ (accessed 9/2/2018).

Bibliography

Abrahamsson, M., & Becker, P. (2010). *Scoping study for partner driven cooperation in disaster risk management between Sweden and Botswana*. LUCRAM, Lund: Lund University.

AccountAbility. (2006). Partnership governance and accountability, reinventing development pathways: The PGA Framework. *PGA General Report*. London: AccountAbility.

Acland, A. F. (1995a). *Resolving Disputes without Going to Court*. London: Century Books.

Acland, A. F. (1995b). Mediators as Leaders, *Course Materials*. University of Cambridge. Unpublished.

Acland, A. F. (2011). Working with uncertainty, *Working Paper*. Wotton-under-Edge, Gloucestershire, UK: Andrew Acland & Associates.

Andersson, M, Svensson, L. Wistus, S., & Äberg, C. (Eds.). (2006). *On the art of developing partnerships*. Stockholm: The National Institute for Working Life.

Ansell, C., & Gash, A. (2007). Collaborative governance in theory and practice. *Journal of Public Administration Research and Theory, 18*(4), 543–571.

Arnstein, S. (1969). A ladder of citizen participation. *Journal of the American Institute of Planners, 35*, 216–224.

Austin, J. E. (2000a). Strategic collaboration between nonprofits and businesses. *Nonprofit and Voluntary Sector Quarterly, 29*(1), 69–97.

Austin, J. E. (2000b). *The collaborative challenge. How nonprofits and business succeed through strategic alliances*. San Francisco, CA: Jossey-Bass.

Austin, J. E. (2010). From organization to organization: On creating value. *Journal of Business Ethics, 94*, 13–15.

Austin, J. E., & Seitanidi, M. M. (2012a). Collaborative value creation: A review of partnering between nonprofits and businesses: Part I. Value creation spectrum and collaboration stages. *Nonprofit and Voluntary Sector Quarterly, 41*(5), 726–758.

Austin, J. E., & Seitanidi, M. M. (2012b). Collaborative value creation: A review of partnering between nonprofits and businesses: Part 2: Partnership processes and outcomes. *Nonprofit and Voluntary Sector Quarterly, 41*(6), 929–968.

Australian Public Service Commission. (2012). Tackling wicked problems: A public policy perspective. Retrieved February 9, 2018, from http://www.apsc.gov.au/publications-and-media/archive/publications-archive/tackling-wicked-problems

Babiak, K., & Thibault, L. (2009). Challenges in multiple cross-sector partnerships. *Nonprofit and Voluntary Sector Quarterly, 38*, 117–143.

Bardach, E. (1998). *Getting agencies to work together: The practice and theory of managerial craftsmanship.* Washington, DC: Brookings Institution Press.

Battisti, M. (2009). Below the surface, the challenges of cross-sector partnerships. *Journal of Corporate Citizenship, 35*, 95–108.

Beeger, H. (2017). Self-management blogs about self-leadership and co-creation. BMC Consultancy. Retrieved February 9, 2018, from https://bmc-consultancy.be/wp-content/uploads/Hans-BegeerCreating-stakeholders-value-through-commitment-blogs-May-2017-1.pdf

Beimborn, D., Martin, S., & Homann, U. (2005). Capability-oriented modeling of the firm. Retrieved from http://www.is-frankfurt.de/publikationenNeu/CapabilityorientedModelingoft1256.pdf

Bendell, J. (2011). *Evolving partnerships: A guide to working with business for greater social change.* London: Greenleaf Publishing.

Benefiel, M. (2008). *The soul of a leader: Finding your path to fulfilment and success.* New York, NY: The Crossroad Publishing Company.

Bennis, W. (2007). The challenges of leadership in the modern world. *American Psychologist, 62*(1), 2–5.

Bettelheim, B. (1988). *A good enough parent, a book on child-rearing.* New York, NY: Vintage.

Bezanson, K. A., & Isenman, P. (2012). Governance of new global partnerships: Challenges, weaknesses, and lessons. *Center for Global Development Paper* (p. 014). Washington, DC: Center for Global Development.

Block, P. (1996). *Stewardship: Choosing service over self-interest.* Oakland, CA: Berrett-Koehler Publishers.

Bollier, D., & Conaty, P. (2014). A new alignment of movements? *A Report on a Commons Strategies Group Workshop*, August 29–September 1. Meissen, Germany: Supported by the Heinrich Böll Foundation and the Charles Léopold Mayer Foundation. Retrieved February 9, 2018, from https://www.boell.de/sites/default/files/report_-_a_new_alignment_of_movements_february_2015.pdf

Bradford, A. L., & Cohen, A. R. (1998). *Power up: Transforming organizations through shared leadership.* New York, NY: Wiley.

Brass, D. J., Galaskiewicz, J., Greve, H. R., & Tsai, W. (2004). Taking stock of networks and organizations: A multilevel perspective. *Academy of Management Journal, 47*(6), 795–817.

Brass, D., Butterfield, K., & Skaggs, B. (1996). Relationships and unethical behaviour: A social network perspective. *The Academy of Management Review, 23*(1), 14–31.

Bresnen, M. (2007). Deconstructing partnering in project-based organisation: Seven pillars, seven paradoxes and seven deadly sins. *International Journal of Project Management, 25*(4), 365–374.

Brinkerhoff, J. M. (2002a). Assessing and improving partnership relationships and outcomes: A proposed framework. *Evaluation and Program Planning, 25*, 215–231.

Brinkerhoff, J. M. (2002b). *Partnerships for international development: Rhetoric or results?* Boulder, CO: Lynne Rienner Publishers.

British Overseas NGOs for Development (BOND). (2003). Partnerships with the private sector, *BOND Guidance Notes Series* 2.

Brouwer, H., & Woodhill, J., Hemmati, M., Verhoosel, K., & van Vugt, S. (2015). *The MSP guide, how to design and facilitate multi-stakeholder partnerships.* Wangeningen: Centre for Development Innovation, Wangeningen University.

Brown, D. L. (1999). Development bridging organizations and strategic management for social change. *IDR Reports, 10*(3), 1–26.

Brown, D. L. (2015). Bridge-building for social transformation. *Stanford Social Innovation Review, Winter,* 34–39.

Bryson, J. M., Crosby, B. C., & Middleton Stone, M. (2006). The design and implementation of cross-sector collaborations: Propositions from the literature. *Public Administration Review, 66*(1), 44–55.

Burton, J. (1990). *Conflict: Resolution and provention.* New York, NY: St. Martin's Press.

Cabaj, M., & Auspos, P. (2014). *Complexity and community change: Managing adaptively to improve effectiveness.* Washington, DC: The Aspen Institute.

Caplan, K. (2003a). The purist's partnership: Debunking the terminology of partnerships. *Practitioner Note Series.* London: Building Partnerships for Development.

Caplan, K. (2003b). Plotting partnerships: Ensuring accountability and fostering innovation. *Practitioner Note Series.* London: Building Partnerships for Development.

Caplan, K. (2005). Partnership accountability: Unpacking the concept. *Practitioner Note Series.* London: Building Partnerships for Development.

Caplan, K. (2006). Creating space for innovation: Understanding enablers for multi-sector partnerships. *Partnership Matters, Current Issues in Cross-Sector Collaboration 4,* 11–14.

Caplan, K., & Stott, L. (2008). Defining our terms and clarifying our language. In L. Svensson, & B. Nilsson (Eds.). *Partnership–As a strategy for social innovation and sustainable change* (pp. 23–35). Stockholm: Santérus Academic Press.

Caplan, K., Gomme, J., Mugabi, J., & Stott, L. (2007). *Assessing partnership performance: Understanding the drivers for success.* London: Building Partnerships for Development.

Chambers, R. (1995). Poverty and livelihoods: Whose reality counts? *Environment and Urbanization, 7,* 173–204.

Chambers, R. (1997). *Whose reality counts? Putting the last first.* London: IT Publications.

Collins, J. C. (2001). *Good to great.* London: William Collins.

Cooke, B., & Kothari, M. (2001). *Participation: The new tyranny.* London: Zed Books.

Crosby, B. C., & Bryson, J. B. (2010). Integrative leadership and the creation and maintenance of cross-sector collaborations. *The Leadership Quarterly, 21,* 211–230.

Cullen, K., Willburn, P., Chrobot-Mason, D., & Palus, C. (2014). *Networks: How collective leadership really Works.* Cincinnati, OH: Center for Creative Leadership.

Damasio, A. R. (1994). *Descartes' error: Emotion reason and the human brain.* London: Penguin.

Davies, J. S. (2008). Against 'partnership': Toward a local challenge to global neo-liberalism. In J. Gross & R. Hambleton (Eds.). *Governing cities in the global era* (pp. 199–210). Basingstoke: Palgrave Macmillan.

Dixon, I. (2006). Funding approaches for external partnership brokers. In PBA (Ed.) *Café conversations: A compendium of essays on the practice and theory of brokering multi-sector partnerships for sustainable development.* London: IBLF and Overseas Development Institute. 67–79.

Dixon, I. (2013). How to build effective partnerships between the business, government, community and education sectors. *White Paper.* Adelaide SA: Dixon Partnering Solutions.

Dryzek, J. S. (2006). *Deliberative global politics: Discourse and democracy in a divided world.* Cambridge: Polity Press.

Earl, S., Carden, F., & Smutylo, T. (2001). *Outcome mapping: Building learning and reflection into development programs.* Ottawa, ON: International Development Research Council.

Edmonson, J. (2013, October 31). Using feedback loops to move from collaboration to collective impact. *Forbes.com.* Retrieved November 16 2013, from http://www.forbes.com/sites/ashoka/2013/10/31/using-feedback-loops-to-move-from-collaboration-to-collective-impact/

Eisler, R. (2007). *The real wealth of nations: Creating a caring economics.* Oakland, CA: Berret Koehler Publishers.

Eisler, R. (2008). Our great creative challenge: Rethinking human nature – and recreating society. In R. Richards (Ed.). *Everyday creativity and new views of human nature: Psychological, social, and spiritual perspectives.* Washington, DC: American Psychological Association.

Eisler, R. (2014). Cultural transformation: Building a partnership world. *Kosmos,* Spring Summer, 50–54.

El Ansari, W., Phillips, C. J., & Hammick, M. (2001). Collaboration and partnerships: Developing the evidence base. *Health and Social Care in the Community,* 9(4): 215–227.

Elworthy, S. (2015, January 7). The tools for a radical new kind of leadership. *The Guardian.*

Environment Agency. (2002). *Environmental impact assessment (EIA) a handbook for scoping projects.* London: EIA.

Escobar, O. (2015). Scripting deliberative policy-making: dramaturgic policy analysis and engagement know-how. *Journal of Comparative Policy Analysis: Research and Practice,* 17(3), 269–285.

European Commission. (2010). *Europe 2020: A strategy for smart, sustainable and inclusive growth.* Brussels: EC.

European Commission. (2014a). *European code of conduct on partnership in the framework of the European structural and investment funds.* Brussels: European Commission, Directorate-General for Employment, Social Affairs and Inclusion.

European Commission. (2014b). Community-led local development, cohesion policy 2014–2020, *Factsheet.* Brussels: EC.

European Structural & Investment Funds Guidance for Member States and Programme Authorities. (2014). *Guidance on community-led local development for local actors,* Version 1. Brussels: EC.

Fife, E., & Hosman, L. (2007). Public private partnerships and the prospects for sustainable ICT projects in the developing world. *Journal of Business Systems, Governance and Ethics, 2*(3): 53–66.

Findlay Brooks, R., Visser, W., & Wright, T. (2007). Cross-sector partnership as an approach to inclusive development. *University of Cambridge Programme for Industry Research Paper Series*, No. 4. Cambridge: Cambridge Programme for Industry.

Fisher, R., & Shapiro, D. (2005). *Beyond reason: Using Emotions as You Negotiate*. New York, NY: Penguin Books.

Fisher, R., & Ury, W. (1991). *Getting to yes – Negotiating agreement without giving in*. New York, NY: Penguin Books.

Fisher, R., & Ury, W. with Patton, B. (2011). *Getting to yes – Negotiating agreement without giving in*. New York, NY: Penguin Books. (Revised ed.).

Fordelone, T. Y. (2009). *Triangular co-operation and aid effectiveness: Can triangular co operation make aid more effective?* Paris: OECD.

Fordelone, T. Y. (2013). *Triangular cooperation: What's the literature telling us?* Paris: OECD.

Friedman, R. A., & Shapiro, D. L. (1995). Deception and mutual gains bargaining: Are they mutually exclusive? *Negotiation Journal, 11*(3), 243, 244 & 247.

Freire, P. (1970). *Pedagogy of the oppressed*. New York, NY: The Seabury Press.

French, J. R. P., & Raven, B. (1959). The bases of social power. In D. Cartwright & A. Zander (Eds.). *Group dynamics*. New York, NY: Harper & Row.

Friend, J., & Hickling, A. (2005). *Planning under pressure* (3rd ed.). Oxford: Elsevier Butterworth-Heinemann.

Frost & Sullivan. (2013). *Growth process toolkit – Strategic partnerships*. Mountain View, CA: Frost & Sullivan.

Fry, L., & Altman, Y. (2013). *Spiritual leadership in action: Achieving extraordinary results through ordinary people*. Charlotte, NC: Information Age Publishing Inc.

FSG: Collective Impact. (2015). *Living cities cross-sector partnership assessment: group planning and discussion guide*. Retrieved February 9, 2018, from www.fsg.org/publications

Gazley, B. (2010). Linking collaborative capacity to performance measurement in government-nonprofit partnerships. *Nonprofit and Voluntary Sector Quarterly, 39*(4), 653–673.

Geddes, M. (2000). Tackling social exclusion in the European Union? The limits of the new orthodoxy of local partnership. *International Journal of Urban and Regional Research, 24*(4), 782–800.

GIZ. (2011). *Capacity WORKS – The management model for sustainable development*. [e-book] Eschborn: Deutsche Gesellschaft für Technische Zusammenarbeit (GTZ) GmbH.

Gladwell, M. (2000). *The tipping point*. London: Abacus.

Glasbergen, P. (2011). Understanding partnerships for sustainable development analytically: The ladder of partnership activity as a methodological tool. *Environmental Policy and Governance, 21*, 1–13.

Glasbergen, P., Biermann, F., & Mol, A. P. J. (2007). *Partnerships, governance and sustainable development: Reflections on theory and practice*. Cheltenham: Edward Elgar.

Glasson, J. (1999). The first 10 years of the UK EIA system: Strengths, weaknesses, opportunities and threats. *Planning Practice and Research, 14*(3), 363–375.

Gombra, N. (2013). How the "partnership brokerage" concept could address management expectations & create new opportunities for the MMF. *Partnerships for International Sustainable Development*. Reflection Essays, University of Applied Sciences, Leiden & Partnership Resource Centre, Rotterdam School of Management, Erasmus University.

Googins, B. K., & Rochlin, S. A. (2000). Creating the partnership society: Understanding the rhetoric and reality of cross-sectoral partnerships. *Business and Society Review, 105*(1), 127–144.

Gould, R. V., & Fernandez, R. M. (1989). Structures of mediation: A formal approach to brokerage in transaction networks. *Sociological Methodology, 19*, 89–126.

Gray, B. (1989). *Collaborating: Finding common ground for multi-party problems*. San Francisco, CA: Jossey-Bass Publisher.

Gray, B., & Purdy, J. (2014). Conflict in cross-sector partnerships. In M. M. Seitanidi & A. Crane (Eds.). *Social partnerships and responsible business: A research handbook*. London: Routledge. 60–78.

Greenleaf, R. K. (1977). *Servant leadership – A journey into the nature of legitimate power and greatness*. New York, NY: Paulist Press.

Greenleaf, R. K. (1998). *The power of servant leadership*. Oakland, CA: Berrett-Koehler.

Grönlund, J., Rönnberg Sjödin, D., & Frishammer, J. (2010). Open innovation and the stage-gate process: A revised model for new product development. *California Management Review*. Spring 52(3), 106–131.

Guba, E., Lincoln, Y., Hesse-Biber, S., & Leavy, P. (2004). *Approaches to qualitative research: A reader on theory and practice*. Oxford: Oxford University Press.

Hafeez, K., Malak, N., & Zhang, Y. (2007). Outsourcing non-core assets and competences of a firm using analytic hierarchy process. *Computers & Operations Research, 34*(12), 3592–3608.

Halper, E. (2009). *Moving on: Effective management for partnership transitions, transformations and exits*. London: International Business Leaders Forum.

Hamdi, N. (2010). *The placemaker's guide to building community* (Earthscan Tools for Community Planning). London: Routledge.

Han, C. (2017). *Trilateral cooperation with China: Sharing China's development experience through innovative partnerships* (p. 3). Beijing: UNDP China.

Hanleybrown, F., Kania, J., & Kramer, M. (2012). Channeling change: Making collective impact work. *Stanford Social Innovation Review*, 1–8. Retrieved February 9, 2018, from https://ssir.org/articles/entry/channeling_change_making_collective_impact_work

Harvard Business Review. (2016). The four phases of project management. Retrieved February 9, 2018, from https://hbr.org/2016/11/the-four-phases-of-project-management

Harwood, R. (2014, April 7). Putting community in collective impact. *Stanford Social Innovation Review*, 5. Retrieved February 9, 2018, from https://ssir.org/articles/entry/putting_community_in_collective_impact

Heifetz, R. A., Linsky, M., & Grashow, A. (2009). *The practice of adaptive leadership: Tools and tactics for changing your organization and the world*. Boston, MA: Harvard Business Press.

Hundal, S. (2016). The value of reflective practice for partnership brokers. *Betwixt & Between, The Journal of Partnership Brokering*, (6). Retrieved February 9, 2018, from http://partnershipbrokers.org/w/journal/the-value-of-reflective-practice-for-partnership-brokers/

Hurrell, S., Hussain-Khaliq, S., & Tennyson, R. (2006). *The case-study toolbook, partnership case studies as tools for change*. London: International Business Leaders Forum.

Huxham, C., & Vangen, S. (2000). Leadership in the shaping and implementation of collaboration agendas: How things happen in a (not quite) joined-up world. *Academy of Management Journal, 43*(6), 1159–1175.

Huxham, C., & Vangen, S. (2004). Doing things collaboratively: Realizing the advantage or succumbing to inertia? *Organizational Dynamics, 33*(2), 199.

International Association for Public Participation. (2007). IAP2 Spectrum. Retrieved February 9, 2018, from http://c.ymcdn.com/sites/www.iap2.org/resource/resmgr/imported/spectrum.pdf

Ivanova, M. H. (2003). Partnerships, international organizations, and global environmental governance. In J. M. Witte, C. Streck, & T. Benner (Eds.), *Progress or peril? Partnerships and networks in global environmental governance: The post Johannesburg agenda* (pp. 9–36). Washington, Belin: Global Public Policy Institute.

Kahlen, T., & Van Tulder, R. (2015). How do partnership brokers actually broker? From interest-based scoping to vision-based negotiation. *Paper*, Rotterdam: Partnerships Resource Centre at RSM Erasmus University.

Kahlen, T. (2014). *Improving the tools of cross sector partnership brokers*. MA Thesis, Rotterdam School of Management, Erasmus University, Rotterdam.

Kaner, S. (2007). *Facilitator's guide to participatory decision-making* (2nd ed.). San Francisco, CA: Jossey-Bass, Wiley.

Kaner, S. (2014). *Facilitator's guide to participatory decision making* (3rd ed.). San Francisco CA: Jossey-Bass, Wiley.

Kalungu-Banda, M. (2006). *Leading like Madiba, Leadership Lessons from Nelson Mandela*, Cape Town: Double Story Books.

Kania, J. & Kramer, M. (2011). Collective impact. *Stanford Social Innovation Review*, Winter: 36–41.

Kohlrieser G. (2006). *Hostage at the Table – How Leaders Can Overcome Conflict, Influence Others, and Raise Performance*, San Francisco: Jossey-Bass.

Kolk, A., Van Tulder, R., & Kostwinder, E. (2008) Business and partnerships for development. *European Management Journal, 26*(4), 262–273.

Krznaric, R. (2014). The Empathy Effect, How Empathy Drives Common Values, Social Justice and Environmental Action, *Paper for Friends of the Earth*, London.

Lackey, S. B., Freshwater, D., & Rupasingha, A. (2002). Factors influencing local government cooperation in rural areas: Evidence from the Tennessee valley. *Economic Development Quarterly, 16*(2), 138–154.

Laloux, F. (2015). *Reinventing organisations: A guide to creating organisations inspired by the next stage in human consciousness*. Leuven, Belgium: Nelson Parker.

Leadbeater, C. (2014). *The frugal innovator, creating change on a shoestring budget*. London: Palgrave Macmillan.

Leal Filho W., Mifsud M., Shiel C., & Pretorius R. (Eds.). (2017). *Handbook of theory and practice of sustainable development in higher education* (Vol. 4). World Sustainability Series. Cham: Springer.

Lee, G. (2006). *Courage: The backbone of leadership*. San Francisco, CA: Jossey-Bass.

Lee, L. (2015). Understanding the role of the broker in business non-profit collaboration. *Social Responsibility Journal, 11*(2), 201–220.

Legler, R., & Reischl, T. (2003). The relationship of key factors in the process of collaboration. *The Journal of Applied Behavioral Science, 39*(1), 53–72.

Lipman-Blumen, J. (2000). *Connective leadership, managing in a changing world.* Oxford: Oxford University Press.

Macdonald, S., & Chrisp, T. (2005). Acknowledging the purpose of partnership. *Journal of Business Ethics, 59,* 307–317.

Maiese, M. (2004). Interests, positions, needs and values in moving beyond intractability. Retrieved February 9, 2018, from http://www.beyondintractability. org/essay/interests/ (updated in October 2012 and again in April 2017 by Heidi Burgess)

Manning, S., & Roessler, D. (2014). The formation of cross-sector development partnerships: How bridging agents shape project agendas and longer-term alliances. *Journal of Business Ethics, 123*(3), 527–547.

Marsden, P. (1982). Brokerage behavior in restricted exchange networks. In P. Marsden & N. Lin (Eds.). *Social structure and network analysis* (pp. 202–218). Beverly Hills, CA: Sage.

Mataix, C., Romero, S., Mazorra, J., Moreno, J., Ramil, X., Stott, L., Carrasco, J., Lumbreras, J., & Borrella, I. (2017). Working for sustainability transformation in an academic environment: The case of itdUPM. In W. Leal Filho, M. Mifsud, C. Shiel, & R. Pretorius (Eds.), *Handbook of theory and practice of sustainable development in higher education* (Vol. 4, pp. 391–428) World Sustainability Series. Cham: Springer.

McCahon, M., & Mitchelmore, N. (2013). Using a review process to strengthen partnerships: A heritage partnership in Newfoundland, Canada. *Betwixt & Between, The Journal of Partnership Brokering* (2). Retrieved February 9, 2018, from http://partnershipbrokers.org/w/journal/using-a-review-process-to-strengthen-partnerships-a-heritage-partnership-in-newfoundland-canada/

McEvily, B., & Zaheer, A. (2004). Architects of trust: The role of network facilitators in geographical clusters. In R. Kramer & K. Cook (Eds.), *Trust and distrust in organizations* (pp. 189–213). New York, NY: Russell Sage Foundation.

Meyer, M. (2010). The rise of the knowledge broker. *Science Communication, 32*(1), 118–127.

Megginson, D., & Clutterbuck, D. (2004), *Techniques for coaching and mentoring.* London: Routledge.

Miller, E. (2014). Partnership brokers as leaders. *Betwixt & Between, The Journal of Partnership Brokering,* (3). Retrieved February 9, 2018, from http://partnershipbrokers.org/w/journal/partnership-brokers-as-leaders/

Minahan, M., Vogel, J., Butler, L., & Taylor, H. B. (2007). *Facilitation 101: The basics to get you on your feet.* Chicago, IL: Organization Development Network, *The OD Practitioner, 39*(3).

Miraftab, F. (2004). Public-private partnerships. The Trojan horse of neoliberal development? *Journal of Planning Education and Research, 24,* 89–101.

Mulvihill, P. R. (2003). Expanding the scoping community. *Environmental Impact Assessment Review, 23*(1), 39–49.

Mundy, J. (2006). Risky business: Removing barriers to effective partnerships for development. Risk management for the Broker's toolbox. In PBA (Ed.) *Café conversations, a compendium of essays on the practice and theory of brokering multi-sector partnerships for sustainable development* (pp. 105–118). London: IBLF and Overseas Development Institute.

Mundy, J. (2013). Progressive review and evaluation as a trust building mechanism in partnerships. *Betwixt & Between, The Journal of Partnership Brokering* (2). Retrieved February 9, 2018, from http://partnershipbrokers.org/w/journal/progressive-review-and-evaluation-as-a-trust-building-mechanism-in-partnerships/

Neal, J. (2006). *Edgewalkers: People and organizations that take risks, build bridges and break new ground.* Westport, Ct: Praeger.

Nelson, J. (2002). *Building partnerships: Cooperation between the united nations system and the private sector.* New York, NY: United Nations.

Nelson, J., & Zadek, S. (2000). *Partnership alchemy, new social partnerships in Europe.* The Copenhagen Centre: Copenhagen.

Nitsun, M. (1996). *The anti-group: Destructive forces in the group and their creative potential.* London and New York, NY: Routledge.

Nixon, N., & Mundy, J. (2017). *Partnering agreements: Effective relationship management in complex development programs.* Development Policy Centre, Australian National University. Retrieved February 9, 2018, from http://devpolicy.org/partnering-agreements-effective-relationship-management-in-complex-development-programs-20170523/

North, D. (1993). Institutions and economic performance. In B. Gustafsson, C. Knudsen, & M. Uskali (Eds.). *Rationality, institutions and economic methodology* (pp. 242–261). Oxon, NY: Routledge.

Nyanti, S. (2016). Dealing with ethical dilemmas – A partnership brokers personal perspective. *Betwixt and Between, The Journal of Partnership Brokering,* (6). Retrieved February 9, 2018, from http://partnershipbrokers.org/w/journal/dealing-with-ethical-dilemmas-a-partnership-brokers-personal-perspective/

Östengren, K. (2004). The logical framework approach: A summary of the theory behind the LFA method. *POM Working Paper* Stockholm. Sida. Retrieved February 9, 2018, from www.sida.se

OECD. (2015, April). Due diligence guidance for meaningful stakeholder engagement in the extractives sector. *Draft for Comment.* Retrieved February 9, 2018, from https://www.oecd.org/daf/inv/mne/OECD-Guidance-Extractives-Sector-Stakeholder-Engagement.pdf

Patscheke, S., Barmettler, A., Herman, L., Overdyke, S., & Pfitzer, M. (2014). Shaping global partnerships for a post-2015 world. *Stanford Social Innovation Review,* Spring, 2–9.

Pattberg, P., & Widerberg, O. (2016). Transnational multistakeholder partnerships for sustainable development: Conditions for success. *Ambio, 45,* 42–51.

Patton, M. Q. (1990). *Qualitative evaluation and research methods* (2nd ed.). Newbury Park, CA: Sage.

PBA. (2006). *Café conversations, a compendium of essays on the practice and theory of brokering multi-sector partnerships for sustainable development.* London: Partnership Brokers Association & Overseas Development Institute.

PBA. (2011). *Appointing a partnership broker, guidance for those involved in making the appointment & assessing the performance.* London: Partnership Brokers Association. Retrieved February 9, 2018, from http://partnershipbrokers.org/w/wp-content/uploads/2010/09/Appointing-a-Partnership-Broker3.pdf

PBA. (2012). *What do partnership brokers do? An enquiry into practice.* London: Partnership Brokers Association.

PBA. (2016). *Weaving threads, an exploration of key principles and themes that underpin all PBA training.* London: Partnership Brokers Association.

Pearce, C. L., & Conger, J. A. (2002). *Shared leadership – Reframing the hows and whys of leadership.* London: Sage Publications.

Peltier, B. (2009). *The psychology of executive coaching.* London: Routledge.

Pinto, J. K. (2010). *Project management.* Upper Saddle River, NJ: Pearson/Prentice Hall.

Poncelet, E. C. (2001). A kiss here and a kiss there: Conflict and collaboration in environmental partnerships. *Environmental Management, 27*(1), 13–25.

Poupart, E. C. (2014). Value for money in partnerships – A challenge to partnership brokers. *Betwixt & Between, The Journal of Partnership Brokering,* (4). Retrieved February 9, 2018, from http://partnershipbrokers.org/w/journal/value-for-money-in-partnerships-a-challenge-to-partnership-brokers/

PrC. (2015). Cross-sector partnership formation – What to consider before you start, *Paper.* Rotterdam: Partnership Resource Centre.

PrC. (2016). *Wicked problems plaza.* Rotterdam: Partnerships Resource Centre.

Preskill, H., Parkhurst, M., & Juster, J. S. (2013). *Guide to evaluating collective impact: Learning and evaluation in the collective impact context.* Boston, MA: FSG, Collective Impact Forum.

Provan, K., & Kenis, P. (2008). Modes of network governance: Structure, management, and effectiveness. *Journal of Public Administration Research and Theory, 18*(2), 229–252.

Pyres, J. (2013). Good for business? An enquiry into the impact of Microsoft's investment in partnership brokers training, Enquiry, unsRWS.

Quinn, R. E. (2004). *Building the bridge as you walk on it – A guide for leading change.* San Francisco, CA: Jossey-Bass.

Raven, B. H. (1965). Social influence and power. In I. D. Steiner & M. Fishbein (Eds). *Current studies in social psychology* (pp. 371–382). New York, NY: Holt, Rinehart, Winston.

Raven, B. H. (2008). The bases of power and the power/interaction model of interpersonal influence. *Analyses of Social Issues and Public Policy, 8*(1), 1–22.

Raworth, K., & Wren-Lewis, L. (2008). *How change happens in the private sector. From poverty to power case study.* Oxford: Oxfam International.

Rein, M., & Stott, L. (2009). Working together: Critical perspectives on six cross-sector partnerships in Southern Africa. *Journal of Business Ethics, 90*(1), 79–89.

Rein, M., Stott, L., Yambayamba, K., Hardman, S., & Reid, S. (2005). *Working together, a critical analysis of cross-sector partnerships in Southern Africa.* Cambridge: University of Cambridge Programme for Industry.

Rittel, H., & Webber, M. (1973). Dilemmas in a general theory of planning. *Policy Sciences, 4*(2), 155–169.

Rogers, C. R. (1980). *The way of being.* Boston, MA: Houghton Mifflin Company.

Rogers, C. R., & Farson, R. E. (2015). *Active listening.* Eastford, CT: Martino Publishing.

Sanyal, P. (2006). Capacity building through partnership: Intermediary nongovernmental organizations as local and global actors. *Nonprofit and Voluntary Sector Quarterly, 35*(1), 66–82.

Schneider, A. (2012). Teaching a new negotiation skills paradigm. *Washington University Journal of Law and Policy, 39*, 13.

Scharmer, C. O. (2007). *Addressing the blind spot of our time: An executive summary of the book by Otto Scharmer: Theory U: Leading from the future as it emerges.* Retrieved February 9, 2018, from https://www.presencing.com/sites/default/files/pagefiles/Theory_U_Exec_Summary.pdf

Scharmer, O. (2016). *Theory U: Leading from the future as it emerges* (2nd ed.). Oakland, CA: Berrett-Koehler Publishers.

Scharmer, O., & Kaufer, K. (2013). *Leading from the emerging future: From ego-system to eco-system economics.* San Francisco, CA: Berret Koehler Publisher.

Schon, D. A. (1983). *The reflective practitioner: How professionals think in action.* New York, NY: Basic Books.

Seitanidi, M. M., & Crane, A. (Eds.). (2014). *Social Partnerships and Responsible Business: A Research Handbook.* London: Routledge.

Selsky, J. W., & Parker, B. (2005). Cross-sector partnerships to address social issues: Challenges to theory and practice. *Journal of Management, 31*(6), 849–873.

Sen, A. (1999). *Development as freedom.* Oxford: Oxford University Press.

Senge, P. (2008). *The necessary revolution: How individuals and organizations are working together to create a sustainable world.* New York, NY: Crown Business.

Senge, P., Hamilton, H., & Kania, J. (2015). The dawn of system leadership. *Stanford Social Innovation Review,* Winter, 27–33.

Sennett, R. (2013). *Together, the rituals and pleasures of cooperation.* London: Penguin Books.

Serafin, R. (2006). Five key things I have learned about partnership brokering: Over 20 years of professional practice in Canada, UK, Poland and other countries of central and Eastern Europe. In PBA (Ed.) *Café conversations, a compendium of essays on the practice and theory of brokering multi-sector partnerships for sustainable development* (pp. 41–52). London: IBLF and Overseas Development Institute.

Shapiro, D. (2016). *Negotiating the nonnegotiable: How to resolve your most emotionally charged conflicts.* New York, NY: Viking.

Sharma, A., & Kearins, K. (2011). Interorganizational collaboration for regional sustainability: What happens when organizational representatives come together? *The Journal of Applied Behavioral Science, 47*(2), 168–203.

Snell, T., & Cowell, R. (2006). Scoping in environmental impact assessment: Balancing precaution and efficiency? *Environmental Impact Assessment Review, 26*(4), 359–376.

Spears, L. (1995). *Reflections on leadership.* New York, NY: John Wiley and Sons.

Spillane, J. (2006). *Distributed leadership.* San Francisco, CA: Jossey-Bass.

Stadtler, L. (2016). Scaling up tripartite social partnerships, insights from the becoming perspective on change. *The Journal of Corporate Citizenship, 63*, 96–118.

Stadtler, L., & Probst, G. (2012). How broker organizations can facilitate pub-lic-private partnerships for development. *European Management Journal, 30*(1), 32–46.

Stahl, A. K. (2012). *Trilateral development cooperation between the European Union, China and Africa: What prospects for South Africa?* Stellenbosch: Cen-tre for Chinese Studies, Stellenbosch University.

Stott, L. (2009). Stakeholder engagement in partnerships. Who are the 'stakehold-ers' and how do we 'engage' with them? *BPD Research Series.* London: Building Partnerships for Development.

Stott, L. (2014). *Partnerships for innovation in access to basic services.* Madrid, NM & Washington, DC: itdUPM & MIF/Inter American Development Bank.

Stott, L. (2016). Partnership: Exploring the terminology. *Paper for the Thematic Network on Partnership.* Brussels: ESF Transnational Platform. Retrieved Febru-ary 9, 2018, from https://ec.europa.eu/esf/transnationality/filedepot_download/564/24

Stott, L., & Keatman, T. (2005). Tools for measuring community engagement in partnerships. *BPD Practitioner Note.* London: Building Partnerships for Development.

Stott, L., & Scoppetta, A. (2013a). Promoting local economic development through partnerships in Europe. *Skills@Work: Theory and Practice Journal, 6,* 2–12.

Stott, L., & Scoppetta, A. (2013b). Adding value: The broker role in partnerships for employment and social inclusion in Europe. *Betwixt & Between, The Journal of Partnership Brokering,* (1). Retrieved February 9, 2018, from http://partner shipbrokers.org/w/journal/employment-social-inclusion-partnerships-in-europe/

Stott, L., & Tennyson, R. (2016). *Improving our learning from practice: An emerg-ing case study framework for partnership brokers.* London: Partnership Brokers Association.

Stott, L., & Van Kampen, H. (2015). Reviewing, revising and reflecting on part-nerships, the partnership broker's role. *Level 1 training: reviewing and revising session' slides* 3, 5. London: Partnership Broker's Association.

Strauss, A. L., & Corbin, J. (2008). *Basics of qualitative research: Techniques and procedures for developing grounded theory.* Thousand Oaks, CA: Sage.

Strive Together. (n.d.). *Theory of action: Creating cradle to career proof points.* [e-book] Retrieved February 9, 2018, from https://www.strivetogether.org/wp-content/uploads/2017/03/StriveTogether-Theory-of-Action-2017.pdf

Svensson, L., & Nilsson, B. (Eds.). (2008). *Partnership – As a strategy for social innovation and sustainable change.* Stockholm: Santérus Academic Press.

Synergos. (2012). *Ten lessons on multi-stakeholder partnerships.* New York, NY: Synergos Institute.

Tariq, H., & Tennyson, R. (2010). *In the bank's best interest – Case study of an ambitious partnership.* London: International Business Leaders Forum.

Teece, D., Pisano, G., & Shuen, A. (1997). Dynamic capabilities and strategic man-agement. *Strategic Management Journal, 18*(7), 509–533.

Tennyson, R. (1998). *Managing partnerships: Tools for mobilising the public sec-tor, business and civil society as partners in development.* London: International Business Leaders Forum.

Tennyson, R. (2003). *Institutionalising partnerships: Lessons from the frontline* (1st ed.). London: International Business Leaders Forum.

Tennyson, R. (2004). *The partnering toolbook* (1st ed.). London: International Business Leaders Forum & Geneva: Global Alliance for Improved Nutrition.

Tennyson, R. (2005). *The brokering guidebook, navigating effective sustainable development partnerships.* London: The Partnering Initiative, International Business Leaders Forum.

Tennyson, R. (2007). The imagined conversation. In S. MacManus & R. Tennyson. *Talking the walk: A communication manual for partnership practitioners* (pp. 43–44). London: International Business Leaders Forum.

Tennyson, R. (2011). *The partnering toolbook: An essential guide to cross-sector partnering* (4th ed.). London: The Partnering Initiative, International Business Leaders Forum.

Tennyson, R. (2013). *Dealing with paradox stories and lessons from the first three years of consortium-building.* London: Partnership Brokers Association. Retrieved February 9, 2018, from http://partnershipbrokers.org/w/2559/dealing-with-paradox/

Tennyson, R., & McManus, S. (2007). *Talking the walk, a communication manual for partnership practitioners.* London: International Business Leaders Forum.

Tennyson, R., & Mundy, J. (2017), *Partnership brokers in action, skills, tools, approaches, partnership brokers training, course workbook* (2nd ed.). London: Partnership Brokers Association.

Tennyson, R., & Wilde, L. (2000). *The guiding hand: Brokering partnerships for sustainable development.* Turin: United Nations Staff College & London: Prince of Wales Business Leaders Forum.

Tennyson, R., & Wood, E. (Eds.). (2013). *Dealing with paradox: Stories and lessons from the first three years of consortium-building.* London: Partnership Brokers Association.

Tennyson, R., Stott, L., Marhubi, A., & Wood, E. (2016). The necessity of transformation, emerging partnership lessons from diverse contexts. *Report for the Promoting Effective Partnering (PEP) Facility.* London: Partnership Brokers Association. Retrieved February 9, 2018, from http://partnershipbrokers.org/w/wp-content/uploads/2010/08/Emerging-Partnership-Lessons-from-Diverse-Contexts-sm2.pdf

United Nations. (2014). The road to dignity by 2030: Ending poverty, transforming all lives and protecting the planet. *Synthesis report of the Secretary-General on the post-2015 sustainable development agenda.* New York, NY: United Nations.

UN General Assembly. (2016). *Resolution adopted by the general assembly on 22 December 2015 70/224. Towards global partnerships: a principle-based approach to enhanced cooperation between the United Nations and all relevant partners,* Seventieth session, Agenda item 27. New York, NY: United Nations.

UNDESA. (2015). *SD in Action – Special report on voluntary multi-stakeholder partnerships and commitments for sustainable development.* New York, NY: United Nations Department of Economic and Social Affairs.

UNGC. (2013). *UN-business partnerships: A handbook.* New York, NY: UN Global Compact Office.

Utting, P. (2001, July 27). UN-business partnerships: Whose agenda counts? *Third World Network*. Geneva: UNRISD.

Utting, P., & Zammit, A. (2009). United Nations-Business partnerships: Good intentions and contradictory agendas. *Journal of Business Ethics, 90*, 39–56.

Van Tulder, R. (2010). Partnering skills – The basic philosophy. *Working Paper Series* (p. 005). Rotterdam: Partnership Resource Centre.

Van Tulder, R. (2011). From platform to partnerships. *Paper*. Rotterdam: Partnership Resource Centre.

Van Tulder, R., & Keen, N. (2018). Capturing collaborative complexities – Designing complexity sensitive theories of change for transformational partnerships. *Journal of Business Ethics* (forthcoming).

Van Tulder, R., & Pfisterer, S. (2014). Creating partnering space – Exploring the right fit for sustainable development partnerships. In M. M. Seitanidi & A. Crane (Eds.). *Social partnerships and responsible business: A research handbook* (pp. 105–124). London: Routledge.

Van Tulder, R., & van der Zwart, A. (2006). *International business-society management*. London: Routledge.

Van Tulder, R., Seitanidi, M., Crane, A. W., & Brammer, S. (2016). Enhancing the impact of cross-sector partnerships. Four impact loops for channelling partnership studies. *Journal of Business Ethics, 105*(5), 111–130.

Von Schnurbein, G. (2010). Foundations as honest brokers between market, state and nonprofits through building social capital. *European Management Journal, 28*(6), 413–420.

Waddell, S. (2011). *Global action networks, creating our future together*. London: Palgrave Macmillam.

Waddock, S. (2010). From individual to institution: On making the world different. *Journal of Business Ethics, 94*, 9–12.

Waddock, S. (2015). Reflections: Intellectual shamans, sensemaking, and memes in large system change. *Journal of Change Management, 15*(4), 270.

Wang, C., & Ahmed, P. (2003). Organisational learning: A critical review. *The Learning Organization, 10*(1), 8–17.

Warner, M. (2002). Monitoring tri-sector partnerships, *Working Paper* No. 13. London: Business Partners for Development Natural Resources Cluster.

Warner, M. (2003). Partnerships for sustainable development: Do we need partnership brokers? *Paper for Overseas Development Institute*. London: Overseas Development Institute.

Warner, M. (2003). *The new broker: Brokering partnerships for development*. London: Overseas Development Institute.

Warner, M. (2007). *The new broker, beyond agreement brokering partnerships for development*. London: Overseas Development Institute.

Warner, M., & Sullivan, R. (Eds.). (2004). *Putting partnerships to work; strategic alliances for development between government, the private sector and civil society*. London: Greenleaf Publishing.

Weisbord, M., & Janoff, S. (2007). *Don't just do something, stand there!* Oakland, CA: Berrett Koehler Publisher.

Western, S. (2013) The eco-leadership discourse: Connectivity and ethics. In S. Western (Ed.) *Leadership; A critical text* (2nd ed., pp. 243–280), London: SAGE Publications Ltd.

White, S. C. (1996). Depoliticising development: The uses and abuses of participation. *Development in Practice, 6*(1), 6–15.

Williams, P. (2010). Special agents: The nature and role of boundary spanners. *Paper to the ESRC Research Seminar Series-Collaborative Futures: New Insights from Intra and Inter-Sectoral Collaborations.* Birmingham: University of Birmingham.

Winnicott, D. W. (1964). *The child, the family, and the outside world.* London: Pelican Books.

Witte, J. M., Streck, C., & Benner, T. (Eds.). *Progress or peril? Partnerships and networks in global environmental governance: The post Johannesburg agenda.* Washington, DC and Berlin: Global Public Policy Institute.

Wolski, B. (2012). The 'new' limitations of Fisher and Ury's model of interest-based negotiation: Not necessarily the ethical alternative. *James Cook Law Review, 19,* 127–155.

World Bank. (2014). *Strategic framework for mainstreaming citizen engagement in world bank group operations, engaging with citizens for improved results.* Washington, DC: World Bank.

World Economic Forum and Deloitte Consulting. (2016). *Building partnerships for sustainable agriculture and food security: A guide for country led action.* Geneva: World Economic Forum.

World Health Organisation. (2016). *World malaria report 2016.* Geneva: World Health Organisation. Retrieved February 9, 2018, from http://www.who.int/malaria/publications/world-malaria-report-2016/report/en/

World Vision. (2013). *Local partnering for development programmes – The essentials.* Monrovia, CA: World Vision International.

Yambayamba, K. E. (2006). "Do it for us?" The challenges of replicating a partnership. *Partnership Matters, Current Issues in Cross-Sector Collaboration, 4,* 69–70. London: The Partnering Initiative.

Yunus, M. (2007). *Banker to the poor: Micro-lending and the battle against world poverty.* New York, NY: Public Affairs.

Zadek, S. (2007). Collaborative governance: The new multilateralism for the 21st century. *Global Development* 2.0. Washington, DC: Brookings Institute.

Zhang, D. (2015). *In-brief: China-Australia-Papua New Guinea Trilateral Aid Cooperation on Malaria Control.* Canberra: Australian National University. Retrieved February 9, 2018, http://bellschool.anu.edu.au/sites/default/files/publications/attachments/2016-05/ib-2015-14-zhang-online.pdf

Zhang, D. (2017). Why cooperate with others? Demystifying China's trilateral aid cooperation. *The Pacific Review, 30*(5), 750–768. Retrieved February 9, 2018, http://www.tandfonline.com/eprint/EZv8eYceC6HHvi3iZ9Z4/full

Index